WALKING FOUR DIRECTIONS

WALKING FOUR DIRECTIONS

A Journey for Regeneration in the Land of Enchantment

ROBB YOUNG HIRSCH

SUNSTONE
PRESS
SANTA FE

Illustrations and cover by AuPalette Illustration & Design, Audrey Ann Taylor

Sunstone books may be purchased for educational, business, or sales promotional use.
For information please write: Special Markets Department, Sunstone Press,
P.O. Box 2321, Santa Fe, New Mexico 87504-2321.
Printed on acid-free paper
∞
eBook 978-1-61139- 690-4

Library of Congress Cataloging-in-Publication Data

Names: Hirsch, Robb Young, 1970- author.
Title: Walking four directions : a journey for regeneration in the Land of
   Enchantment / Robb Young Hirsch.
Description: Santa Fe : Sunstone Press, [2023] | Includes index. | Summary:
   "Walking, the author journeys to four destinations in New Mexico and
   explores life forces key to humanity's restoration, presenting a way to
   solve the climate crisis by using our own two feet in teamwork with
   non-violent direct action"-- Provided by publisher.
Identifiers: LCCN 2022048963 | ISBN 9781632933911 (paperback) | ISBN
   9781611396904 (epub)
Subjects: LCSH: Walking--New Mexico. | Climate change mitigation--New
   Mexico. | Social justice.
Classification: LCC GV199.42.N49 H57 2023 | DDC
   796.5109789--dc23/eng/1112022
LC record available at https://lccn.loc.gov/2022048963

WWW.SUNSTONEPRESS.COM
SUNSTONE PRESS / POST OFFICE BOX 2321 / SANTA FE, NM 87504-2321 /USA
(505) 988-4418

DEDICATION

To humankind's best friends: our dogs.

To my parents and ancestors past and to my children and young people forward who have the courage we've thus far lacked to stand up for a livable climate; may we have the wisdom to walk in their shoes and be likewise inspired so that all together we heal the world.

CONTENTS

SECTION I
FINDING STRIDE

"Maybe what matters is that we embark."
—Barbara Hall

1
STEPPING OUT

"Raise your paw. Who's up for an adventure?"

Walking my dogs Coaster (a black lab) and Gary (a French bull dog) for several months during the heart of the Coronavirus sparked in me not only an appreciation for walking (and a continued appreciation for the dogs) but also a craving to walk beyond the confines of our regular routine. We have a handful of standard walks in different directions around the neighborhood (including dirt roads, paved roads and arroyos) which are all pleasant, but they get a bit dull after a thousand repetitions.

Let me step back a moment to say I wasn't just taking occasional mini dog walks here and there. I was doing a lot of dog walks and relatively long ones to the point where I was beginning to wonder if the dog walking was getting to my head. But I had two excuses: Firstly I was not swimming at that time, preferring to stay out of indoor work out facilities, and so I was needing an outdoor alternative. Secondly Coaster had surgery at that time which required rehabilitation so I was taking lengthier dog walks than normal. I was told by the vet to build up to a half an hour three times per day, and then the vet said they can be "unlimited leash walks." Is it an oxymoron to say "unlimited" and "leash" in the same sentence?

Anyhow, it was the word "unlimited" that resonated with my soul and compelled me to do something greater. And I don't mean something greater in terms of walking Coaster and Gary greater distances with a leash. I mean something greater with my life through walking.

It hit me late during a sleepless night in February 2021. I envisioned walking from my home in each of the four directions, heading in one distinct direction in each of the four seasons upcoming. I had a compelling reason for going in every direction, all with a unifying and connected purpose: to restore. Restoring my own health and well being was an integral part of this, but the main purpose was to contribute to the healing of humanity and the planet. This is a big task, especially because I am so small, just a drop in the boundless bucket. I'm also a bald then 50 year old white man on my second hip replacement (not to mention many other shortcomings and limitations of mine). But contributing to the healing of humanity and the planet was the reason that kept me up dreaming about this walking quest. While it may be a big stretch that someone like me can have an outsized influence. Who knows. It may just be possible by putting one foot in front of the other, especially if life forces come together.

This was a good time to embark on a journey for regeneration and healing. In fact it was an urgent time! In February 2021 we were well into the COVID 19 pandemic, the worst public health crisis in over a century. People all around the world were suffering. I didn't know the least of it. But the aching and human agony was palpable. Meanwhile the climate crisis is even more agonizing and harmful to our civilization, and it is looming out there unresolved. We have a narrowing window of time by which we must come together and meaningfully address this man made emergency. The UN's Intergovernmental Panel on Climate Change (the IPCC) says by 2030 we'll need to have adopted a full scale global and domestic transformation. And so the time to act boldly for restoration was right then and is still right now! Furthermore, the United States should lead the world in solutions—given that we have majorly caused and perpetuated this crises as the greatest historic and highest per capita emitter of greenhouse gasses. But it was and remains hard for the US to lead when we are in denial, not to mention so polarized in what seemed like a cold civil war after experiencing an insurrection at our nation's capital. We had and have a terribly divided country which has come apart at the seams, and our human and racial relations were and are direly being strained from intolerable acts of white supremacy and systemic racism. And to top it off we had and have a deeply corrupt and dysfunctional politics. So, as I was saying, if there were ever a time to embark on a quest for restoration this was and is it.

2
WHY WALKING

"Walking is man's best medicine"
—Hippocrates

Why is walking a good way to draw light on the promise of regeneration? Because walking itself is regenerating, in multiple ways. For starters it is great for our physical health. It can for example lower high blood pressure and help prevent against diabetes (two underlying conditions that led to so many more deaths during the pandemic). Walking is very effective physical fitness and good exercise which doesn't take a toll on the body. Running, on the other hand, on pavement especially, can take a toll on your joints. Walking is soothing on the joints.

Walking is also amazing for our mental health. I read a book called *Keep Sharp* by Sanjay Gupta (Reference) which is all about nurturing the well being of the brain and the number one thing that is recommended (before sound sleep, a nutritious diet, new experiences, mindfulness practices, social connectedness and a good attitude) is exercise. Walking in particular is singled out as an excellent way to support brain fitness. Sanjay Gupta says "movement can increase brainpower by helping to increase, repair, and maintain brain cells, and it makes you more productive and more alert throughout the day." He writes at length about "the tremendous physical healing power of exercise" including walking. Dr. Ron Peterson, a world leading neurologist from the Mayo Clinic, likewise recommends "brisk walking" as a way to fortify our mental health. The compelling truth is that the physical and mental health benefits of walking are very impressive and closely intertwined as this list by Sanjay Gupta reveals. Backing this up is a recent study from the Harvard School of Public Health that confirms not only that walking extends our lives but it helps stave off depression (Reference).

Sanjay Gupta's list of benefits from exercise including from walking:

Stronger immune system;
Increased stamina, strength, flexibility and energy;
Decreased inflammation and age related disease from cancer to dementia;
Increased muscle tone and bone health;
Increased heart health, with lower cardiovascular disease and high blood pressure;
More restful and sounder sleep;
Stress reduction;
Increased self esteem and sense of well-being;
Release of endorphins, the brain chemicals that act as natural mood lifters and pain relievers;
Increased blood and lymph circulation and oxygen supply to cells and tissues;
Decreased blood sugar levels and decreased risk for insulin resistance and diabetes;
Lower risk of death from all causes;
Ideal weight distribution and maintenance.

It is true, as I have been experiencing personally, that taking a walk makes us feel better. I recall a story of Larry David, the creator of the hysterical and self deprecating HBO show called Curb Your Enthusiasm, who advises his family in real life—if they're feeling down or depressed—to "take a shower!" It's very similar kind of advice my wife Numi got from her grandfather "Opa." When she wasn't feeling well he would encourage her to "take a walk outside." There is a lot of wisdom in that. Walking outdoors gets the blood flowing, gets our mind contemplating and gets our spirits up (especially when we have four legged furry creatures leading us).

Walking Coaster and Gary on the road by my home.

Being outdoors and walking in the fresh air is healthy at anytime in our history but of course it was advisable even more so then as we looked to avoid unventilated rooms and seeked to get out more to recover from the Coronavirus. An equally compelling factor in the value of walking extends beyond our human health into the realm of healing our planet. Obviously when we are walking places, we are not driving, and thus not spewing tailpipe emissions and greenhouse gasses into the atmosphere, and we are in other fundamental ways not polluting the environment. That's really important because one of our sacred responsibilities is to strive to do no harm. Walking not only does no harm to the environment and is a clean mode of transportation but it is also empowering. When we walk we put each foot down step after step. Touching the ground time and time again with the soles of our feet is literally connecting us to the Earth. This experience of connection, contacting the ground stride after stride, seeps into our consciousness. Naturally by walking we become less self centered and more grounded as well as aware of the atmosphere around us. Walking, therefore, presents a transformative opportunity for us to develop a regenerative mindset that lends itself to humankind healing rather than harming the planet.

Another cool thing about walking is the ease and fun of tracing our progress on any hand held devise. I can readily see on the health app of my I phone a summary of my walking statistics and the progress I am making each day. That winter I averaged 10,394 steps per day which translates to about 4.3 miles/day and my walking speed was just over three miles per hour. There are other charts and statistics I can look at but the one that most resonates is steps per day. I am not obsessed. I just check it occasionally and it's kind of nice to keep track of. Speaking of I phones and health apps, Apple founder Steve Jobs was big on walking. He'd have "walking conversations" with people interviewing for the company and he was known to walk long distances. He attributed walking to thinking better, greater productivity and more creativity. In fact there is a study that was done that compared people trying to think of new ideas while sitting down in comparison to walking. People did resoundingly better while walking, particularly while walking outdoors (Reference).

Another compelling point is that, when you compare it to other exercise activities, walking doesn't cost much if anything. All of us can afford it. You don't have to pay a gym membership. You don't need fancy equipment (that so often requires updating). You don't need a Peloton. You can just head out the door for a stroll. You can even go bare foot if you want to. And I do want to, but I thought it was about time I got myself a new pair of walking shoes. The running shoes I had in the closet were over ten years old and were beyond repair. So I went to a local shoe store and picked out new comfortable shoes which I could use for the increasing dog walks I was taking and for my four direction journey. It's a big deal for me to get new shoes because, as my wife likes to point out, I don't usually buy clothing and stuff for myself. My wardrobe is static (she would say worn out). And instead of replacing the old with new, I take my clothes to a seamstress shop where they are sown and restored for many more months of use to come (to my wife's chagrin). But in this case, I figured a new pair of walking shoes was worth the investment (my feet and joints were celebrating after years of neglect).

Before I conclude this chapter on why walking is the right thing to do for our restoration, I want to share the perspective of someone who has walked circles around me and circles around the most avid walkers of modern humankind. A man named Dr. John Francis spent over 20 years exclusively walking. He made an extraordinary commitment to walking and not ever using any fossil fuel based transportation in response to an oil spill in 1971 near the Golden Gate Bridge where a half a million gallons of crude oil leaked from a tanker polluting the majestic waters there. He ended his ban on motorized vehicles 22 years later after earning his doctorate degree in environmental studies, after criss-crossing the Northwest and walking across the country and after being hired by the US Coast Guard to help develop regulations for oil spills. He wrote a book about his journey called *Planet Walker: How to Change Your World One Step At A Time* (Reference).

John Francis personally dedicated himself to the healing of the planet by always walking instead of using fossil fuel vehicles. (Illustration by AuPalette)

From all his years of walking (and from his silence: for 17 of the 22 years he remarkably took a vow to not speak in order to listen better) John Francis certainly gained a deeper understanding. He said "there is something spiritual and sacred in the ordinary act of walking" (p. 31). He felt that walking made him connect to the present and he noted that every moment "contains the seeds of opportunity for change" (p. 36). "In the walking," John explains, "I discover a thread that runs through time, beyond the need of personal protest, connecting me to...life" (p. 38). By walking, he noticed aspects of nature that he never noticed before; he grew more aware of all that was around him (p. 41); his senses came alive including a "constant sense of place" (p. 104); "moving slowly on the ground, feeling every rock and stone" (p. 169); "sensing our environment...is necessary for our survival (p. 193)."

These are all compelling attributes and outcomes of walking from someone who has a wealth of experience. But there is more to it. He said during his pilgrimage, "for a moment I feel like a kid again, feeling the mud...between my toes." As an impressionable kid growing up in Philadelphia he was impacted by a car running over a young robin bird. As an adult in the midst of his walking journey—reflecting on loved ones lost, the bird, the oil spill and his relative short lifespan—he said "in facing death we experience the whole of life, and in that experience we find meaning and are obligated to act" (p. 91). By his action of walking and otherwise, John Francis learned a new sense of freedom (p. 183), creativity (p. 182) and a diversity of human life (p. 172).

Perhaps most of all he gained a comprehension of and appreciation for relationship: "the spirit of generosity" (p. 226) from the communities he passed through; a "kinship" all around (p. 109): "the deepest level of communication is not communication, but communion" (p. 172); a taste of harmony: "I think I feel ecstasy sometimes. It is a fleeting moment of being in touch with all the pleasures and the pain, the vacant stares and touches, the clapping hands, and the stars, the music and the rain" (p. 229); and reciprocity: "sometimes we have to give something up to find something else" (p. 231). He chose Earth Day 1990 to start speaking again to commemorate that from that day forward he would be "speaking for the environment" (p. 250). Some of his first words were: "The environmental crisis is an outward manifestation of a crisis of mind and spirit… the crisis is concerned with the kind of creatures we are and what we must become if we are to survive" (pgs. 251-252).

John Francis was humbled by those who had walked before him like Peace Pilgrim Mildred Norman who dedicated over half her life to taking the pathway of peace. She thought true peace was only attainable through inner peace which she thought came from four kinds of steps: the first was "right attitude toward life;" the second step was living a harmonious life in connection with the natural environment; the third was finding your place in God's plan; and the fourth step, according to Peace Pilgrim, was "the simplification of life" which for her meant dedicating her life to service and giving up material things. She walked just with the clothes on her back.

John was in awe that she walked 28 years in such modesty. And of course I am blown away by all these walking champions—many of whom, including these two, I will feature in a compilation of "walking heroes" that I will update throughout this journey of mine (see Appendix 1). In comparison with these great ones, my quest to go in four directions in the upcoming four seasons is minuscule, but there is deep purpose and integrity to it nonetheless.

Peace Pilgrim walked over 25,000 miles for her cause and among other feats she became the first woman to walk the Appalachian Trail which spans 2,050 miles. (Illustration by AuPalette)

What is my rationale for walking in four directions? Like I said, I did not plan this out rigorously; it came to me kind of like a vision while I was lying awake in bed. I pondered: what will it take for us to heal as a society? Four foundational concepts came to mind: spirit, nature, heritage and community. I think of these as the regenerative cornerstones. Human Spirit because we're deeply wounded and we are wounding each other and the planet as a result; we need a combined sense of humbleness and can do spirit to rise to the occasion and usher in our healing. Mother Nature because there are vital restorative forces there that can guide us, that we can interact with and that can stand on their own. Heritage Values because we should heed and learn wisdom from those who have come before us. And Beloved Community because we must develop and enact hopeful solutions in teamwork with others; if we all start acting locally, in grassroots fashion, our actions will flow into a mass movement that reverberates throughout civil society and can propel the nation which can move the world. In pondering all of this I thought what better way to explore, bring attention and hopefully give testament to these four tenets than to walk four directions in their honor. If I do, I thought, walk four directions for each of these four cornerstones maybe they will become more concrete and we can actualize them and assemble them into the wholeness we need to successfully combat the human climate crisis.

3
FAMILY WALKS

"If you want to walk fast, walk alone,
but if you want to walk far, walk together."
—Ratan Tata

On a personal and family level, which is where I start my journey, I am striving to embody enduring integrity and natural spontaneity. I have a sense of seriousness about me but a sense of humor too, as I have learned not to take myself too seriously. In my upbringing, and in many ways throughout my life, I feel the duality of my existence. In one sense I feel as though I am on a mountaintop, because I feel so lucky to be alive with the love that has uplifted me and the chance I have to give back which inspires me. But I also feel like I am trapped in a maze where the walls of the maze represent contrasting feelings: whole and broken, calm and irritable, connected and solitary, loving and grieving, ease and disease, levity and intensity. I have not yet found my way out of this maze, and I am not even sure I want to leave because there is something compelling and very real about seeking harmony in contradiction. But I do have ambition in the sense that I want to tear down the walls that confine me and divide us; I want us all to break free from our self imposed limitations. I want us all together to stand un-trapped and unobstructed on the mountaintop and see, yes even get to, the promised land, not in an afterlife but in our immediate lifetime.

I will elaborate on this restrictive maze and promising mountaintop by taking a walk down memory lane recalling the sentiments from memorable walks with loved ones past and present...

In late February 2021 I took a walk with my daughter Tabatha at a place I call Little Pequeno. I know the name may sound silly because both words mean little, first in English and then in Spanish. It is fitting that we went there. First of all because humbleness is apparent in the name of the place: we are not just little in the grand plan, we are little little. Tabatha is no longer little. She was nineteen years old and half way out the door.

She is as cheerful, radiant and warm as sunshine. Truly thoughtful. Strong and adventurous. But also tender. I remember the night she was born, the umbilical cord was wrapped around her neck and the heart monitor was going berserk while the doctors kept rushing in. I was a mess, but she and her mom were glowing. Sixteen years later she was diagnosed with Crohn's disease and it was similarly tumultuous. But with a Specific Carbohydrate Diet (SCD) and mindfulness work, among other fruitful ways of being, she has regained and even improved her gut health and her immune system is now stronger than it was before the diagnosis.

Among many gifts she brings to the world, she is a singer and song writer. One of the first songs she wrote when she was in 8th grade is called "Together," which is an ode to the environment and an appeal for humanity. When I listen to it or contemplate the lyrics (below), I find clear references to the foundations of healing that I am exploring starting with being humble and raising up the human spirit.

Lyrics to Tabatha Rose's song titled "Together:"

Have you ever seen the sky, not just looked but wondered why
People here we are so small, when you look above us all
Have you ever felt the tide, floating upon the ocean wide
Don't be afraid to lose control, when you let go you become whole

I don't know if we should be crying, screaming, fighting, acting
I don't know should I be breathing or gasping

So can we come together, fix our future, take these problems, find solutions, this is dire, we'll get through this, find the fire, we can do this, we can do it

Have you ever touched the ground, when you stand up, put your foot down
We can't just keep walking in the same place, we've got to run toward change…

We know everything there is to know, but we don't know anything at all

So can we just come together, fix our future, take these problems, find solutions, this is dire, we'll get through this, find the fire, we can do this, we can do it

Have you ever changed the world!

Nature of course comes alive in the song as it does on the Little Pequeno walk which starts along a dirt road and becomes a lovely trail winding up alongside the Santa Fe river. There is no greater sound for me than naturally trickling water which I can hear along the way. Throughout the riparian areas is a bosque, which shelters us from the stiff New Mexico winds. Sunlight weaves through the canopy. Eventually we come to a big cottonwood tree with a tire swing hanging from it's branch, and soon after there is a tree growing sideways at a 40 degree angle that kids love to climb. My then ten year old son Holden loves the tree swing. The dogs love to run along the little river, Coaster in particular because she loves to wade in water. I love it because I come here with my loved ones, including on this walk with my daughter. I knew she would be heading off to college in the Fall after the gap year that she was on and so I knew it was not every day that I would be able to walk with her like this.

Little Pequeno has heritage value to me. It is an intersection place: my mom past, my children heading into the future and me present. My mom (named Holly, nick named "Nama"), my step father (nick named "Stampa") and I used to walk Little Pequeno when they visited from Colorado. My mom was frail then as she was facing the later stages of Parkinson's. But she would always plod along putting one foot in front of the other. She sometimes had a strain on her face but on a good day you could also catch the twinkle in her eye. We relished our time together in this little wonderland; and when she got tired, there was even a bench we could sit on to talk, to hear the stream go by and listen to "the Quiet Voice"—which Nama always encouraged us to do. My mom passed away some years ago. To this day I am inspired by her gentleness and some day I will be a gentleman thanks in large part to her influence (I still have a ways to go).

My mom, Holly (known as "Nama" by my kids), loved meadows
and she loved nature, and we love her so.

During our walk together at Little Pequeno I told Tabatha about the vivid dream of my mom that I had the very night before. I very seldom remember my dreams but when I do, especially when I dream of either of my parents who have both passed, it's special. In the dream, I told Tabatha, my brother and I were running and playing with my mom in a meadow (Nama loved meadows so much that for her second marriage with Stampa she got married in one). At the end of the dream my brother and I were sitting in a parked car with my mom. Next thing I knew a handsome young man came into the car with us and when he saw Holly he cried in a cathartic way reflecting a deep sense of closeness with my mom. I told Tabatha I didn't know who the young man was who got in the car, but immediately, she said "Robin, was it Robin?" Robin was my mom's late brother who had died of a drinking and driving accident long before I was born. And yes, Tabatha was absolutely right, it was Robin. It must have been. I think it is amazing Tabatha knew that because she hardly ever heard of Robin, not to mention all of us in my immediate family never meeting him.

I think my mom had always quietly struggled with the loss of her brother. He was so young—with his whole life ahead of him—when the fatal crash happened. It plagued my mom I think that she was powerless to prevent his passing, that she couldn't be there for him to protect him from this fate. But what the dream makes clear is that there was no love lost and they are bound together even long after their respective passing. There was an emotional clearing that morning, a touching sense that my mom was somehow reconciled: a hopeful idea that grief never completely processed in her lifetime was being processed now through her son and granddaughter. A weight was being lifted from our family, and Tabatha on our walk together at Little Pequeno, helped bring clarity to this prospect and prompted it along.

Now that I think of it there have been several walks with my family that have meaningfully processed hardship and or faced the duality of brokenness and wholeness in our lives. This represents further the benefit of walking: it can be therapeutic, a conducive and safe venue for sharing feelings and facing adversity.

A walk with my mom comes to mind. I was a junior in high school and we were staying the weekend at Aunt Anne's in Buffalo Bay, a magical place in Connecticut by the shore of the Long Island Sound. My mom invited me on a walk and I went along. I generally didn't like to walk or hike so much when I was young. I preferred ball sports and more physical activity. (My two sons are the same way. The only way they will join me in walking the dogs is if we bring a football or play frisbee golf along the way.) My mom and I took a walk along a dirt road through the late fall color trees. Midway into it she told me how she made mistakes in her first marriage with my dad. It was more on her that the marriage ended she said as she revealed she had had an affair before they split up. I was troubled to hear this—less at the time and more over time into my early twenties when I became a bit disillusioned by the idea of marriage. At the time I was—and to this day I am—proud of my mom for telling me her role in things. As a parent now I think kids can handle more than we realize and need to hear as they come of age the truth about their parents' shortcomings. But despite what she said, I know that marriage is a two way street, and there are mutual dynamics that go into a healthy or unhealthy marriage. I know too that my mom got married when she was very young and I understand people change. I do think though that infidelity is cowardly; I would hope people could have the decency to break things off before they fool around. On the other hand, I also think my mom ultimately acted bravely for leaving a comfortable life back east and carving out her own exhilarating path in the mountains out west.

On my wedding day my mom told me, "the mountain is in you," and that always stuck with me. My mom instilled in me, along with her spiritual gentleness, a deep appreciation for nature. Meanwhile my dad instilled in me a sense of integrity and a deep appreciation for people. He taught me at a core level to do my best and treat others with respect. I am very sad that my children didn't get to know my parents in their healthy vibrant state. But I am so grateful to both of them for all that they taught me and for the unwavering love they gave us which I never take for granted and try to pass on to my kids.

I recall a walk with my father in Central Park in New York. It took place right after he was diagnosed with Pick's disease at the ripe age of 60. Pick's is also known as Frontal Temporal Dementia (FTD). It is a degenerative disease in the brain affecting the frontal lobes and increasingly impairing one's executive functioning. My dad, having just learned this fate, walked with me around the reservoir. On this circular walk he told me the passage from his favorite movie with Paul Newman about a boxer named Rocky Barbella. He said "Toope (he always had the best nicknames for us), Somebody Up There Likes Me!" He went on to explain that even though his life hadn't always been rosy, his divorce with my mom was very troubling as was this health diagnosis, but he said how he was extremely grateful for so much and felt so strongly that his life was a gift. He said the greatest gift of all for him was his three sons, all so unique and incredible in our own ways he said. He told me on our walk that he was the happiest and proudest in life fathering us and watching us run toward whatever made us tick.

My dad holding his newborn granddaughter Tabatha.
I called him "Daddles" which is fitting because he was the best father I could ask for.

My dad passed away ten years later but in that time I grew to experience what he meant about being grateful as a father. I became a father to my three children and have been loving seeing them grow up into the unique, amazing and caring people that they are. While I couldn't fix the brokenness from my parents' divorce, I could at least strive for wholeness as I grew up.

And when I grew up, I fell faithfully in love with Numi. We had known each other from high school but we were reacquainted eight years later on the eve of Thanksgiving in 1997. I had literally just pedaled into New York City that day right after doing a three month bike ride called the "Climate Ride." I wasn't planning to go out that night but my brother convinced me, and she wasn't wanting to go out either but her friend convinced her. Fate happened I like to think and I knew there was a magic feeling between us because we couldn't leave each others' sides—which has remained the case. One year later, again on the eve of Thanksgiving, I asked her to take a walk with me that night, first along La Barbaria Trail and then up a steep incline. She was up for it and went along with me not asking questions, just trudging up the mountain together. When we got to a look out point, I knelt down and asked her to marry me. She was speechless but Sam, her Labrador Protector as I call him, barked affirmatively and so she nodded. Even though it was dark, the terrain was tough and the hill we climbed was rough, I will always love that walk and likewise I will always love this woman.

Sometimes I feel like our loving marriage is a testament to our parents. Numi's late father was named Ronald. We named our first son after him—Ronald Fisher Hirsch (and we call him Fisher). When Numi was only nine years old her father Ronald took his own life. He did so for mental health related reasons we don't fully know; and part of it was the anguish he felt from his impending separation with Numi's mother, and another part of it had to do with feelings of inadequacy professionally. The most anguishing part though was how Numi's immediate and extended family reacted by blaming and not talking to each other—not only in the immediate aftermath but for decades to come. Nonetheless, I think Ronald, or "Ronnie" as he was called, would be smiling as would my parents at how Numi and I are so far going the distance, and I don't say that cavalierly. Like any relationship, things aren't perfect—as you will see—but we feel very lucky to be in love and so thankful to be able to be present for the whole precious growing up time with our kids.

The walk I will never forget is walking down the aisle with both my parents on my wedding day. They hardly ever spoke and interacted after their divorce but at my wedding all our arms were interlocked. The memory is as soothing as the sound of water rippling under a bridge. I knew then that there can be healing from one generation to the next. No perfection in this imperfect world but a passing of the baton in the journey of love.

Walking down the aisle.

Personally and in our families I think we all have wounds that need healing. Thinking of Ronnie, I know I feel inadequacy. Not in a dire or drastic way that I would ever entertain taking my own life but in a very human way. For example, while I can fall asleep at night no problem (it helps knowing that "I'm not a terrible person" which is a joke my wife and her best friend Erin and I say to each other), I often wake up in the middle of the night and have a hell of a time falling back asleep. And the reason for that is a number of things some of which I am not aware of. But one thing is the feeling of inadequacy and anxiety about the state of the world and my measly role in it. I can't stand it that I am part of the current generations causing the climate crisis. I know we have dropped the ball, and even with all the boundless opportunities for solutions in our midst, we are not doing our part to pick up the ball we have fumbled. Rather we are unjustly straddling our children and future generations as well as present marginalized communities with tremendous burdens that are unbearable. I feel that unbearable weight on my shoulders and I feel like I am not making a meaningful impact and not doing enough to help turn the tide. And so I toss and turn.

I may other times be sleepless from family and health related grief bubbling up to my consciousness: my mom's Parkinson's, my dad's Pick's, Numi's father's suicide, and to a lesser but still important extent our daughter's Crohn's and my son's Celiac...these mental health, degenerative and/or autoimmune diseases in our immediate family and increasing in the wider public make me angry, and stir anxiety in me that can keep me from falling back asleep. But on the flip side, it was on a sleepless night that I envisioned this journey I am taking. The difficulty of reconciling my life and the climate crisis and the challenges of my family's health energized me to wake up and do something about it. Difficulty falling back asleep and coming to terms with my inadequacy propelled me on a journey for regeneration, which if fruitful could ironically help remedy my sleep disorder—and potentially much better yet, could help rekindle and awaken our fellow humanity.

When we live asleep or are numb to our negative impacts on life, human degeneration and environmental degeneration feed off one another harmfully. Here's an example. The widespread use of pesticides and toxic fertilizers pollutes clean water from run off, harms the soil and the microbial life in the soil, endangers our gut health from the tainted foods we eat, and can penetrate our neurological pathways contributing to the spread of autoimmune disorders and degenerative diseases like Parkinson's. So on one hand, we and the environment are mutual victims in a dangerous spiral. But the more rejuvenating point to me is the corollary: when our attention is keenly on life giving principles, human health and environmental health go hand in hand in a mutually regenerative way. We can choose to eat healthy food grown from farms and ranches run without the use of toxic chemicals but managed with healthy soil principles instead. Healthy soil principles include minimizing soil disturbance, maximizing biodiversity, keeping the soil covered, maintaining a living root and integrating animals. All of these deployed together enable farmers to overcome the need for pesticides or nitrogen based fertilizers because the soil on its own develops healthy defense mechanisms to pests and extreme weather risks. From soil health, nitrogen is produced naturally, saving producers money from not needing to use external inputs, lessening pollution including nitrous oxide which is one of the most potent greenhouse gasses. From soil health, more water and carbon are stored in the ground and all together we become more resilient to climate change.

So, the point I am making is, we all have it in us to bring forth that which is lacking in the world. Where there is human illness and harming of the planet, we can bring forth healthiness and regeneration, just as the Prayer of St. Francis encourages.

When my mom visited us in Santa Fe, she and I—while we waited for a table at our favorite restaurant, Cafe Pasqual's—would walk to the St. Francis Cathedral. Tucked away on the outside of the cathedral is a tribute to St. Francis and written on the wall is the Prayer of Saint Francis. Reading the prayer (below), as we always would, inspires the idea of making whole that which is broken.

The Prayer of Saint Francis

Lord make me an instrument of Your peace.
Where there is hatred, let me sow love;
where there is injury, pardon;
where there is doubt, faith;
where there is despair, hope;
where there is darkness, light;
where there is sadness, joy.

O Divine Master,
grant that I may not so much seek
to be consoled as to console;
to be understood, as to understand;
to be loved, as to love.

For it's in giving that we receive;
and it is in pardoning that we are pardoned;
and it is in dying that we are born to
eternal life.

St. Francis de Assisi is one of the founding fathers of environmentalism.
He was so in tune with nature, birds would land on him. He was named the
Patron Saint of Ecologists because he thought all creatures including humans are
brothers and sisters. He also actively cared for the poor and sick. "Remember"
he said, "that when you leave this earth, you can take with you nothing that you
have received—only what you have given." He renounced his family's wealth
and devoted himself to God and the service of others. You could definitively
say he walked the walk. For all these reasons and more he is relevant for this
journey for regeneration, and he is certainly a walking hero (Appendix 1) to
appreciate. As far as walking and St. Francis are concerned, on October 4th there
is a worldwide commemoration of his environmental teaching when people do
nature walks in his memory, and there is a 342 mile trail from Florence to Rome,
through Assisi where St. Francis was born, going along refurbished paths where
he would walk with only his robe, staff and girdle.

Gary contemplating the meaning of life beside a statue
of St. Francis at Cerro Gordo park.

There can be harmony in duality, like my family life has taught me and like St. Francis advised, as long as we offer up what is lacking. At the end of the day, we can either be crumbling or we can be soaring. Both are in motion and are happening at once. The soaring suits our soul while the crumbling fits what happens eventually to our body, but that eventuality doesn't seem so worrying because in crumbling we simply rejoin the earth below our feet.

SECTION II
NORTH: HUMAN SPIRIT

"When you pray, move your feet."
            —An African proverb often recounted by
      John Lewis

4
INTROSPECTION

I thought the spring would be the right time to start this journey for regeneration because the spring represents new hope and possibility. I also felt that if my four direction walk was genuinely going to be about healing, the first direction I walk should be dedicated to finding and mending the human spirit, which is so key to our greater recovery. Humility is a prerequisite to recovery. Admitting to—and committing to turn away from—our life threatening mistakes can help set us on a pathway to health. If, on the other hand, we stay the course and stubbornly perpetuate our misguided behavior, we will most likely end up irreparably destroying ourselves and the very sources of life. To locate and build up the human spirit we need to confront our misguidedness head on. A walk, one that directly faces our folly, genuinely seeks redemption, and honestly commits to changing direction with help from God—or, if we are not comfortable with religion, from a spiritual force greater than our selves—could be just what the doctor ordered.

Raising up the human spirit is essential as one of the cornerstones of what I believe is needed to restore our well being and solve the climate crisis. But what does human spirit really mean? According to *The Decoding of the Human Spirit: A Synergy of Spirituality and Character Strengths Toward Wholeness* (Reference) the spirit component of the human spirit means connecting with the sacred to derive meaning and purpose in life; and the human component of the human spirit connotes an aspiration of character. And they feed off one another. Human character development lends itself to deepening our spiritual connection and spirituality leads naturally to the evolution of human character strengths. The two come together in the notion of human spirit as a vigorous quest toward wholeness.

Vigor is key. The idea that when we bring vigor or our best selves to the table, we can bring out the best in others. I recall my high school motto: "It is the spirit that quickeneth!" This resonates with me. And it reminds me of the meaning of Obama's campaign slogan: "yes we can!" Holden, my youngest son, has his own similar kind of phrase that he summons especially during a hard task: he says "you got this!" So there are different expressions that all amount to uplifting our fellow belief and capability. This is what invigoration is all about: raising up our can do spirit and our vision of what is possible. But in order to be uplifted and uplifting, we need to first face the music and assess our true role in creating the situation we find ourselves in. Honoring this combined calling for honesty and inspiration is what my first walk is all about.

The Chimayo Pilgrimage naturally came to mind as the right venue. It takes place from Good Friday to Easter Sunday. People do the long walk from Santa Fe, as well as places nearer and farther away, to El Santuario—a beautiful chapel in the Northern New Mexico town of Chimayo. This year and last year because of COVID the community walk was cancelled. But I figured if I did it quietly without company (regrettably) and at a different time than Easter weekend, so as not to be violating the COVID restrictions, then hopefully it could still work wonders. Doing the pilgrimage on Earth Day, just a few weeks away from the customary time, felt like a fitting alternative.

Because the pilgrimage is a spiritual journey, I thought it was incumbent on me to do some foundational thinking and spiritual introspection before I set out. And because the pilgrimage to Chimayo is supposed to take place on Easter weekend, I figured it was necessary to take the occasion to reflect on the religious aspects including the story of Easter and how it all ties into the quest for human spirit. In past years on Easter, I practiced a tradition of going to a different service each year to witness the variations. Sometimes I would go on my own and other times with my kids and/or with a good friend named Tim who likes this tradition. One year we went to an Easter service in Colorado with a stunning view of the Rocky Mountains in the background and a memorable sermon the pastor gave in the foreground. He talked about when Mary Madeleine discovered that the body of Jesus was no longer in the tomb after the crucifixion. She was Earth shaken and went out to the garden perhaps to compose herself and while she was outside she met up with someone she thought was the gardener but who was none other than Jesus who said to her: do not despair for I am rising up in redemption. He told her to tell the disciples and encourage them to go onto to Galilee and he would meet them. And on their walk to Galilee, Jesus joined them but they did not recognize him. In that moment they were downcast and too stuck in melancholy and conventionality to believe what was truly happening—like the way we are still stuck in a fossil fuel world and lack the imagination and courage to burst out of it.

But God still walks with us even when we are weak, misguided and/or living a lie. We may, like every mortal in life, be faint of heart or going down a mistaken path but there is still hope for us during these times. At the end of the Easter story, the ultimate story of restoration, Jesus says, "surely I am with you always." Which brings to mind a parallel story about Jesus walking on water. The disciples were in a boat at night crossing a body of water that was volatile in the midst of a storm. They saw what appeared to be a ghost coming their way; they did not recognize or they failed to believe that it really was Jesus walking on water toward them. Then, only after the weather calmed, waters became placid and Jesus joined them in the boat, they finally believed. What I take away from this story is to have faith from the get go, knowing God, or a calming force greater than ourselves, is present and human fortitude is possible even in—and perhaps especially during—turbulent times, like we find ourselves in today.

On Easter morning in early April 2021 without an in person service to go to because of COVID, our family walked instead to a swimming hole along the river and we plunged into the chilling water. The cold was excruciating and exhilarating at once. A sort of baptism. And as it turns out, plunging into a cold river, besides serving as an act of faith, is actually very good for our health. This is proven by the Ice Man, who takes freezing water swimming to a whole other level. He is a testament to the notion that putting our body into the abruptness of cold water strengthens our immune system and wakes up our mind and spirit!

Taking a Cold Plunge.

In terms of being awake in any formal religious sense, beyond attending a few different Easter services over the years, I should be clear that I am not religious. I have some Protestant and Jewish background but I never observed and I never regularly or irregularly even attended church or synagogue. You could certainly say I am lacking religious structure. Nonetheless I follow a spiritual path unfolding before me. I believe in God, aka the Great Spirit, and feel like we are all an integral part of a greater purpose. It is not always clear what the interwoven deeper purpose is. But I know it is incumbent on me in concert with others to find out.

One of the only structured religious steps I have taken to contemplate these questions of faith, spirit and purpose was attend Beit Midrash for a few years. Beit Midrash means house of exploration. It is a class dedicated to "walking in the footsteps of the prophets"—both old school, Old Testament prophets, and modern day prophets like Martin Luther King. We explored the wisdom of the prophets and tried to apply it to our every day lives and the current times. Rabbi Nahum Lev conducted the study group exquisitely and the participants were diversely aged with enlightening perspectives. Nahum, in facilitating the conversation, said to us that "the goal is not that we know something more but rather that we be something more." And this ties into the character aspect of building up our human spirit which is so important to our restoration.

Here are some take aways from Beit Midrash: God wants a relationship with us; God gives us free will in order that we actively choose our direction; love is the answer even though we are not told so explicitly, and love is not just some romantic notion but rather it is a transformative force through which we can restore and raise up our human spirit; there is a dynamic living presence and on-going creative energy that we can always tap into; the prophets aim both to lift up our consciousness and break down dominant, oppressive structures; ultimately they encourage us to achieve collective liberation; and we are all called to embark on a journey. Abraham at the ripe age of 75, broke with convention and went on a courageous journey toward monotheism. Moses left the comfortable palace of the pharaoh and traveled with his people for 40 years through the desert toward the promised land. There are so many poetic exemplars of breaking from conventional norms and seeking a brighter, more just path. For a closer look at these and a deeper understanding of the prophetic stream I encourage Nahum Ward Lev's wonderful, insightful book, *The Liberating Path of the Hebrew Prophets: Then and Now* (Reference). Knowing that—like the hierarchical societies from the polarizing times of the Hebrew prophets—we are off track, Nahum's message is sobering. But it is also rousingly hopeful in that, as he writes, "we are a world moving toward Tikkun (healing)."

As I was soon to be setting out on my pilgrimage and four direction journey I was grappling with the question: what is required of us to heal? I got a pretty direct clue from the prophet Micah who said: "what is required of us is to act justly and to love mercy and to walk humbly with God (6:8)." To act justly means among other things that we call out the corruption by the powers that be and instead honor 'the power of the powerless,' as Vaclav Havel encouraged. We do our part to create a society that uplifts those who are struggling. This embodies the message of the prophets and the story of Jesus. In *Staying Awake, the Gospel for Changemakers* (Reference), Reverend Tyler Sit writes about social justice as a river and how one of Jesus's central organizing principles is to look after marginalized voices. Another is to turn and actively move in another direction from the one that is misguided.

We are acting unjustly in our society today—especially when it comes to the treatment of those living in poverty, the treatment of people of color and the treatment of the Earth. The climate crisis, like John Francis said about the environment, is a crisis of human spirit and it is a matter of justice that we turn in a different direction. The fossil fuel industry, the elected leaders who perpetuate it and our society at large still subscribing to it are perpetrating injustice. The brunt of the resulting pollution falls on the backs of poor people and people of color who live in frontline communities. And as a world community, it is the poorest people, island nations and least developed countries who suffer most from the resulting flooding, decertification, wild fires, toxic water and air degradation. Since the late 20th century when we have known the science of the greenhouse effect and that humans cause global warming, we have had no excuse not to turn away from such harmful pollution toward a clean future. But especially since the 21st century when we have increasingly and readily available to us cost effective alternatives—in the forms of electric cars versus gas guzzling cars, renewable energy and battery storage versus natural gas and coal power, plant based packaging instead of plastics, soil health principles instead of nitrogen based fertilizers, heat pumps instead of propane and gas heating—not transforming our economy is not only uneconomical in the long run, it is unfathomable.

Who gives us the right to pass on to the next generation the dirty externalities of all the hidden public health, economic and environmental costs? We should have been and should now be paying the real price in goods of these costs rather than passing the buck to the future. At minimum, polluters should pay for the pollution they cause. In the most fair way possible, based on income and consumption level, we as a society should pay a carbon tax. We in the United

States, as the chart indicates, are the greatest historical emitter of greenhouse gas emissions, causing the most harm yet doing not nearly enough about it.

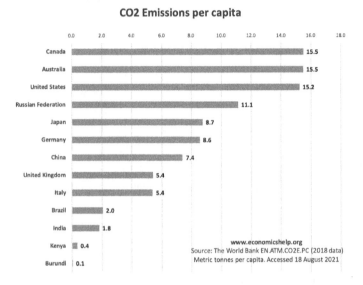

CO2 Emissions per capita

This is merely 2018 data but for all time the US is the greatest emitter of greenhouse gasses.

My dogs and I tried to do something about it by attending a relevant environmental protest held the second week of April outside the entrance to the New Mexico Governor's mansion. We walked from our home to the site of the rally. And then I listened. Only young people gave remarks and they all spoke very articulately about the urgency for action on climate change. They spoke solemnly and clearly about injustice. How their generation and those in frontline communities bear the brunt of our political cowardice. All the youth, who came from different backgrounds—from New Mexico pueblos and tribes, from regional high schools and elementary schools, from frontline communities—said half steps will not suffice. They were upset about the lack of any bold steps in the state legislature and particularly upset about the Governor's lame request for an exemption to President Biden's proposed moratorium on issuing any new oil and gas drilling and fracking permits on federal lands. "No exemptions. No waivers. No excuses!" Including the excuse about jobs, because as the young people pointed out there are many more jobs in the clean energy sector than in fossil fuels and they said astutely that as a society we can and must retrain blue collar fossil fuel workers for the new jobs in clean energy and sustainable technologies.

A climate protest outside the Governor's mansion.

These youth, along with the youth movement building around the world, reminded me of the prophets of old and made me think of the abolitionists. Think about taking half measures when it came to abolishing slavery and preserving the human right of freedom. Slavery isn't half wrong. It is all wrong and should have been abolished from the outset of our country, a nation supposedly founded on liberty. But we came up with half measures like the Three Fifths Compromise and the Missouri Compromise which only perpetuated a morally compromised half free and half slave society. Tragically and unjustly the legacy of unethical compromise continued since the Emancipation Proclamation and the 13th, 14th and 15th Amendments in the form of Jim Crow laws, segregation and more recently racial discrimination, police brutality and voting restrictions.

The climate crisis is playing out similarly. Is it okay to compromise on pollution: for the oil and gas industry to purchase offsets to go on emitting carbon dioxide, methane and nitrous oxide from the extraction, combustion and use of their products; for the fossil fuel industry to have immunity from liability in return for a carbon tax? No. We need to hold the oil and gas industry fully accountable and increasingly keep all oil and gas reserves in the ground as we fully transform our economy. We need a major push to sequester carbon in the soil, in expanding forests, and in the "forests of the sea." And we need a major push to phase out, boycott and soon ban fossil fuels and other leading greenhouse gas emission sources. We need full scale conservation and true carbon insetting where companies really lead by example instead of green washing. We need to do more than carbon neutrality, we need negative carbon emissions to reverse the climate impact we have been having.

We need to adopt the full on strategies illustrated in Paul Hawken's *Draw Down* (Reference) and the *Global Green New Deal* by Robert Pollen and Noam Chomsky (Reference). These solutions are not pie in the sky. They are achievable within the context of a capitalist economy. They can achieve the transformation needed in the urgent time frame that we have. The urgency is crystal clear. As the young people say, "We can't afford to wait!" "Half measures and exemptions will only hold us back!"

If we care to go forward, we would be wise to actively listen to the young people today and resolve the unethical dilemma of our climate and race relations. To do so we need to learn how to "walk humbly with God" as the prophet Micah advised. Isaiah, one of the most well known of the prophets, took this guidance to heart. He spent three years walking and not only that but walking barefoot dressed in rags. Walking in this manner to the extent he did showed his humility and the lengths he would go to earn the trust of ordinary people who were not easily convinced by the prophets' urgings. He gained credibility in the street to the point where not only is he a walking hero (Appendix 1) but for time immemorial humankind has been inspired by his words, the most famous of which are as follows:

> "Behold the nations are as a drop in the bucket
> and are counted as a small dust of the balance…
> But those who wait upon the Lord will renew their strength;
> They shall mount up with wings like eagles;
> They will run and not grow weary;
> They shall walk and not faint."
> —Isaiah 40

It is stirring and inspirational to read this prophetic poetry; it is heartening to know there is hope for the least among us and thereby hope for the restoration of all humankind. It is hard hitting to face that our nation is just a drop in the bucket, especially if we don't uphold our promise of liberty and justice for all.

Empires, like the Roman Empire past, along with the richest and most powerful countries in the world today, of course including the United States, may amount to nothing but dust if we don't transform ourselves. Neither our might nor our wealth will really matter in the end. They won't last. Rather, those who have nothing shall inherit the Earth. Maybe the time has come when out of humility we heed this message and orient our society, not around the greed of the well off, but around service and the rise of the downtrodden. What a beautiful prospect.

One week from departing on my walk northbound, while I was driving my then ten year old to school (he had just started in person learning after over a year being on-line), we saw the man we often see walking his dog up the hill who waves at everyone going by including us. It's a nice way to start the day receiving a wave from the man. The sad thing was one of his dogs was no longer with him, but the nice thing was that he was walking with a woman friend who had a dog of her own so there was hope. Speaking of which, my wife and I had a drink together that night at a restaurant (which by the way was the first time I was inside a restaurant since the COVID situation; since we were vaccinated it felt like a real treat to be dining out). Among other things we discussed that evening, she told me, kind of out of the blue, that it matters how we walk (in other words what we look like when we walk or the appearance of our stride). She said her mom waddles like a duck. She said we all have distinct gaits. It's important, Numi continued, that when you walk into places that you command the room (but without coming across as arrogant); rather being graceful and sure of yourself in your stride. It never occurred to me what I look like walking. I thought of my late grandfather Chet Robinson Young (CRY) who accentuated his bold legged-ness when he walked. He had a wry smile as he ambled along, demonstrating a lot of hand and knee action and often complaining about his "aching knee bones." I wondered if that was my destiny. That wouldn't be so bad, especially if I also carried on his extraordinary sense of humor.

Something that is not humorous but solemn happened two days before my pilgrimage. On April 20th the jury in Minnesota unanimously convicted Derek Chauvin on all counts for the murder of George Floyd that happened nearly a year earlier on May 25th 2020. The family spoke so bravely and eloquently after the ruling. George Floyd's Aunt said how dark that fatal day in May was and how the world came crashing down but she also said how touching it has been since because of the outpouring of love they received from so many—and she wondered if we could see that kind of love on an on-going basis. Reverend Al Sharpton spoke about how the current movement to bring an end to police brutality and guarantee equal justice under the law was in confluence with all the movements that have come before including the Underground Railroad. Hopefully this was not an end to a chapter but—as George Floyd's daughter said "my Daddy is going to change the world"—the beginning of something sustaining: the eradication of systemic racism in this country and the fulfillment of racial justice.

One day before my walk I read the announcement that President Biden would host a Climate Summit on Earth Day on-line with countries from all around the world. This news was bitter sweet. Sweet that the President of the United States was taking the climate crisis seriously. Trying to position the US to lead the world in climate solutions and setting a more ambitious goal than previous administrations by pledging to reduce greenhouse gas emissions 50% from 2005 levels by 2030 were good things. Sue Biniaz who worked with John Kerry, the climate emissary, said "knowing that we have an opportunity to actually make what I hope is a pretty big step forward, and almost a step change, really feels exciting." And it was exciting to have a rallying cry by the United States President, to know that the executive branch was trying to ramp into action, and to hear the words of Avril Haines the director of national intelligence that climate change should be the "center" of our foreign policy and national security. But the bitter part of all of this for me is the domestic side of the equation. The fact that, here at home, pledges don't get the job done. We need demonstrable action domestically. We need to actually change and enact laws! Can you imagine the efficacy of a voting rights and civil rights "pledge" instead of the Voting Rights Act and the Civil Rights Act? I just don't think it is appropriate that we tell the world what to do about the climate crisis until we step up and inspire the world by our own example. I think it is more appropriate at this stage to be humble about our leadership and showcase the leadership of others until that day comes when we put our money where our mouth is, when we make this a central organizing principle of American society, and when the United States congress passes bold and meaningful laws on climate change in response to the overwhelming urging of the American people. Then through our deeds we will change the world. We need to humble ourselves, not beat our chest.

The night before my departure the wheels started coming undone on my domestic front. My daughter, who had previously and happily agreed to help with Holden (drop him off and pick up from school and take him to his after school activity), started to back track; she asked Numi if she could do some of it, which made me upset because I knew Numi had a lot of work obligations. Then Numi and I got into a fight. She was disturbed about what I was doing and she criticized me for how I was doing it. She thought I was being self involved by not including anyone else on my first walk. I said that was merely because the state had cancelled the Easter pilgrimage because of COVID and I wanted to be low key out of respect for that. I said how the fourth walk was a community walk that I would invite people to. In the meantime through the newsletter for my non profit organization called Climate Change Leadership Institute (CCLI) I invited people to do their own walking project in solidarity.

Numi was also justifiably worried that I would try to fast during my long walk. Honestly the idea did occur to me. I thought it would be in the spirit of a pilgrimage to do that. Plus my doctor, who is super supportive of healthy living, and Sanjay Gupta even, had both said that intermittent fasting is a great way to strengthen our immune systems, but I acknowledge they did not suggest to fast in conjunction with walking long distances. And so I relented and agreed to take some power bars and bananas along with an ample amount of water. While she was right about making sure I didn't fast, and I conceded that, the arguing aspect of our interaction aggravated my sleeping disorder. This time, as I was trying to drift off to sleep, my mind was racing thinking about Numi not approving of my endeavor and I was beginning to feel insecure about the whole thing. Around midnight I turned to her and told her that I would have preferred her to be supportive, especially the night before my departure. She came over to my side of the bed and curled up with me. She said that she was very sorry, that she was just concerned about me and thrown off by my bewildering ways. And at the end of the day, she said she really did support my journey. As far as me not being able to sleep though, she deservedly gave me a hard time saying it's not like I was doing an Iron Man or flying a space ship in the morning. "You're just walking!" she said, and then we both laughed. It was good to be humbled by my wife the night before a quest for humbleness and human spirit.

I finally fell asleep and woke up four hours later at 4:30am. It was April 22nd, Earth Day! I got up, took a hot shower (Larry David would be pleased) and got outfitted, which consisted of: a comfortable tee shirt, long sleeve layer, an athletic style collared shirt (I like that I could raise the collar to protect my neck from the sun because my skin doctor said the back of the neck is where a lot of people get skin cancer), breathable pants with handy pockets, special edition CCLI tube socks, bandana (to add a layer of warmth on my bald head during the morning cold), broad brimmed hat (with a sun symbol on the front), and, sorry to say this, a fanny pack (packed with water, snacks, sun glasses, a mask, lip balm and sun screen and a little journal). Notably missing from my gear was my wallet which I was delighted to leave behind. I would have liked to leave behind my smart phone too but I put it in my lower pant leg pocket to have handy for some pictures. Finally set, I went to open the door and there placed above the knob was a note with hearts drawn on it from my daughter saying: "good morning and welcome to this exciting day. WALK ON. Love Feepers (the nick name I have for her). P.S. Very sorry to have complicated things. Don't worry though. It's all worked out." So with my domestic affairs resolved, I departed my house at 4:50 bound for Chimayo in Northern New Mexico about 26 miles away.

5
JOURNEY 1: THE CHIMAYO PILGRIMAGE

Stepping outside, I appreciate the darkness and the stillness in the air. It is surprisingly pleasant. I expected it to be chilly in the early morning. I walk down the driveway and turn right onto the gravel road heading upward. At the top of the dirt road less than a mile up I turn on to Bishops Lodge Road and I walk just to the right of the white line on the right side of the pavement. I prefer gravel but my running/walking shoes have poorly designed soles in the sense that pebbles keep getting stuck in them. There are no cars in sight. No sounds at all. I was expecting to hear birds but it is too early I guess.

The sign near the top of Bishop Lodge Road.

Soon I come to this sign that says I am on the very beginning (the northbound section) of the Old Spanish Trail. This was a 700 mile historical trade route that connected the trading hub of Santa Fe to other major western commerce destinations including ultimately Los Angeles. It was one of the most arduous of all trade routes and was traveled by Spanish explorers in the 1500s. I think these histories are cool on one hand but I am cautious. The rich cross cultural history of New Mexico is extraordinary and vitally compelling but on the other hand the deep wounds of colonialism inflicted by the Spanish and the White people on the Pueblos and other Native American tribes here have not really healed. Furthermore, the gentrification of Santa Fe has led to understandable resentment by Spanish, Mexican and other Latinx Americans whom used to live here much more affordably.

After a mile climb from my house, I get to the top of Bishop Lodge Road, an elevation of about 7500 feet, and I then descend into the Tesuque Valley. I was hoping to see stars, in particular the North Star, given that I am on the northbound direction of my journey. But I see no stars in the darkness. Instead I see lights leading to the entrance of a newly revamped five star Bishops Lodge Resort. It looks like it's about to open. I am sensing that the long economic pause of COVID 19 is about to end and the bustling is about to be back. Of course it is good for jobs and livelihoods to "be back" if that's what happens. But I wonder if just rebounding to the normal bustling economic activity is sufficient for the predicament we are in. Have we learned anything or are we just going to fly around and drive around and fuel our economy in the same manner as before? I think of the Jerry Maguire movie, when he stands up to his sports agency firm for not having values and makes a grand departure and then the elevator door closes with him in it and everyone in the office immediately gets back to business like nothing happened.

I pass a speed limit sign with a sensor that shows my pace at five mph. I do have a spring in my step but it must be because I am heading down hill now. I am liking this walking business. Soon I make it to the Tesuque River and I pause to listen. I take a deep breath in and exhale. The birds are out now, especially near the river and they are making their beautiful good morning sounds. It's delightful to walk along the river for a while. The sky has gone from black to a lovely pinkish color in the western horizon. I am thankful that I rose early enough to experience the beautiful transition from dark to dawn. What a precious time of day that I rarely notice because I am usually lying (often sleepless) in bed.

I pass the Tesuque Elementary School which features a bright sign that is flashing: "pre K is now open." More indication of the COVID restrictions fading. I pass the Tesuque Market, which is where my family and I and some friends are planning to have dinner tonight. I am happy to see along the way some signs like this one that helps for safety and raises consciousness about walking. Some cars are finally stirring and passing me on the road. I think of the man who waves to everyone while walking with his dog. And then I decide to start waving to the cars going by. I chuckle thinking that they must wonder "who is this walking nerd

Tesuque, New Mexico.

with a broad brimmed hat and his fanny pack waving at me and what is he doing outside before sunrise?" But for the most part, besides those in tinted windows whom I can't see, the drivers wave back at me. Waving is such a nice gesture that humans do back and forth, a gesture of our fellow humanity.

I go through the underpass below and then walk along the frontage road, with the peaceful Tesuque Pueblo on one side and the busy highway on the other. It's much noisier. People are getting going and heading to work. The sound of the cars is almost deafening compared to the stillness and quiet when I first started. Electric cars would be quieter, I am thinking, but there aren't enough of them on the roads yet. But just wait, that will change soon. I pass an abandoned, weed infested baseball field. The spring season comes to mind and I am hoping kids will go outside and play ball. Just then as I am thinking about playfulness, I see a worn white and black striped ball in the drainage area of the frontage road I'm on. I kick it loose and see that it's a MacGregor volleyball. And it occurs to me that perhaps God wants us to play in the Great Outdoors. So I kick the ball along with me as I walk. At first it feels awkward and it's upsetting my stride. But as I go along experimenting, dribbling, walking in pace with the ball, or tapping it so that it stays in pace with me, the ball and I come together and find relative harmony. I laugh thinking of my son Fisher's high school soccer team and how they should do this as a drill: walk dozens of miles on end dribbling an old volleyball. I laugh again thinking of Tom Hank's friend Wilson from Cast Away and my new friend MacGregor.

Encountering the MacGregor volleyball on the frontage road
along the Pueblo of Tesuque.

We pass the Buffalo Thunder Casino. It's been ages since I have been there. I like to play poker. I remember years ago on Good Friday I was there and one of the players had just returned from doing the Pilgrimage to Chimayo. Faith in God and playing Texas Holdem are not incongruous perhaps. Soon I am in the town of Pojoaque passing by the Roadrunner Diner, Julian's Barber Shop and El Parasol which has some good Mexican food. Since I don't have my wallet nor hardly any hair it doesn't make sense to visit any of these local establishments.

What is beautiful is that in being focused on dribbling the volleyball instead of the noise from the highway I have rather pleasantly made it through this rather unpleasant eight mile stretch along the highway. It's great when you can take your mind away from noise pollution. Music can do that too. I recall Holden saying that he learned from his music class at school that music is really soothing for the mind because it is one of the few things that integrate our left and right brains. Nathaniel Rateliff & The Night Sweats' Redemption song comes to my mind: "just set me free…while redemption seems far away, while I stumble though every day, just set me free…" and then and there I decide to assemble a walking related playlist for songs that come to mind during my four direction journey (Appendix 2). I ponder the Ecclesiastes song, "for everything turn, turn, turn, there is a season turn turn turn and a time to every purpose under heaven" (Appendix 2), and I make up a culminating line: "a time for playing and a time for seriousness."

So right after turning on to the beautiful Nambe/Chimayo Road, I stash the ball in the bushes and I get into a different mode. According to the signs, I am now on the High Road to Taos, heading eventually to some classic northern New Mexico communities like Truchas and Penasco. I am not going that far. El Santuario de Chimayo is ten miles ahead. Going through Nambe is lovely with large trees (including purple flowering trees) lining the road and views of the mountains in the distance. The cross cultural heritage is noticeable just by looking at the street names like "Camino la Familia" and "Poechunu Poe Road" which is Tewa language. The Nambe pueblo, an anglo American community and a Spanish speaking community are all in the same vicinity and to some degree intermixed.

The High Road to Taos.

After I go for several miles past the residential areas, the landscape changes, it becomes drier, hillier and more desolate. The walk becomes longer and more tedious. Since the shoulder on the road becomes much more spacious, when cars aren't passing, I start closing my eyes for periods at a time and focusing more inward. I am wondering if this pilgrimage is masterfully designed in that the more arduous it becomes physically, the more tired we become of our old selves, and the more ready we are for new possibilities. Now I have entered the Badlands of New Mexico, and the cold hard fact is there is no where to hide here. I am alone with my soul. One part of me is feeble and puny and another part of me is enduring and expansive. It's all mixed together. Walking on in some natural rhythm helps sooth me but I know I can't escape from the inevitable and two pronged truth that we go on and we perish.

The Badlands.

After making the turn toward Chimayo, now about three miles away, as I am still walking up the desolate road, a funeral procession comes past me in the opposite direction. A hearse leads the long string of cars. I check my phone for the time: it is exactly 12:00, high noon! Just then I pass a sign that says "Do Not Pass." And besides the obvious meaning for cars not to pass at this dangerous point in the road, my mind starts racing struggling with a potential deeper message. Does this mean do not die, do not die frivolously; does this mean—do not pass, in the spirit of Jesus—that when are body passes away our soul shall not pass but instead become everlasting? I do not know what the sign at this high noon hour means exactly, but I think of my good friend Lee when we used to take road trips around New Mexico together with our boys, we made a point of paying attention to the signs around us. I am paying attention now on this walk. On the hillside along the road I see a memorial with a cross. There is all this death and never dying imagery and it feels almost like a rite of passage. I am climbing the remaining uphill portion before reaching the plateau and descending into the valley of Chimayo.

A memorial cross right before the descent into Chimayo.

At the very top I see yet another sign: "Pass with care." This makes more intuitive sense to me on many levels. One level is: don't take life for granted, don't be careless. Another sensation that jumps to mind, from one of the Raiders of the Lost Ark movies, is: "only the penitent shall pass." Indiana Jones heeds the message to avoid getting his head chopped off. He bows down and passes through the gauntlet successfully and eventually makes it to the chamber with the Holy Grail containing the healing water of everlasting life. On queue I take out my water container and take a sip but it goes down the wrong wind pipe; I cough it all up and it sprays out of my mouth onto the ground. I realize then and there that I need to fast while I am in this sacred valley visiting El Santuario. And with all these heedings—the precession, the cross on the hill, the do not pass and pass with care signs, I understand that I need to be humble and to pass through this special place of the chapel with genuine consideration and respect.

I begin my descent. Only about a mile to go now. I see homes sprinkled along the hillside and other features of this quaint community. I arrive at the turn off and then proceed onto a little dirt road that meanders to El Santuario. It meets up with a lovely acequia flowing toward the destination. I pause again, close my eyes and listen to the water flowing. My mind is in synch with my body and spirit. I am ready. A few more paces and I come to the chapel. I have been here a few times before (once by bike and once by car), but this third time really is the charm. It really is one of the more charming places I have seen.

The picturesque and sacred Chimayo Chapel.

The adobe chapel was built in 1816 to honor Nuestro Señor de Esquipulas. Not surprisingly it was designated a National Historic Landmark in 1970 (which happens to be the year I was born and the first year Earth Day was celebrated). I take my time taking it all in and experiencing the layout. I then make my way to the Chapel and before I get there I meet two women at the statue of Father Casimiro Roca who was the first priest assigned to El Santuario back in 1954. He served the wider community, he served the church goers and he welcomed all the pilgrims for over a half century. The women's names that I met are Sharon and Maria Lisa (in the picture Sharon is standing and Maria Lisa is in a wheelchair). I ask the ladies if they knew Father Roca and Sharon says very much so: she has been coming here since she was a child, and loved it even more then because there was dirt all around. She did communion there and she says Padre Roca was an instrumental part of her and her late husband's life. She tells me a story of how Padre Roca joked with her late husband, both of whom were bald, that it is a good thing birds don't land on their heads because they would just slide right off. I took off my hat and showed Sharon my bald head and we laughed. Sharon says she would walk here from Española every Easter weekend. I ask her what the pilgrimage means to her and without missing a beat she says: "hope!" I thank the two of them for visiting with me and then just as we part, as I am about to enter the Chapel, Sharon calls over to me, "I will pray for you."

Sharon and Maria Lisa beside the statue of Father Roca.

I walk into the dark but cozy chapel. In the entrance is a hand written note on the wall that reads: "God = Love." Some visitors are inside sitting down, so I take the queue and take a seat. The moment I sit down, strain is lifted from my body. I bend over, close my eyes and unthinkingly take a little cat nap. I wonder if that's okay to do. Soon after I am feeling rejuvenated, I think about Sharon praying for me and I consider reciprocating in the sense of doing a prayer for others. I am in the perfect spot for it. So I keep my eyes closed and what comes to mind is to pray for those who have been harmed as well as those who have done harm (the Catholic Church could be included in this category). As far as climate change is concerned I am in the latter category, the harmer. We are all the former, the wounded, but those who have the least are being hurt the most. I think the wounded sooner than later are not going to take it any more and they are going to rise up like Isaiah prophesied. But those who have been wounding others—through a modern day version of colonialism, the culture of consumption and all the resulting pollution—I pray for us and our society to find the honest humility and strength to acknowledge the pain we have caused, to actively turn in a humane direction and redeem ourselves.

I stand up. I walk a little further ahead and look inside a small room adjoining the chapel: there are pictures of families covering the walls and there is a long row of crutches hanging from the ceiling. I think of Maria Lisa in the wheel chair. And I think, not everyone can walk but we all can be moved whether by acts of faith, restorative deeds or displays of humanity like Sharon is doing by wheeling Maria around.

A testament to New Mexico's multicultural heritage.

I head out of the chapel and outside I make my way around and down the stairs to check out the remaining aspects of the site. I pass a statue in tribute to New Mexico's three cultures—Native American, Spanish and Anglo—which of course is simplistic but still nice to give homage to a plural society. Further behind the chapel I come to the river, which is beckoning me. I find a shady spot under a tree. I take off my shoes and socks, sit down on the riverbank (again I feel the ahhh of relief in my body). I put my feet in the water and rest them on the mossy river floor. At first the ice-cold river water is startling but very soon it is soothing.

In honor of Earth Day I extend my prayer that started inside the chapel to the outside world. I pray for all living creatures/beings many of whom are being terribly impacted by humankind. The Greek Aeschylus phrase Robert Kennedy would quote comes to mind: "make gentle the life of this world." Birds are not landing on my head, like would be the case for St. Francis, but an insect is crawling on my hand. I find a twig that it can crawl on so that it can return to the bank safely.

My few hours at El Santuario are almost drawing to an end. With my shoes back on and my feet rejuvenated, I walk up the steps to the far side of the chapel and I see the pilgrim statue that is featured at the beginning of this section and I read the compelling tribute below:

> "Come Pilgrims from the four corners of the earth.
> The lord has invited us to walk to his shrine of love in Chimayo.
> Here we will find the 'holy dirt' that strengthens us
> and purifies the faith that takes away our pain."

El Santuario.

I reflect on this for a while next to the acequia which runs by the front of the chapel. I feel like this phrase—in conjunction with the experiences of this visit—hold clues to the journey I am on for personal, human and planetary restoration. A source of our regeneration is giving and receiving the 'holy dirt' that can heal and uplift us all. I think of the hand written sign at the entrance of the chapel: God equals love. Transformative love. I think of Micah's statement about what is required of us: to act justly, to walk humbly…and to love mercy. I am grateful. I feel in some senses restored but I also feel moved to turn around—not only to turn around my harmful impact, but turn around my way of thinking. At that moment I get up and I literally turn around to begin going back the way I came but with a new perspective.

Once I climb out of the valley, I resume eating what is left of my power bars and drinking water. I am pleased that sometimes there is a third way other than yes or no. In other words, I didn't have to fast the whole way and risk my health (and my relationship with my wife) and I didn't have to abstain from fasting the whole time. I could fast during the most sacred time in the Chimayo valley. In life we can look for and find a third way more often than we might think—if we are thinking transformatively.

I can see things in a new way going in the opposite direction. I have seen the ground. I have closed my eyes. I have seen both immediately in front of me and far ahead of me. I have even walked backwards for some moments and so in that way I have seen behind me. But I have not really taken the time to look

straight up. And so on my return I do just that. I look up and really see the sky above me. It's sensational with the striking blue and compelling clouds. I wonder why I don't look up more often.

We continually look forward, sometimes glance back or stare down but how often do we look straight up?

I make it back though the "challenging stretch" of wind and loneliness and badlands. I come back to the outskirts of the residential community. I pay attention to the large warehouse, which is part of the USDA funded food distribution center for the Eight Northern Pueblo communities. It has been getting a lot of use especially during these times. I think of the food depot in northern New Mexico where I have been periodically volunteering over these last few months. When I started in February there were lines of cars that went on for miles in order to pick up donated food. When I went in mid April, there was still definite need but the lines had subsided significantly and hopefully that trend continues.

Back in the village of Nambe, I pass a piñon fence through which I can see the most beautiful green pastures. I fanaticize about sneaking through the fence and finding a shady spot in the clean tall grass and going to sleep. I think better of it. The people who own the property also own the *Santa Fe New Mexican* newspaper and I laugh at the prospect of them either doing a story about my journey for the paper or arresting me for trespassing. I pass another speed sensor sign and this one flashes the message "slow down!" I look behind me to see if a car is racing toward us but there is nothing in range. I know I am not going fast so I chalk it up as a warning sign. I am getting close to the highway frontage road section and my feet are aching, one with a blister about to burst, the other with my big toe nail coming off. It may be that my walking has run its course for the day and my time is up.

I have taken 63,500 steps, I've gone about 36 miles and this is the longest I have walked in one day in my lifetime. I text my buddy Lee who said if I need him he would happily pick me up at the highway intersection and so while I wait for him to come I take a little rest along the river bank and then soon thereafter meet up with Lee at the coordinated spot. He kindly brings some Neosporin and bandages for my battered feet. Better yet he brings me a beer, which I gotta say tastes out of this world. We have a spontaneous and fun-loving conversation as he drives me to the Tesuque Village Market where I am having dinner; Lee drops me off deciding not to join, but until we meet again I take a parting picture.

My dear friend Lee and my new friend MacGregor.

6
REFLECTION

With the walking portion of the first leg of my journey complete, I spent some time following the walk in reflection. On Saturday midday, two days after the walk, I participated in a few hour workshop called "Walking with the Earth." The New Mexico Interfaith Power and Light organization facilitated the program on zoom. I happened to be the only guy participating, with Sister Brown, whom I really respect and some other women whom I had not met before whom were very thoughtful and kind. I participated in this because it sounded relevant and interesting and I thought it would help bring some closure from my first walk. I found the subject matter of the workshop compelling. The essence of it was to collectively explore aspects of grief and healing in nature as well as in our lives. I did not know I was feeling grief, although as I have said we are all broken and whole to varying degrees, but when it was my turn to share it all came out. We were asked to walk in our environment and look for a wound in nature and think about a wound in our own lives. We were then invited to commemorate some form of healing that could grow out of the grief.

Walking up the little hill behind my home I found the remains of a small tree which had been removed to make room for a walking and biking trail. All that was left above the surface was a little stump just a few inches off the ground. I felt it with my hand. I wondered about the roots that I could not see below and if they were still alive. It felt harsh to have cut down the tree, but then I thought, as far as healing goes, if we thank the tree for making room for the trail and if we appreciate the giving of the tree when we walk past that would help make some amends. When I told the group of women on zoom about this reflection, I proceeded to share a personal wound that came up for me. I shared about my mom and dad and how their lives were prematurely cut down—like the tree—by Pick's and Parkinson's respectively. As I was sharing this, I was sobbing in front of my computer screen. I could barely get the words out. I mustered the wherewithal to say that: "even though I am deeply hurt by the loss of my parents to these harsh diseases and while I miss them dearly, the healing part is that they carry on in me and I can live my life in a way that honors them and hopefully makes them proud." Still crying with every word, even more now, I said "I know in so many ways I come up short in my life, but notwithstanding that, in memory of them and the future of my kids in mind, I am seeking to help resolve the human crisis of climate change and assemble [from the cornerstones] a foundation for our restoration."

The workshop started and ended with a prayer in combined appreciation of Earth Day, Indigenous traditions and the collective work that we did that day. Paraphrasing a portion of the passage, it went like this:

> We offer a prayer to the Great Spirit, our Father Sky and Earth Mother
> In doing so may we understand that we are not the center of the universe
> but rather we dwell in a humble and hopefully balanced place
> Let us take every step with respect and humility before all our relations
> whom we honor by living lightly on the Earth
> Great Spirit, let us consider not what we say but how we walk
> whether we nourish paths for all creatures
> and give thanks for the mystery of it all
> Help us see that all beings are sacred and may we not take our lives for granted
> May we seek healing through grieving
> and redeeming the wounds we inflict on nature and one another

This prayer and all prayer is beautiful in its own right and serves a wonderful purpose. However our prayers if left alone may not take us to where we need to be. In *Walking with the Wind: A Memoir of the Movement* (Reference) written by the late John Lewis, he reflects on the importance of prayer and recites an old African Proverb that goes "when you pray move your feet." His lifetime was a prayer backed up by thoughtful preparation and momentous action. In this autobiography, John Lewis chronicles his upbringing in rural Alabama all the way though to his distinguished and dedicated public service as a congressman. The heart of the book is his participation in the Civil Rights Movement. When he was in between boyhood and manhood he witnessed the Montgomery bus boycott which moved him to take action more than any other event in his lifetime. He said "50,000 black men and women in Montgomery were using their will and their dignity to take a stand, to resist. They weren't responding with their fists; they were speaking with their feet…that kind of protest appealed to me, that felt very, very right (p. 59)."

John Lewis participated in extensive training from Jim Lawson and others in non-violent action. These were highly disciplined workshops imparting the non violent methodology. But these lessons flowed much deeper than just to be used as a vital strategy. He and his colleagues were learning "love in action," and "a way of life" going well beyond self determination. This was about "soul force" and "redemptive suffering" which are transformative ideals (p. 86) that are needed now with the human climate crisis as they are needed in our race relations. John Lewis in this book periodically quotes relevant passages of the Bible like: "Blessed are they who are persecuted for righteousness's sake, for theirs is the kingdom of heaven" and "Fear not them who kill the body but are not able to kill the soul." These are meaningful messages. But such biblical values only meant something to John if they were not reserved for hollowed church halls but actually flowed "out into the streets" (p. 382).

He was less interested in words and divinity and more interested in deeds (p. 141). Along with a fellow generation of courageous change-makers, John Lewis quietly and bravely took a leadership role in epic moments throughout the civil rights movement including the Freedom Rides and ultimately the Selma March in Alabama. There he led a peaceful march across the Edmund Petus Bridge which was met by brutal violence from the Alabama State Police. "Bloody

Sunday" as it was called, aired on tv networks throughout the nation, prompting indignance and compassion by the public at large and ultimately prompting the passage of the Voting Rights Act, signed into law by President Johnson just a few months after.

John Lewis, a champion for civil rights and a walking hero.
(Illustration by AuPalette)

The turbulent story of change-making carries on now when tragically the constitutional and legislated voting rights that were secured by the epic sacrifice of so many brave souls are not secure today because state legislatures in Georgia and Texas and elsewhere are wrongly limiting the unrestricted right to vote by BIPOC communities. The reason why John Lewis is included here as a walking hero (Appendix 1) is not only because the present day John Lewis Voting Act must be enacted and the civil rights movement revitalized. It is also because his and others' extraordinary dedication to mass movement epitomizes the power of the human spirit and the regenerative force of love. The enduring protest was faithful not only to the great cause of civil rights, but our common humanity and the path of non-violent action to achieve these aims. "Prayer is one of the most powerful ways of reaching out that humankind has" John Lewis says at the very end of the book, but he adds, to bring it into being "as a nation…we must move our feet, our hands, our hearts, our resources to build and not to tear down, to reconcile and not to divide, to love and not to hate, to heal and not to [destroy]" (p. 475).

The same goes for our prayers for the environment and a healthy resolution to the man made climate crisis. We need to mobilize in a mass movement to transform our society and adopt a more gentle invigorating footprint. It won't just magically transpire. We have to both step up to make it happen and, with equal regard to the restorative power that comes from nature, we have to step back to let it happen.

SECTION III
EAST, MOTHER NATURE

"Walk along the river, sweet lullaby, it just keeps on flowing
They don't worry 'bout where it's going', no, no
Don't fly, mister blue bird, I'm just walking down the road
Early morning sunshine, tell me all I need to know."
        —The Allman Brothers Band (Appendix 2)

7
PRELUDE

Nature along with the human spirit are powerful sources and cornerstones of regeneration. With her and our fellow humanity exist life forces and lessons that can restore the health of people and the planet alike. When we act in symmetry with nature, a pathway opens to solving our own spiritual crisis and the human climate crisis. We and the earth may ultimately thrive respectively when nature and humankind are intertwined in equilibrium. Being in interaction is key, and it is much different than us being driven by human nature or nature being left apart.

I am pivoting to the second stage of my quest which involves journeying east toward the sunrise to explore the remarkable realm of Mother Nature to gain insights for our collective well being. Before August when I will embark on my hike into the Sangre de Cristo mountains, I took some warm up hikes. Late in May I ventured out with my wife for several hours including a portion of the walk in an aspen grove. We gained a lot of elevation at the outset. Part way through, during the steepest part of our climb, she asked me, facetiously, if I brought her water. She knew the answer was no but she wanted to give me a hard time. As I said, I am not a gentleman yet. I am not the best (yet) at being proactive in my consideration. We have taken many outdoor adventures on which I failed to bring water and snacks. One time we did a cross country ski outing for a good five hours without any nourishment and all I can say is I heard about my shortcomings on the way home. I know I should think ahead just for the sake of being a good husband, but also I should do it to avoid the dog house where I spend unnecessary amount of time.

Gary leading us through an aspen grove.

Back to this current hike in May, I was considerate to Gary our French bull dog who I knew would have ample opportunity to hydrate at the midway creek crossing. The water from all the snow melt was moving along and rushing quickly. But not so quickly that I couldn't hear Gary slurping it up which is a wonderful sound that makes me very happy. Numi said "how come you don't take pride and joy—like you do with the dogs—watching me drink water and have the thoughtfulness to bring me some?" I said "we both should be ashamed (a standing joke of hyperbole between us that we use) that we forgot to bring water." And she said "no, it's your job to take care of me!"

Numi's actually very independent and not needing to be taken care of but like anyone, having some nurturing is important. I thought about Numi's mother, and how she has not been the most caring to Numi over the years, which unfortunately is an understatement. Numi for well over a year from that point had decided not to talk to her or engage with her until her mom stepped up to the plate and took responsibility by forging a loving, instead of a negative, relationship. I said to Numi that she was handling the tough situation with her mom in the best way she could by not engaging in the negativity and certainly not enabling it. Perhaps someday her mom would get the message and come around. Numi said she's not counting on it.

I extrapolated to the bigger picture and was thinking then that it doesn't bode well for humankind if we can't count on us as a human race to change and become more care giving to the planet. But I also thought, more hopefully, that those who are more able can fill in for those who may not be ready yet. We can be stand in care takers: both in my case for Numi and in our case for Mother Earth. We can reach a critical mass where society changes on the basis of a growing collective to the point where laggards will have no choice but to come around to the new way of being that will emerge. But I'm not naive about what we are dealing with here.

Human nature is a deep seated epistemology that regrettably and tragically has kept us more self centered, more severed from nature and has held us back from collective regeneration. Human nature so often inclines us to be more self involved to the point of digging in our heals rather than giving in for love sake. Human nature also seems to make us more focused on accumulating rather than accommodating, enveloping us to get ahead rather than encouraging us to come together. Consumption and convenience seem king in this way of thinking despite the harm caused by so much of our materialism. Polluting the planet is a byproduct of human nature's endless drive for more: more money, more things, more comfort, more conquest. But more is not real nourishment nor lasting fulfillment. We (mis)think that our security comes from having more rather than being more or tending more to the common good.

Our biological nature may be driving us—as it did for so many empires and dynasties that have become obsolete. We're also driven by the dominant culture, replete with the pressure of assimilation, the pride of colonization and the lure of conventional thinking. But are the prominent culture and our biological nature really our primary driver, our fundamental nature? To be a society so centered on getting ahead and rising up in a way that so much and so many are left behind in our wake? What kind of security is it if our mainstream epistemology coupled with our exorbitant lifestyle lead to a climate, human health and equity crisis fundamentally destabilizing and endangering modern civilization? This is not true security but rather the antithesis.

Rather than allowing our human nature to dominate our way of thinking leading to widespread insecurity, we could adopt a transformative way of thinking that works with nature and collectively secures our well being as well as a vibrant future. Composting is a good example of transforming to a more nature oriented way of living. When we let our food waste go into the trash bin and send it along to solid waste facilities as part of a wasteful food culture, this food waste converts into and exacerbates methane pollution at our landfills and methane, even though it stays in the atmosphere less than carbon dioxide, is a more intense greenhouse gas that of course majorly contributes to global warming. If on the other hand, instead of sending it to solid waste facilities, we collected our food scraps, the egg shells and the banana peals and all the spill overs and convert it into compost and use it to replenish the land, we help heal rather than hurt the world. Those food scraps mightily contribute to lush organic matter in the soil, feeding the microbiology below the ground and supporting healthy top soil which can grow food anew with greater nutrients supporting our sustenance. Pictured here in front of some mounds of compost is Tejinder Ciano who along with his wife created Santa Fe's very own Reunity Resources which is a farm and a major compost operation. For several years now I have been collecting my family's food scraps and delivering them in bins once a month to Reunity Farm, where it recirculates back into the Earth in our local community. Tejinder says it is all part of a virtuous "loop" further strengthening "our bond with nature" in contrast with the habits of our industrialized society. The restorative potential is compelling: "we're taking food waste, we're making compost, and we are using that compost to create healthy soil and that healthy soil helps create healthy food."

Tejinder Ciano, founder of Reunity Resources.

Another way of integrating nature into what we are doing, and a way of integrating our thinking, is by utilizing biodegradable or plant based packaging instead of using plastics. The oil and gas industry has pulled a wool over us convincing us to think somehow because it is so widespread that plastic packaging is a given, that it is somehow good like Apple Pie, and that it is a necessary part of our economic life. But the truth is not only are plastics very harmful to the planet, we don't need them anymore. There are more respectful, biodegradable and cost effective alternatives. The same goes for styrofoam, aluminum and many other energy intensive, nature harming products.

We also need to look at our consumption levels which are way off the charts and way out of synch with a healthy natural world and humankind. And that's a whole other discussion that is worth having. But if we are going to consume, which we have to do to a certain reasonable extent, we should pay for the true cost of our consumption and we should consume products that are made responsibly in terms of ensuring humane labor practices and minimizing the environmental impacts. We should also choose products that are more inherently natural. Renewable energy is an example of a much more naturally restorative product to meet our electricity needs as opposed to gas and coal which are destructive. Sunshine and wind as well as geothermal energy are powerfully enduring and readily available sources of energy. They don't create pollution. We can harness these clean and natural energy sources in combination with energy storage for 100% of our electricity needs, which will increasingly include all electric cars for the roads and heat pumps to warm and cool our homes.

Tabatha told me on a bike ride we took about the book she was reading at the time. Being on her gap year so far away from academics she thought it might be a good idea to read occasionally to keep her mental capacities humming. From the sound of it she chose a good book: *Sapiens, A brief History of Humankind* by Yuval Noah Harari (Reference). She told me the gist which is that as a human species we made a major miscalculation bringing forth the agricultural revolution. We as a species were in stride as foragers. As hunters and gatherers, we were very fit physically and mentally. We were more dialed in nutritionally. Our mindset was much more present and we were very alert in the moment. We were not controlling nature as our way of life but rather we were living more in confluence. We attended to the seasons and followed migratory patterns like so much in wildlife does. Not that we were devoid of problems. Not that we were perfect environmentalists; for example we preyed upon and brought on the extinction of many large mammals throughout the world. But we valued and relied more on vegetation and forests for our food including root vegetables, berries, nuts, protein rich meet.

With the agriculture revolution, we burned down the forest and the prairie grasses. We plowed the soil. We became sedentary. Domineering. Less healthy. More centralized. Less liberated. More at odds with, less in synch with, nature. It cost us then and it plagues us to this day—economically, physically, and climate wise. Just look at the implications of industrialized agriculture: the mono-cropping, tilling, wide scale spraying, the massive yields that come at a massive cost to the health of humankind and the natural world. Society's taking mentality is also costing us spiritually.

My then seventeen year old son Fisher, seemingly out of the blue one night, asked me to read out loud *The Giving Tree* (Reference) to him and Holden. Of course I obliged, knowing in the back of my mind what a fleeting opportunity this was to read to him, then a junior in high school, and to his younger brother at once. And in the reading of this epic book of course it is so striking how mankind takes so much from the Tree and gives back so little: we take her apples for money, we take her branches to refurbish our homes; we take her trunk for transportation; and to top it off we take her for granted, resting on her stump after we have cut her down.

There is a highpoint in *The Giving Tree* when there is a deeper, interactive and more harmonious relationship at work: when the man is a boy and the boy plays with the tree, gathers her leaves, climbs up her trunk, swings from her branches and even takes a nap above her roots. The boy and the tree love each other.

Similarly there was a time in my life when I freely engaged with and played in nature. When I was a boy growing up in the little mountain town of Gold Hill, Colorado, I played outdoors all day long and into the night. We explored the abandoned gold mine shafts. We played in tree forts hidden under the golden autumn leaves. In snow storms we'd go sledding on Suicide Hill or play hockey when the Pond was frozen over. In springtime I would catch tadpoles there and have picnics in the meandering meadows on the way back to town. We would play softball games above town on a field covered with wild grasses. In summer we would stay up late finding fun: whether sneaking into the Gold Hill Inn which we thought was haunted or sneaking up to the Trojan Ranch. Sometimes we'd sleep out under the stars. During the school year I would walk or bike to the two room Gold Hill School, where we spent as much time outside in recess, running around the school yard, as we did inside studying in groups. And while I did not master the three R's, we definitely mastered the art of playing outdoors, exploring and being care-free. We smiled in our surroundings and our little mountain town responded in kind.

Gold Hill, Colorado.

It turns out Fisher's request for me to read *The Giving Tree* was not out of the blue. For his school's English class he had listened to a podcast called On Being by Krista Tippett featuring Robin Wall Kimmerer (Reference). I was so glad he told me about the podcast because listening to it, as I did afterwards, is gravitational.

Robin is a member of the Citizen Potawatomi Nation and founding director of the Center for Native Peoples and the Environment. She says she was born a botanist because she loves trees and plants so much. As a child—as is the pattern—she played vigorously outside, and as she grew she become increasingly drawn to nature traditions and ecological knowledge. As a professor at the SUNY College of Environmental Science and Forestry in Syracuse, she has been intrigued about the different ways of knowing the natural world. While she knows the scientific names of plants and trees, she prefers learning their stories, which is a shift in worldview emphasizing mutuality. She resists calling a tree or plant an "it" because she knows that plants are not objects for our possession: they have consciousness and being-ness.

Taking what we need to survive and thrive is a necessary part of being homo sapiens she says but taking too much, much more than our share, like in The Giving Tree, is exploitation. "We have been captured by a world view of dominion and it doesn't serve us [or the world] well." But she says we humans have gifts that can be given in reciprocity. One of Robin's gifts is writing, and another is her way of giving attention to, listening to and learning from nature. "Do you love the Earth [think about how we could show that] and does the Earth love you back?" she asks. "It is a really liberating idea that the Earth could love us back." That's how the Earth treats us—"with the love and regard"—shown to us in the foods the Earth provides us like sweet strawberries for example. But with her love "comes a really deep responsibility" to live in symbiosis.

The podcast was so compelling that I decided to read in full Robin Wall Kimmer's majestic book *Braiding Sweetgrass: Indigenous Wisdom, Scientific Knowledge, and the Teachings of Plants* (Reference). Everyone should read it and would immensely appreciate it I believe. In her preface she writes about how Sweetgrass, called Wiingaashk in her native language, "belongs to herself" in that it is both wild and free. In other words it cannot belong to or be owned by us. But it needs us too. We can be interactively instrumental in braiding sweetgrass for basket making, spiritual ritual and/or a healing ceremony. In care-fully and creatively doing so "people and the land can be good medicine for each other." She goes on to say, "When we braid sweetgrass, we are braiding the hair of Mother Earth, showing her our loving attention...in gratitude for all she has given us" (p. 5).

She writes about the western world notion of land ownership versus the Indigenous way of sacred ground, land held in common (p. 17). Science pulled and pressured her to stand objectively apart from nature. Whereas her grandfather, despite being sent to a white peoples' assimilating boarding school to strip him of the native worldview, inspired her to connect with land and her Indigenous cultural roots. Her Potawatomi grandfather as it turned out walked from the Wisconsin forest to the Kansas prairie with her grandmother and she writes "the world has a way of guiding...our steps" (p. 44) just like she is guided by her native culture. But it is possible—as she embodies in her career and her books—to integrate science and Indigenous wisdom to the point where "...a whole human being...finds the beautiful path" (p. 47).

She writes that nature and humankind "are linked in a co-evolutionary circle...a sacred bond" (pgs. 124-5). She elaborates that if we can build our economy on ecology then our future can flourish (p, 153). With a graduate student she did a case study that reveals how sweetgrass thrives when it is harvested respectfully more than when it is not harvested at all (p. 162), in other words human beings are integral to nature flourishing just like nature is integral to humans flourishing. It's a regenerative two way street, a circular revitalizing path, and "all our flourishing is mutual" (p. 166), a confluence of "life flowing into life" (p. 194).

As we learn to walk in a way that each step is a tribute to Mother Earth, we can learn how to be human (pgs. 206-208). "This is our work, to discover what we can give" (p. 239), rather than just taking too much. The walking journey I am on is something I am seeking to give, and it can serve as a gateway to discover what I may be able to offer in a deeper on-going way. I think my natural way of being integrating is a part of the answer. I suspect the more giving we are the more whole we become, and the more whole we are the more clearly we know what we have to offer. But on the flip side, as we struggle and wander in between broken-ness and wholeness there is gift giving in the making by our being more understanding of the many people who are struggling likewise.

"We need acts of restoration, not only for our polluted waters and degraded lands, but also for our relationship to the world. We need to restore honor to the way we live, so that when we walk through the world we don't have to avert our eyes with shame, so that we can hold our heads up high and receive the respectful acknowledgement of the rest of the earth's beings" (p. 195).

"If grief can be a doorway to love, then let us weep for the world we are breaking apart so we can live it back to wholeness again" (p. 359). Robin says that a sweetgrass braid can be burned in ceremony for the sake of healing the body and the spirit (p. 301). Humankind could benefit from that ritual along with the many other steps of reconciliation; and of course in turn the healing of humankind would greatly benefit nature. I am drawn to Robin's point that, unlike the elements and compounds like water that do what they do, "people… have a choice" (p. 315). We can understand ourselves as students of nature, not the masters." We can consider the land as a teacher. Further still, we can actively engage in a new era of restoration which would enable a remarkable opportunity for partnership (p. 333). "It is not the land that has been broken, but our relationship to it…if we restore our relationship with the land, both nature and ourselves can be restored at once (p. 336).

One of Robin's main points is when we step back from our tendency to control "it" how much we can learn from and be in a rejuvenating alliance with "her," with Mother Nature. Let's consider Earthworms, for example. They can do what we so far have been incapable of doing. They can regenerate themselves and the world around them. Worms have a remarkable ability of living on even if they are split in half. If the animal is split behind the clitellum, the original tail parishes but the head of the worm may survive and the remaining body can regenerate a new tail. It is good that they can survive because alive they do wonders for the soil. They are considered keystone species because of how beneficially they influence the physical, chemical and biological properties of the soil. Among other stewardship wonders they perform, worm casts measure up to five times more in the amount of key nutrients compared to the surrounding soil. Worms heal degraded soil and healthy soil enables healthy food for us to eat, a vibrant ecosystem for us to live as well as resiliency for us to persevere. The list of their capabilities goes on and because of these and other compelling reasons I list Earthworms as a unique kind of walking hero for our world (Appendix 1).

We are not taking care of these incredible creatures whom take such good care of us. Rather we are harming the keystone species and their critical habitats. As proven in recent studies (Reference), the widespread use of pesticides is causing major harm to organisms like Earthworms, Beetles, Springtails, as well as to vital pollinators like Bees, that are all so essential for soil health and for our lives. Researchers found that farm chemicals are having an alarmingly negative impact on these unsung heroes.

So not only are we not learning from and working with nature like we could be, we are systematically harming nature. We have also been harming people who work in nature on the land tending to the crops and the harvest. The farm workers work so close to the land and the plants, to the point that they are intermingled, but we are not respecting them; rather we are severing them and systematically harming their health.

Holden regularly reads out loud with me for reading practice and one of the books he read aloud just before summer break was: *Who Was Cesar Chavez?* (Reference). For one thing, Cesar Chavez is another walking hero (Appendix 1). He together with many brave change-makers raised the level of humanity by raising awareness of the mistreatment of migrant farm workers. Not only have migrant farm workers been significantly underpaid, they have worked in grueling conditions, endured intolerable health risks from exposure to pesticides and other dangers and have faced a litany of unfair labor practices. Chavez and others did not stand for it. They organized, they formed unions, they picketed, they led strikes ("Huelgas"), they led boycotts (of grapes and other fruit and produce that were grown unethically. Cesar said that the boycott helped the public understand the value of food and the people who help bring it to our kitchen tables). Furthermore they fasted, they were incarcerated acting in accordance with their constitutional right to protest ("they can jail us" Cesar said, "but they can never jail the Cause")…and of course they walked to make life better!

In protest they walked all the way from Delano to the California Capitol in Sacramento. The local police chief and officers in Delano tried to block the walkers but Cesar Chavez who was leading the walk said they will stay the course as long as it takes and the police relented. The 300 mile walk took 25 days in all. During it Cesar's leg was seriously swollen, he had a fever and his back was in pain but he persevered and all the marchers persevered to the capitol. The march earned national media attention, new worker contract rights and thousands of new union members joined the cause. At the conclusion of the march Martin Luther King Jr. sent Cesar Chavez a telegram that said: "Our separate struggles are really one—a struggle for freedom, for dignity and for humanity."

Cesar Chavez. (Illustration by AuPalette)

What stood out and bothered Holden the most while reading the book aloud was how the landowners tried to intimidate the farm workers who were on strike by shouting at them, turning their dogs on them, threatening them with guns and, most glaringly to Holden and me, spraying them with pesticides! Completely inhumane. In converse, it is our humanity that MLK alludes to, that Cesar Chavez rose up in the farm workers struggle and that we must raise up in responding to the human climate crisis. What inspired Holden most about Cesar Chavez's story was how dedicated he was to the movement, and how "Cesar helped people not be brainwashed," Holden said, which is such an astute observation. Many of us in our society have been brainwashed into thinking that the degradation of people and the environment is a necessary part of our economy, and that we don't have agency to do anything about it. Cesar Chavez showed we do have agency. Our humanity, not human nature, can rise to the occasion to ameliorate the human and environmental condition.

I took another warm up nature hike with my wife. This time we went up to a waterfall. And this time I was more considerate to her ahead of time by having a water bottle with crisp cool water all filled up and ready to go. She said later that she appreciated it but wasn't as thirsty as the last time. Nevertheless, she wound up drinking the majority of it throughout the outing. I mistakenly suggested half way through that we take a longer route home which would have led us up a steep mountain climb and then eventually back down. Numi shot that idea down on the spot, irritated that I would bring that up without having snacks or energy bars on hand. I said it would only take an additional two hours but she said she would get hungry and I should know that. So I was half in trouble again. Brought water yes, brought snacks no. "Baby steps," I told her, at least I was taking baby steps at being a gentleman. My diversion suggestion was a humorous lowlight, but a refreshing highlight of our walk was feeling water droplets on our face when we reached the waterfall. Another highlight was just being together taking in the sheer beauty of the wilderness, the clear blue sky, the snow covered peeks, the lovely forest.

Aftermath of an avalanche in the Rocky Mountains.

One section however made us pause: it was where an avalanche had happened and caused devastation including a vast grove of trees felled in its wake.

It felt like a grave yard of trees, and I could only imagine that if an avalanche could up root these strong trees how it would completely wipe us out. Even though I knew the dead trees would regenerate into the land, and sunlight and nutrients left over would spring new life in the aftermath, I couldn't help but feel loss and feel responsible as a human race. We have heated up our atmosphere to the point where these avalanches, and other such dangerous climate change related weather events, are increasingly prevalent.

On a resilient note, there are many members of humankind that have turned natural disasters into rallying cries for change making. One young woman doing this very thing is Chante Davis, an organizer with the Sunrise Movement. She is among a sea of youthful activists that are rising up and she is another walking hero (Appendix 1). Chante witnessed, up close and personal, the ruthless warnings of nature. She experienced first hand three major hurricanes in her lifetime. She fled from her native city of New Orleans during Hurricane Katrina and moved to Houston where she endured Hurricane Harvey and Hurricane Ike. These "natural" disasters are so often caused or exacerbated by human created global warming and they are devastating. But Chante along with other courageous activists in her generation have responded with demonstrations of dignity. Chante and her companions have led student strikes, marches to Austin, Texas and a series of school walk outs.

Chante Davis was uprooted by several hurricanes and has since become a rising leader in the climate movement. (Illustration by AuPalette)

She said "the urgency is now." On why youth including her are having to lead this movement she says the youth are inspiring but she poses to us older generations, "why wasn't this done before?!" More recently she has been leading a 400 mile walk over 40 days from New Orleans to Houston. "We're going to march. It is time to set the movement in motion…I am marching to stop the climate crisis" she says and to "make sure we are prepared and protected from natural disasters." She continues: "This march is a symbolic gesture of me claiming agency over my future and as a climate refugee." Chante underscores how BIPOC and low income communities are getting hit the hardest from the climate crisis living in "unprotected areas when it comes to tornados, wildfires, snowstorms and hurricanes." Instead of being under siege from storm water or leading the gulf south climate movement, she would much rather older generations would have led the movement and she could pursue her passion of swimming in clean calm waters.

The summer was sailing by but not without incident. I was going to do my eastward bound hike sooner but I felt a little under the weather. I was feverish and felt achiness in my muscles and joints. (Does that sound familiar?). Even though I was vaccinated my family thought I should be tested for COVID, given how much the Delta Variant at the time was wreaking havoc. I took a home test which was negative. Then my wife was worried about Lyme disease because I had had a tick bite and so I took antibiotics (as well as probiotics) as a precaution. The spread of Lyme disease and COVID are alarming reminders of how we have been relentlessly encroaching on nature and how nature is biting us back. Reverberations are being felt all around including in the form of fire. Smoke was prevalent in the New Mexico sky when I was writing this book. There were no major wildfires in New Mexico that year thank goodness but the smoke was being transported in the weather from the latest California "Dixie" fire and other raging wildfires out west. Apparently seven of the then last eight major wild fires in California were more devastating than all the wildfires that raged during the previous hundred years. The warnings have not been subsiding. The writing on the wall is getting larger.

On August 9th 2021 the UN IPCC reported not just that the human race is clearly the cause of the climate crisis but that the window to avert catastrophic warming is rapidly closing. Greta Thonburg responded that we must be "brave", rise up from our slumber and treat the crisis like an actual crisis. Another of the books that Holden read out loud to me this summer was a biography about Greta Thornburg (Reference). She has ancestors that date back to an original scientist that founded theories on climate change back in the early 1800s. She has a condition known as Asperger's syndrome and while it plagues her, in so many ways it makes her stronger. For instance what is remarkable about her is how she is the polar opposite of being equivocating. From such a young age she has always taken this matter of the climate crisis with the utmost seriousness it deserves and has resolutely been calling for the bold action we need to meet the moment that we are in. All the old guard politicians and crony capitalists stare back at her blankly. They are desperate to maintain their feeble stranglehold on the world, a power grab that's built on corruption and denial, that offers only the lame responses of more status quo "blah, blah, blah," or at best compromise and incrementalism.

It's time I breath in some fresh air in order to think clearly and unequivocally. It's time to wake up from my slumber. It's time I take my eastward walk, on the Winsor Trail into the Sangre de Christo mountains and the Pecos Wilderness.

Of course before my departure, as there were before my first north direction walking journey, there were a few complications. The first complication came a few days earlier. I had just walked the dogs in the morning as usual and while walking home I had an idea. When I came into the kitchen to eat some granola for breakfast, Numi was at the counter next to me and I told her the plan I had conceived: we wake up at dawn the next day and hike the first leg of the Winsor Trail together from Tesuque to the Ski Basin (in time to take the blue RTD bus down I added). Arguing ensued. That night we were supposed to go out with our friends and Numi thought it was ridiculous to go on a long hike after being out late the night before. Furthermore she didn't believe me that I had her genuinely in mind for the hike; she thought I had come up with this for my own agenda and that she was an afterthought. Arguing about it wasn't getting us anywhere but things calmed down after I had a drink of Kombucha and read the words on the bottle: "There is power in who we really are that we don't need credentials for." Long story short: I let down my guard and became flexible—something I don't always do. It was not my way or the highway. It was not throw up our hands and do nothing. We decided, after I sincerely conveyed that I wanted to do this with her, that we would together do the first leg of the Winsor Trail hike two weeks later when the schedule worked better for everyone involved.

The second complication came the night before departure for the second leg of the Winsor trail which I was now going to do first. As I got into bed I checked my phone to see what time it was and I noticed a missed call and an unread text message. I guess I hadn't seen it earlier because I keep my phone in silent mode and don't check it all the time. Anyhow it was a message from my friend Lee. He was planning to walk to Santa Fe Baldy first thing in the morning with his father in law Peter and kindly they were going to give me a ride up the ski basin and we were going to hike a portion of the way together. But his text said: "Robb, we have to talk about tomorrow. I can't leave my house until 8:14. I'll explain but hope you can still join us. I know your destination is significantly farther and you needed to get an early start. I hope you can still join us. If so, we'll be at your place as close to 8:21 as possible." At first I thought it was a joke because he referenced "8:14" and the meet up time as "8:21" and that's something I do when I am joking around with him is suggest oddly specific meet up times.

But when I called him I learned it was not a joke. He said he had to stay at his house and watch his dogs until just after eight and I said "What the hell, I love dogs but I don't keep my dogs company at all times. We had a plan. You're changing it at the last moment." Lee went on to explain he's not just keeping his dog company but that he needs to supervise the dog because she gets seizures and she could collapse. And at that point, I immediately changed my tune and respectfully calmed down. I understood what I misunderstood a few seconds earlier. The tension eased. I thought about how incredible dogs are and how they always look after us and our well being. The least we could do is treat them with the same kindness and consideration. I apologized and became flexible, again something—like nature shows us—I am learning how to be.

8
JOURNEY 2: THE WINSOR TRAIL

With complications resolved, after a decent sleep and after the early morning organizing was completed, I venture out at 8:14 on August 14th for the second EAST direction of my journey bound for the Pecos Wilderness (doing the second leg of the Winsor Trail hike first). I depart my house with a well packed hip pack (I can't stand the expression 'fanny pack' so I am changing it). I was wearing my broad brimmed hat again and shorts this time. At 8:21, as stated, Lee and Peter pick me up just down the street from my house. We go up Artists Road heading toward the Ski Basin. I am reacquainted with Peter. I had met him at Lee and Brook's wedding some years ago. Peter's from Massachusetts and even though he's been living in New Mexico for a while, he still has a New England accent. He is a former military guy. He is a straight shooter with a good sense of humor. He went to Wesleyan, where my dad went to college, and he appreciates as my dad did one of the famous alumni Bill Belichick, the head coach of the Patriots, Peter's favorite team.

At the end of our thirty minute drive we discuss the ten essentials to have on a hike or camping outing. Holden knew nine of them when we went over it the night before. The list includes: Navigation (I have a map), headlamp (no, I am not spending the night), sun protection (I have sun screen and sun glasses), first aid kit (a concerning no), a knife (Holden cutely lent me his), fire (no, not sleeping over), shelter (this can include a bivvy sack or tent, and sense I am not sleeping out I don't have either), food (I have peanut butter crunch power bars and bananas and an almond chocolate bar that Numi gave me), water (I brought two white Oat Malk containers filled with water and placed in either side of my pack, extra clothes (I only have what's on my back—given that there was only sun and clouds in the forecast I skimped on this; Lee on the other hand brought a rain jacket; he was concerned about my irresponsibility on this one).

All this talk about preparation, I failed not only to bring first aid and rain gear but I also failed to go to the bathroom before I left home. You would think that is one of the most basic essentials to remember. Fortunately there is a public restroom at the ski basin by the trail head. But uh-oh, there is no toilet paper. Thank goodness for the excellently prepared military brass, because Peter has toilet paper and kindly gives me some.

With Lee and his father in law Peter at the Winsor trailhead.

At nine a.m. sharp we have a picture taken at the tail head and we head on our way. It's a climb right out of the gate and right away I am winded. I jokingly tell Lee and Peter that "this was great, but I am going to head back now." But as I catch my breath and quiet down, hiking away from the minor sounds and minor bustle of the parking lot, we emerge into this exquisite natural world all around us. Just moments after the commencement of the hike, I am blown away by the sheer beauty.

There is no better sound than water streaming down in the wild.

The whole of it is beautiful and the particulars of it are beautiful. Wildflowers come into sight. Water is flowing. The trees rise above. Moss grows at our feet. I say to Lee and Peter. "Do you ever fantasize about walking barefoot on moss?" Peter answers first: "no…but I like to walk barefoot on the beach." He tells me about one of his favorite destinations called Ixtapa Zihuatanejo in Mexico. With the ocean in mind, Lee mentions the new Kelly Slater surf ranch in California (and elsewhere) and how you have to pay as much as $10,000 to visit the park and ride some of the perfect—artificially manufactured—waves, which is an oxymoron. It seems increasingly like we are manufacturing nature but hopefully we don't take the real thing for granted.

I think of the documentary Numi and I and Holden started watching the night before called *100 Foot Wave*, about Garrett McNamara's journey to ride the biggest waves ever ridden at Nazaré, Portugal. His wife's statement stands out most in my mind. After she fell off her board while surfing and experienced the life threatening turbulence of the crashing wave, she said somberly and declaratively for her future: "I am not taking breathing for granted!" As we head past the wilderness boundary, departing the Santa Fe National Forest and entering the Pecos Wilderness, I am breathing in and out, not taking Mother Nature for granted!

How now black cow.

We crossed the second and third creek, that magical sound never growing old. We see giant black cows super close to us and to the trail. I think it's peculiar in wilderness lands to see them. In fact I don't think livestock is allowed in the wilderness but I learn later that people who had permits to graze when this was national forest land were grandfathered in. In any case I am marveling at these huge, hearty and healthy cows. Lee says they look "super tranquilo." Two and a half miles along we come to an intersection at Puerto Nambe. Trail 251 heads northeast toward Baldy and Trail 254 heads southeast toward the Pecos. We take a break there in the meandering meadows. I eat a banana and peanut butter power bar, and give one to Lee who eats it along with an apple that I have been eying. He saves his sandwich, "his hiking treasure," for Baldy Peak. Peter snacks on this new gorp he found at Costco. At 10:56 Lee jokes, because I have been making notes along the way, "I think you should write something in your journal before we depart in four minutes." I take him up on it saying and writing at once "I just had the pleasure of hiking the Winsor with you two kind gentlemen."

Camaraderie one way, solitude the other.

And now, after we carry on heading out on our respective trails, I have the pleasure of solitude in nature. Beforehand I reflect on the human interaction in nature that just passed. Bonds were formed. Memories were made. An acquaintance became a companion. A strong friendship grew stronger through the vitality of this experience as well as through our shared good humor.

After I leave Lee and Peter and after leaving the upland area of meadows, I soon arrive in what feels like a new ecosystem all together. I am now descending. I contemplate being on my own in nature which is another oxymoron because we are never truly alone. There is life all around—especially out here. But I see fallen trees off to my right and I think about the conversation I had recently with Holden that he initiated about when we pass away. "What happens then?" he asked. "I don't know" I answered. We talked about different theories. He wondered if we rejoin our loved ones passed? He hoped so, and I hope so too. Is there some luring brightness in the heavens he wondered or is there just darkness that we go to like when we go to sleep he pondered. I mentioned the Buddhist philosophy, the idea of non attachment, the cycle of birth, rebirth and eventual enlightenment. We talked about how patient and Buddhist-like trees are not only during their lifetime but also when they pass; they open up room for other life to grow with the space in the canopy they leave behind.

Fallen trees hold symbolism.

He asked what my intentions would be with my body when I pass away. I said I liked the idea—like a fallen tree—of an out in nature burial, replete with a biodegradable bivy sack. Alternatively I said, since it would be easier for my descendants, I could just have my ashes placed at a special spot. I mentioned Nama in Gold Hill. I mentioned the apple tree in Montauk and the larger tree in Central Park where the ashes of Great Grandma and Great Grandpa and Grandpa Gerry were scattered. I think about how Holden has been emotional lately thinking about Grandpa Gerry. How they share traits in common athletically and otherwise and how sweet it is that he thinks of my dad in a tender way. Mainly I feel thankful that Holden is exploring his emotions and able to talk about vulnerabilities in a non fearful, relaxed manner. It's natural to be pondering these kind of questions.

Just now a bird lands on a tree next to me. I pause my walking. Her head moving up and down repeatedly as if she's checking me out and sizing me up. She comes closer, hopping off the tree limb and landing on her spry feet on the trail immediately in front of me. I sincerely wonder if she's going to fly onto my shoulder or onto my hand because she's standing so close already and she seems intrigued to want to get closer. But before I have the chance to experience for the first time what St. Francis experienced countless times, I spoil the moment by reaching for my phone to take a picture and of course the bird darts away. I learn my lesson: be in the moment rather than try to capture the moment. I learn also from dozens of baby butterflies to stay still when I am observing them rather than move closer because they inevitably fly away when I encroach.

Baby butterflies.

I am realizing with every creature I come across and with every step I take deeper into the natural kingdom how wonderful it is here! It's as if we live 30 minutes from nature's equivalent to Disney Land. And without hoards of people. It is so uncrowded here. I have only seen a few others the entire morning. How is this possible on a Saturday in mid August? I have to pinch myself.

After a steady descent, at about high noon, I arrive to Spirit Lake in all its majesty. The last time I was there it seemed more like a pond. That was with Numi a few decades ago before we were married. We hiked there without any food (my brilliant idea) and with just a bivy sack and one sleeping bag for the two of us (another one of my brilliant ideas). It's a wonder she married me after that. Needless to say we didn't spend the night. We hiked back out before dark and got back to town just in time before the pizza place closed (it was a nondescript restaurant but, with how hungry we were, the pizza tasted like it was from Heaven or Naples if I had to pick a place in this world).

Spirit lake is lovely this time and, as I said, much more full of water which is a good sign. I can see trout swimming below the surface. I take off my shoes and socks and place my feet on a bed of moss, which feels so soothing. I rest a moment and then try to meditate—thinking that's what I am supposed to do at Spirit Lake—but I hear women's voices in the background and I struggle to concentrate. Instead I put my shoes back on and slowly make my way around the lake.

I set off again on the trail heading northeast toward the other lakes in the valley. I realize that the name of the three most prominent ones—Spirit Lake, Lake Katherine and Stewart Lake—all signify tenets for restoration: Spirit Lake for kindling human spirit; Katherine Lake for honoring Mother Earth; and Stewart Lake for summoning stewardship. My hike today is a testament to these regenerative forces, and while it is not an extraordinary length, only about 16 miles, it is accessible to all. We all can connect to places of nature like this and in doing so rise to the occasion. As I am walking and pondering, a young man passes and quietly nods as if he agrees with my thoughts. Simultaneously, a wood pecker makes his customary sound which I take as a sign of approval.

Nature and man can coexist if the latter is unobtrusive.

I cross another soothing creek, and at the crossing point a man sits on a rock bathing his feet in the cool flowing water. I marvel at his disposition while I ask directions to Stewart Lake.

Later on I realize either I did not listen well or he did not guide me well because I find myself three quarters of the way up a trail bound for Katherine Lake instead. I know this because I meet up with a couple led by a trusty old beagle and I ask if the dog had just taken a swim at Stewart Lake. They said no. They say they just came from Katherine Lake and that Stewart Lake is down further southeast of where we were. I thank them, promptly turn around and get back on track. I am now thinking it is best to listen to a combination of people (the couple) and Mother Nature (the beagle) than to listen to just one man alone. It also would be wise I'm thinking to have referred to my map, which would have corrected me sooner. And then I pass the sign where I made the mistaken turn and I realize if I looked at it closer I would have known because someone scribbled, in small writing, that "this trail leads to Lake Katherine."

It's important to pay attention to and carefully read the signs!

As I walk, I carry a little journal and pen in my shorts pocket and when I have a thought that I think is worth noting I take it out and jot it down. I am deciding now to call this Walk Writing: contemplative expressions while ambling along through the great outdoors. It's present tense, spontaneous, reflective and basically stream of consciousness journaling (with the bonus of having actual streams around for inspiration). Whatever I call it, the notion of doing in motion poetry outside appeals to me. I think my mom would appreciate it. She is the original and best poet in the family, although my step dad Stampa should not be discounted. He is a professional writer who in the twilight of his life has turned his writing focus fully on poetry which he's giddy about it.

Creek Walking.

I am now hiking down the Winsor creek trail which feels like "creek walking" because it's so effortless and spectacular like I am a piece of bark floating down, weaving around the mossy rocks with sunlight sparkling off the water; like I am floating barely off the ground with my feet skimming wild flowers and red berry bushes. The breeze on my face, the gracefully flowing water, the sky bound trees, the cooling sensation of shade during the hottest part of the day…The wonder land keeps magnifying step after step.

Stewart Lake.

I arrive at Stewart lake, and of course I am not disappointed. Harmony is a word that comes to mind. Refreshing is another, as I dip my head and face in the gentle run off from a small waterfall at the southeast side of the lake. I re-apply sunscreen and lip balm (with SPF 30), and I take a drink of water from the Malk container. Stewardship, it occurs to me, is caring for and replenishing our environment in the same manner as we tend to our well being.

Just around the bend lies an equally enchanting but hidden lake which has no name that I can find. It features an exceptional reflection. It's low lying location and the trees surrounding it must shelter it from the wind, enabling a greater tendency for glassy waters, and thus reflection. Also the water is alluringly dark. I am happy to be greeted here by a blue dragonfly who is acting like the maitre d' for the lake: welcoming me with a paperless menu of delights to ponder. I am moved by her hospitality, how Mother Nature can still be so inviting to us after the way we have treated her.

Hidden Lake.

At the outskirts of the these waters I see a wild man with a big beard running—In all sincerity he looks like Forrest Gump. He stops for a moment to talk directions with me. While he didn't know the trail names from Adam, he has a clear idea of where we are each going: him in one direction and me in the other. He is kind to pause his long distance run to navigate with me. And as he points the way which is what I needed for confirmation, I feel deeper confirmation that mankind is not a selfish bastard; we like the natural world actually do have the capacity to aid, to guide and to care for each other.

At the fork I turn right and commence the final leg of the journey on the Winsor Ridge Trail. It's hard not to notice the uprooted tree beside the trail. The extensive root system is fully exposed giving me a sense of what goes on beneath the ground's surface. I come to another tree that's hard to miss. This one is standing upright, deeply rooted and massive. I stop to wrap my arms around her trunk but I can only reach so far around.

Rooted and massive.

Further along on this new trail, I again notice changes in the ecosystem. More view-sheds, a drier environment, more meadows, less tree cover, more sun exposure. I am glad I reapplied sunscreen. And I am glad I have experienced so many variations of the Pecos Wilderness: the alpine, the creek line, the lakes, now the ridge-line. What a day I am having. It feels like I have picked the single best day of the year to do this hike. Nature is in full bloom and showing all her glory. It's is not too hot. Clear skies, with only occasional cloud cover.

The different trees create a tapestry.

A tapestry of lime green aspens and dark green pines enlivens the rolling mountain below as I descend past more meadows surrounded by more aspen groves. Silliness comes to mind from my stream of consciousness, and I say out loud, to both myself and the surroundings, "Hello Wellness!" I chuckle because this expression is not just the sensation I am experiencing right now but also the name of our close friend Erin's mental health consulting business. And it's fitting this synergy because there is no doubt that nature heals and rejuvenates our mental, spiritual and physical health. Erin was recently on the radio speaking on the topic of mindfulness and climate change. She said on one hand we can feel dauntingly overwhelmed by the climate crisis, and even under assault, to the point where we either become numb or we react in a fight or flight type mentality—which is not conducive to solving the problem. But on the other hand, she said, if we are calm and in focus we can rise to the challenge, drawing on mindfulness resources and bringing forth our best selves.

An opening to mindfulness.

I take what Erin says to mean, even though we have different degrees of trauma and hurt that can make us more defensive and reactive, which hold us back during times of great need, there is a more invigorating inner power and a deeper reservoir we can all tap into that can help us prevail.

In this moment walking down the trail I encounter a true symbol of this combined strength that can aid and guide us. The symbol is a young aspen tree growing right beside the path. There is promise and gentle pureness in a young aspen. At the same time there is solidarity in the way aspens grow in groups and feed off one another. I reach out and place my hand on the tree. At that moment I am overcome with emotion. Several crosscurrents of feelings and thoughts run through me. My mom comes very much to mind. She always loved aspen trees and I understand why. I feel her spirit as I hold the tree and tears start flowing down. I don't know what to say except that Mother Nature can help heal our hurt souls and work wonders when we connect with her, honor her and listen to her, and when we remember her.

Connectedness.

I feel lighter on my feet, as though I am liberated from the weight of disconnection. I begin to hear music playing in my mind. Vivaldi Four Seasons (Appendix 2) is what my juke box selects and it's a fitting selection for the occasion. It's certainly upbeat as I stride along. It feels right for the surroundings, but when I gaze at the canyon below another fitting song comes to mind: my daughter's song called Canyons. A smile comes to my face, thinking of the serendipity and synergy from one generation to the next. What I love about this song of hers is the interplay of the environment and human beings. The idea that nature's and our own stark divides can come to understanding through relationship. She wrote this song inspired by the Grand Canyon and Zion national park which she visited with her best friend. I sing aloud some of the lyrics: "Our love is up close to understand. We tear our earth apart when we can. And it's simple and it's elegant. And they think it's damage but it's our canyons" (Appendix 2).

Now nature's own music takes over. The sound of the afternoon breeze blowing. Crickets chirping. Endorphins kick in and the rest of my senses come alive. I watch intently every scene that I pass by and presently I am seeing a sea of ferns all around me. Mesmerizing! The ground below my feet comes into greater focus. I am blown away witnessing dandelions (at the stage when you can blow them) the size of baseballs. I smell sweetness in the air. I encounter purple flowers that have sprung up on either side of the trail. I am inclined to touch them so I do: gently reaching out as I walk letting my palms brush the flowers one after another. They are so soft and soothing to the touch. They don't seem to mind me. On the contrary maybe they like me as I like them.

Exiting the Pecos Wilderness.

I reach the final stage of the walk before reaching the Pecos River. I am amazed that over the six mile stretch on this Ridgeline Trail I have not encountered one human being, on such an exquisite day. How on earth can I have this all to myself! I feel lucky, and inclined to be sharing the experience in my walking journal for others to enjoy.

I am glad I started the day off hiking with Lee and Peter. And I am looking forward to doing the first leg of the Winsor with family in a few weeks time. I am also grateful for experiencing some solitude in nature. The bottom line is that nature is restorative and the more who enter this realm—alone or together— the better for our well being; and the more whole our well-being, the better we will treat the environment. I pass the sign exiting the Pecos Wilderness. I descend through the grasslands and eventually I arrive back to civilization witnessing the first of log cabins and homes since I left Santa Fe. Kids are playing in the ponds and creeks below. I hear the voices of families enjoying the outdoors. I feel the anticipation of seeing my three kids. I am so happy to be greeted by them because I am doing this journey for restoration in part for them as well as future generations. They do not deserve to be inheriting a deeply wounded earth.

Reconnecting with my kids
at Cowles Ponds.

I first see Fisher who is setting up his fly rod in front of the car in the parking lot. He is so immersed in what he is doing that he doesn't notice as I sneak up and give him a warm embrace. "No way" he says and I say "yes way!" Embracing my kids, swimming with them in the river, watching them fish at Cowles Ponds and seeing them interact and play together brings joy, hopefulness and a sense of relief as well as a deeper sense of resolve and determination.

I love that Fisher and Holden both love Fly Fishing. What a great way to be out in nature. Holden says, "We have to be quiet and careful and thankful to succeed." That's some wise advice for all of us.

Fisher and Holden fishing.

The second leg of the nature walk was completed and so now for the first leg of the journey which commences from nearby our house in Tesuque and climbs to the Ski basin. This is the beginning of the Winsor Trail.

A week before August 28th, the date Numi and I had planned to do the first half of the Winsor Trail together, we were on a camping trip and I played and defeated Tabatha in a game of backgammon. The stakes were if I won she would join us for this hike. Afterwards she said, quoting a phrase by Rosie Peres that I have used many times, "sometimes when you lose you really win!" On August

25th, however, it seemed like no one was winning. I had another argument with Numi about my stubbornness and selfishness regarding the walking journey. We were like a broken record. In fact I wondered, how on earth was I supposed to advance human and environmental wellness if I can't even keep my own house in order?

When we dug down a bit further she was upset at me that the walk was evidently going to take eight hours instead of four and a half which is what I had told her originally. We went to sleep arguing about the whole thing and that's never a good way to sleep peacefully. But of course she fell asleep no problem and slept soundly while I tossed and turned. I could understand her feeling that a rigorous ascent for four hours is manageable but eight hours would be a whole other story. In the morning (of August 26th) I shared my idea which I thought would help: we go on the Winsor hike but she and Tabatha turn around after an hour or two if they wanted to instead of hiking all the way to the ski basin. But that didn't resolve the matter. The heart of the matter was that Tabatha was leaving to college in a few days and Numi was having concerns related to that, which I can totally understand. I got a text from her that said: "I don't want to fight. I will be positive—I'm just stressed about Tabatha leaving and I don't want her to get sick and overwhelmed before she leaves. I love hiking and being with you and am always up for an adventure. I just need you to be clear that this is really about what you are trying to accomplish, and we can join you for your hike, but it's yours not ours."

It is true that I didn't want to do a different hike with them like Nambe Falls even though it could have been more reasonable. I wanted to do the first section of the Winsor in accordance with the journey I had already initiated (and even altered in order to be flexible). And I was clear and unapologetic about that. At the end of the day, I said to Tabatha and Numi, that I would sincerely love them to come, and I could make accommodations, or they could decide not to come at all and that would be okay too; I wouldn't make them feel bad about it. I just said my piece and suggested they let me know one way or the other by Friday night, which was the eve of the hike.

They got back to me earlier. Numi called me around lunchtime on Friday to say they were up for joining me but on two conditions: the first was they wanted to depart leisurely at around 8am; and the second was they wanted me to spot a car at the ski basin. I was okay with the leisurely departure, even though I preferred to set out at the crack of dawn. On the second matter, I wanted to take the RTD blue bus back down so we wouldn't have to use a car but Numi was saying that they didn't want to feel pressure to have to arrive atop the mountain at one of the three pick up times (12:30, 2:30 or 4:30). I much preferred to have them along on the hike than to be stubborn about the car situation. So I chose to be accommodating, which is what Mother Nature is. The good news was that later that afternoon I was able to drive up the mountain, spot the car and catch the RTD blue bus back without needing a second car and person to take me down.

On Saturday morning, at last the day of this long anticipated hike arrived, I woke up early. I walked the dogs (since they weren't coming on the hike), made sandwiches for us and helped organize the water and gear situation. Maybe I was taking another step toward greater consideration. It's been a slow progression and sometimes a regression. At seven I woke up Tabatha by walking into her room and quoting my mom: "The mountain is in you!" She woke up without complaint but I learned later that she had just had a nightmare earlier in the morning. Numi too, the great sleeper that she is, slept "terribly." It seemed they were both dreading this hike.

Amazingly, even after some milling around time, we manage to set off from the trail head in Tesuque right at eight o'clock.

A map of the Winsor Trail.

The morning sunlight is streaming in from the trees. The air temperature is perfect. Tabatha comments that she didn't realize how nice it is to hike "so early." We talk about how real this outdoor experience is compared to in middle school when Numi and I did something called "Wildcat" which was cracked up to be "adventurous camping" in the "mountains" but really we were just wandering around the hills of New Jersey. We are really lucky to have such great outdoors at our finger tips. We not only revel in it but we acknowledge how much more there is to explore that we haven't experienced yet.

Some people are hiking down past us and they stop to caution us that they saw bear poop on the trail up ahead. Tabatha takes the warning in stride, saying to us if we encounter a brown bear to be big and boisterous compared she says to a grizzly when you are supposed to be still and curl up in a ball if chased. We joke about the fact that if Tabby and Numi didn't join me this morning I would have started at the crack of dawn and probably been mauled already by this or another bear so I thank them for wanting to start later and saving me.

Smell the bark.

The girls go in and out from talking about meaningful things (like Tabby's upcoming college journey) and superficial things (like blow drying their hair). But they also appreciate the nature around us: they pause at the trunk of a large tree to smell the bark. They claim that the aroma is delightful and strong. I have trouble picking up the scent and wonder aloud if I have COVID.

Taking in the magic of morning.

A biker comes by and pauses beside us, curious if we are hiking all the way to the ski basin where he came down from. He is happy to hear that we are going all the way up. He shares that he has been biking this trail for 40 years and that this is one of the more exquisite days he can remember. We appreciate how calmly outgoing and un-jacked he is. There are some people who boast about their adventurousness and he certainly isn't one of them. I let the girls know how quietly hard core and agile they are. They brush it off but it's true; they hold their own out here. I tell Tabatha the story of her mom in college. How she was a city girl, who used to never hike or exercise outside but when she went to CU Boulder all that changed after her freshman year. She went hiking (sometimes running) in the mountains every day and on the weekends she would go on vigorous mountain bike rides with a hard core and fun crew. If it wasn't for that outdoors college experience she and I probably wouldn't have connected and live together out west.

It will be cool to see what new experiences and endeavors Tabatha explores in college, which who knows could help shape her direction. But let's not get ahead of ourselves: the present path and eastward direction is in focus. Tabatha says "with all the shade from the trees, there is no need for sun protection." I did bring sunscreen of course, and sun glasses and a hat. I also was carrying a heavy bowl of fruit salad that Tabby wanted to bring. It is significantly weighing me down and the juice is leaking out. I keep joking about it—how cumbersome it is. Thankfully Tabby wants to take a break and eat the fruit salad. We find a good spot in a little meadow, and I do my best to eat as much as I can to take the carrying weight off. We only manage to eat half of it, but Tabatha finds an opening in her pack to carry it the rest of the way. I have never felt so free. Tabatha on the other hand regrets taking a break because now her legs feel like jello she says.

Changing ecosystems.

The hike to this point has been extraordinarily beautiful. The ecosystems have been unique, even stunning in many places and we have been walking along the Tesuque river the whole time. Now we depart from the river and get to higher and drier ground. The trail is also getting steeper now. Numi says, also perhaps experiencing the jelly legs sensation after our break, "perhaps the novelty has warn off." She asks me what I think about hiking now and I say, because my endorphins have kicked in, "I love it." I also say, "what's weird is I love the feeling

I get from walking but I used to hate hiking when I was young." I ask Tabatha what she thinks of it and she says she doesn't like to talk about it, she likes to just do it. But all the talk we had leading up to this day she says turned out to have a silver lining: it is not nearly as daunting as she was expecting.

The notion of ease and dis-ease enters the fold. Numi mentions that she didn't realize how these two words and their meanings are connected until now. On queue Tabatha shares some of humankind's deeply wounded heritage from the *Slavery and Justice Report* she is reading for Brown (Reference). How a dark history of slavery, grave mistreatment and lack of acceptance of people of color as well as rampant racism was so prevalent at most of the nation's "best" colleges and universities including the Ivy League. There is so much we need to learn about the ramifications of slavery she recounts including what the African continent could have been without the ravages of colonialism and the slave trade. She says there is such a compelling case for reparations not only for African Americans who were so wronged but also for all systemically oppressed peoples. Native Americans too deserve reparations but money is not what they seek: they want their homelands and sacred lands returned and, as Tabby elaborates, "you can't put a price on that!" She reiterates that we have a jailing and criminal justice system (that is so backward) but we don't have a just or fair system to properly deal with the egregious crimes being committed against humanity.

Embracing a new era and leaving time behind.

The time is ticking for us to right our wrongs including right now with such rampant environmental injustice happening. Just today the news is that the more exposure to air pollution there is, the more likely people are to experience brain related illnesses including a much higher incidence of chronic depression. It is not everyone that is equally exposed to air pollution. People of color and low income communities are exposed at much greater rates. Also today the news is that hurricane Ida is about to slam into Luisiana and the Gulf coast as a category four with sustained winds of 140-150 miles per hour. The governor of Louisiana said how this could be the most powerful storm to hit their mainland since before the civil war. And we all remember the visuals of Hurricane Katrina and the communities that were most devastated.

Numi says, while we continue walking upward, that we have overcome a lot of bleak times and grave challenges in the past. She recounts that in the 1980s something poignant in her memory was the threat of nuclear war that kept her and her classmates up at night the way the climate crisis and racial injustice keep Tabby's generation demoralized. But Numi's broader point is hopeful and important to remember. We have overcome a slew of dark periods and major challenges throughout history, like the Black Plague, the Civil War, the Spanish Flew and Nazi Germany for instance, and therefore we can overcome the climate crisis and the crisis of racism plaguing us today.

The conversation turns personal and there is the unspoken feeling that we are at a crossroads with Tabatha given that she is about to set off from our home. We as her parents know that this is an important walk of passage together. Numi says: "Tabby, you are an incredibly strong person and need to know deep inside that you can handle whatever life throws at you." My message to her is similar: "Don't hold back or limit yourself. Soar! We want you to lift off, and we are always here for you and love you so much."

A series of mountain bikers cruise down the trail about to pass us. Tabatha anxiously calls on us to "step back and step aside" so we don't get in their way. One of the bikers tells us that they just came from the blue bus / RTD shuttle which is waiting in the parking lot. I am relishing the fact that I needlessly spotted the car and the fact that the hike took us only four hours as I initially indicated it would. Numi to her credit acknowledges that she over reacted and apologizes for putting me through all that pre-hike torment. I give her a hug in appreciation of her and her acknowledgment.

At a crossroads with Tabatha.

A hug in appreciation.

As it turns out Numi and Tabatha both agree at the end of the day they would have rather done this hike together than one that would have been closer by and more reasonable. We are in agreement that this has become our hike rather than my hike. Numi even says that next year we should do a hike like this together with Fisher right before he heads off to college.

Given that we have the car spotted we have some free time, Tabatha and I seize the opportunity to take a stream plunge and then we all enjoy a leisurely picnic together. Our hunger takes over and we devour the sandwiches and snacks that we packed. The only thing we don't finish is the bowl of fruit salad (which Numi is humorously holding in this picture at the end of the hike)!

At the top.

9
POSTSCRIPT

It is self evident that our hike coupled with my first walk into nature—which together completed the full span of the Winsor Trail—was not at all Herculean. The total steps and miles of the two legs amounted to: 64,645 steps and about 27 miles which is not insignificant especially through the mountains but it certainly is not earthshaking physically. As I have said, this four direction walk—while unique in its own way—is deliberately accessible. It is something the community and our fellow humankind can hopefully wrap their feet around (excuse the pun). That said, there are several members of our human race who have done or are doing extraordinary length nature oriented walks for a deeper cause. While they all deserve acknowledgment, there are of course far too many to mention in this journal. But I do want to highlight a few here to honor what they they have done and to consider what they have said about it.

Connor DeVane a documentary filmmaker who did Hike the Divide.
(Illustration by AuPalette)

For example, Connor Devine is a young man who endeavored on a 3000 mile trek along the entire Continental Divide Trail to raise awareness about the need for climate action. What caught my eye—among other things about this amazing feat—is that he completed his journey right here in the southwest of New Mexico in the Gila Wilderness (Reference).

Lucy Barnard is an Australian citizen trying to become the first woman to walk the length of the world from one pole to the other, from Ushuaia, Argentina to Barrow, Alaska (Reference). Only a few men have walked from pole to pole. What impresses me is not only her endeavor to be the first woman, and the courage that takes, but she is also the first to do this with a dog by her side. Wombat (pictured here) and Lucy are a remarkable team. She said, "Wombat brought purpose to the expedition. We shared the sorrow, fatigue and restlessness, as well as the joy, accomplishment and the greater expanse of the wilderness—who without, I find myself walking alone." It took her three years to traverse about half the way including the length of Argentina, Chile, Peru, Ecuador and into Columbia where she had to suspend the journey due to COVID traveling restrictions. What she reflected on along the way stands out to me as a very important insight:

"It's easy to forget that the whole planet is a system, that all life is part of a biotic web…when you walk a long stretch of land you witness how different ecosystems overlap and ease into one another, you can see that state lines and borders are arbitrary lines…hiking is a window into the reality that the divide between humans and the natural world is just a myth we have been telling ourselves."

Wombat. (Illustration by AuPalette)

Of course there are those throughout history who have done epic nature walks including John Muir, who has been called the father of American conservation but who has also become controversial for reasons I will just begin to explain below. In 1867 he undertook a thousand mile walk to the Gulf of Mexico, going from Louisville Kentucky to Cedar Key Florida (not to mention dozens of other extensive walking journeys he took in homage to the land). At 29 years old, he was "joyful and free," going 20 miles per day, trying to find "the wildest, leafiest and least trodden way." In his written account called the Thousand-Mile Walk (Reference) he wrote that what we don't see matters. "The universe," he said, "would be incomplete without man; but it would also be incomplete without the smallest transmicroscopic creature that dwell beyond our conceitful eyes."

While Muir should be acknowledged for his outsized contribution to helping safeguard the natural world, he and his followers also should be held to account for the troubling disregard for BIPOC communities that they displayed. In fact one of his great legacies—being the establishment of Yosemite as America's first National Park in 1872—also reveals a great stain on his and America's character. This place and other majestic lands pursued for conservation were violently seized and ruthlessly colonized by the United States government and stolen from Native Americans. So many national parks including Yosemite were the original homelands and sacred lands of Native American tribes. There is a legitimate movement underway to return the parks to the management and oversight of the Tribes (Reference) who dwelled on these lands long before this nation was even conceived. I think there is merit and justice in this idea. And there are plenty of counterarguments as well (Reference). Perhaps there is a third way, instead of simply leaving the parks in the control of the US government or rightly returning them to the first peoples inhabiting these sacred places. Perhaps we could establish a collaborative co-management of the national parks by the rightful relevant Tribes in tandem with the United States government and people.

While the governance structure would need to be determined, and there would of course be significant complications that would have to be worked through, there is promise here and precedent in the world for this kind of approach. In New Zealand for example there are designations known as "Mataitai" reserves and "Taiapure" areas which are estuaries and other vital places by the coast which the Maori people have traditional ties to that are now co-managed by local Maori communities and the New Zealand government.

There is a combination of preservation (restrictions on commercial fishing) and traditional harvesting that makes for a dynamic stewardship which I highlighted in my graduate thesis entitled *Kindling Tikanga Environmentalism: the Common Ground of Native Culture and Democratic Citizenship* (Reference). The essence of my graduate work and this more current idea is to take better care of the environment and advance our fellow humanity through shared leadership by Indigenous peoples and democracies collectively managing enchanted lands in common. Reciprocity, a respectful give and take relationship, as Robin Wall Kimmerer encourages, could arise as could the age old and brand new quest for restorative integrity.

The movement, both returning important lands back to Native Americans or co-managing lands, is starting to take root. Jim Robbins wrote a story (Reference) about how this trend is growing with advantageous impact for nature and for people. The story highlights the Salish and Kootenai Tribes who are reclaiming lands near Yellowstone and co-managing the National Bison Range with success because there is more respect for the animal and more intimate knowledge. Likewise, the Nature Conservancy through the Indigenous People and Local Communities program is involved in land and management transfer back to the "original stewards" who have deeper ties and more experience dating back "millennia." Similarly there is an effort underway in Maine called First Light returning to Wabanaki Confederacy Tribes access to lands through land trusts for traditional hunting, gathering and ceremonial purposes. Across the country in California there recently was a transfer of land involving redwood forrest and steelhead salmon back to the Esselen Tribe who will both protect natural values, i.e. supporting the regeneration of salmon populations, and use the land for traditional rituals and plant gatherings. While not all cases prove better for conservation, most do and thinking "holistically" through an Indigenous approach tends to pay dividends long into the future.

The US Department of Interior, which houses the National Parks, Bureau of Land Management and Bureau of Indian Affairs administering the nation's trust responsibility to the 574 federally recognized sovereign tribes, is becoming more actively engaged in the growing initiative of collaborative management of lands by Native Americans and the government. In 2021 the US Department of Interior along with the US Department of Agriculture which houses the National Forest Service began taking more formal and official actions to bolster Tribal co-stewardship of public lands and waters. This growing initiative is incorporating Tribal capacity, expertise and Indigenous knowledge into federal land and resource management.

There is no more fitting Secretary of the Interior for the rise of such developments than the stellar and inspiring one currently in office named Deb Haaland. She is the first Native American to serve as the Department of Interior Secretary and previously she along with a representative from Kansas were the first two Native American women elected to the United States Congress. She represented a swing district in New Mexico no less. Deb Haaland is an enrolled member of the Laguna Pueblo, and comes from a family that served in the United States military. I had the great pleasure of presenting her with a climate leadership award when she was running for Congress. What is so impressive about her is how she has always stayed true to her beliefs, maintaining a strong stance for environmentalism and human rights during her career and throughout her general election when politicians tend to be more mainstream.

Deb Haaland by her example shows the vital importance
of standing up for one's beliefs.
(Illustration by AuPalette)

I am concluding this journal section featuring Deb Haaland because she epitomizes the ideal of honoring and learning from Mother Earth. She is one of my walking heroes (Appendix 1) because she walks the walk. She signed the No Fossil Fuel Money pledge, she opposed Wells Fargo's funding of irresponsible oil and gas projects, and during her run for Congress she left the state and paused her campaign at a crucial time to go to Standing Rock on the Sioux Reservation to join the Dakota Access Pipeline protest. She stood up for all the Water Protectors and protestors who were standing their ground. She served as a volunteer cook and supported the health and well being of those who were present in this vital movement. Before we can truly walk for a purpose greater than our selves, we need to know who we are, understand where we come from, figure out what we believe in and ultimately, like Deb Haaland, we need to stand up for our beliefs and carry forward our heritage.

SECTION IV
WEST, HERITAGE VALUES

"Heritage is our legacy from the past, what we live with today, and what we pass on to future generations. Our cultural and natural heritage are both irreplaceable sources of life and inspiration."

—UNESCO

10
BEFORE

When I started the heritage values section of my journey in the fall there were many coincidences, the first being that September 15–October 15 is Hispanic Heritage Month. This is a national celebration to honor the history, culture and influence of past and present generations who came from Spain, Mexico, the Caribbean and Central and South America. The day of September 15 is significant because it is the anniversary of independence for Latin American countries including Costa Rica, El Salvador, Guatemala, Honduras and Nicaragua. In addition, Mexico and Chile celebrate their independence days on September 16 and September 18, respectively.

This is directly relevant to New Mexico because fortunately there is an active, extensive, and growing presence of these communities here. Our current governor Michelle Lujan Grisham is the first Democratic Latina elected governor in the US and she says this occasion is not only a chance to celebrate culture but also "reflect on our ongoing work toward justice and equality." She's "following in the footsteps" of those before her by, she says, "working to promote equity in every sector of life in New Mexico."

I honor this occasion by highlighting the life of Dolores Huerta, who is another one of my walking heroes (Appendix 1). She, like her parents and grandparents before her, was born in New Mexico and lived in a coal mining town called Dawson. As a little child she grew up wanting to be a flamenco dancer. Her father was a leader in the United Mine Workers Union and Sugar Beet Workers unions which left an indelible mark on her, but for all intents and purposes her mother was the one who raised her. From growing up during the Depression, living responsibly and helping those in need became automatic to her. She said, "the thing about New Mexico is the whole idea of service to others...if someone needed help you had an obligation to help them." And, even though she moved to California when she was still young, she says: "I still have a lot of that New Mexico philosophy in my veins."

Dolores Huerta became a teacher and then went on to become an activist first with the Community Service Organization and then working arm in arm with Cesar Chavez in protesting migrant farm worker conditions and forming the National Farmworkers Association. To say she was hard working is an understatement. She not only worked grueling jobs to provide for her big family, which ultimately consisted of eleven children, but she also found the time to dedicate herself to 'La Causa.'

Delores Huerta is a strong proponent of nonviolence and ardently opposes public apathy, believing that we all have the power to make a vital impact. She said: "Each of us has a voice, how can we use it for social change?" She also said "Walk the street with us into history. Get off the sidewalk" (and off the sidelines). The most important place to march she says is to the ballot box. And, she cautions, "we can (and should) march until the moon turns blue but we must turn our social justice convictions into laws in order to make a lasting difference." Then well into her nineties, Delores Huerta has epitomized the heritage values that can fulfill our country's promise of liberty and justice for all: the values of hard work, service to others, democratic citizenship, dedication to family and many more. At the end of the day, she says, "we are all brothers and sisters, we are all cousins, we are all related." Her belief in solidarity and the other referenced civic virtues are all part of a deeper and more powerful river that we can tap into to heal and restore as a people.

As we honor hispanic heritage and Latinx communities—which again I thank goodness have a strong representation in New Mexico—we should acknowledge the burdens facing them. In keeping with the focus on climate and health, Latinx communities have been and are being disproportionately exposed to pollution in the United States much more than the broader society. There are also so many Central and South American refugees desperately trying to migrate to the United States to flee more dangerous living conditions, increasing drought and food and farm famine, caused and exacerbated by climate change. These frontline communities know too well what environmental injustice means. Because of these dire circumstances and because of their daring values Latinx communities are becoming a unique brand of stewards and have been coined "cultural environmentalists" (Reference). That is, as Evette Cabera chronicles, they regularly tap into the cultural traditions of their ancestors—the ingrained conservation practices of their mothers, aunts, uncles, and grandparents, perhaps dating back even to Mexico's ancient Aztec Civilization that at one point was zero waste and had an elaborate system of recycling all organic waste back into the soil and their food crops. Caring for the commons is part of Latinx heritage which has for so many descendants become second nature: closing the fridge, limiting the AC, turning off the lights, eating all that is on your plate, making use of leftovers, sharing what you have, saving or re-using, sewing your torn clothes rather than buying new clothes, using left over water from the shower to water plants, and so on and so forth. These are heritage values, which we all hopefully will subscribe to because to solve our pollution problem we can't just rely on clean technology, although it is essential, we also need to rely on such habits of the heart.

I had the great fortune of not only being close with, but also learning these kinds of values from, my grandparents. They likewise lived through the Great Depression and could certainly be described as thrifty: they saved, they re-used, they rarely wasted anything, they lived modestly for themselves but were very generous to all of us in the family and to those in need. My grandmother named Mary Strasser Hirsch was barely five feet tall but she was larger than life. My dad, her son, regularly used to recite the quote "it's not the size of the dog in the fight but the size of the fight in the dog" and I equate that to my grandmother. She volunteered for fifty years at the local hospital in her neighborhood. And when I was working with at risk Native American youth, forging trust and encouraging life affirming opportunities involving education, their culture and wellness, she told me to take pride in the work that I was doing. She knew that mutual gestures of humanity, shown day in and day out, overtime make a difference in our collective lives.

Her husband, my grandfather Leonard Coe Hirsch, was a big influence on me as well. He was a gentleman through and through although he called himself "even tempered: always angry." It's likely no coincidence that he was an avid walker. When my older brother and I were staying over he'd walk us to the park where we would play wiffle ball or he'd walk us to a neighborhood building with a brick wall where we'd play paddle ball. I remember him taking a walk every day, like a ritual. He'd bring along a small transistor radio, listening to music some of the time but most of the time listening to current events or public policy which was his passion. He too is one of my walking heroes (Appendix 1).

My grandparents Mary (known as "Pixie") and Leonard (known as "Monk") Hirsch.
She, notwithstanding her small size, had an outsized impact on us
and he is one of my walking heroes.

The picture features my grandparents while they were visiting me in Washington DC when I worked at the US State Department for the Bureau of Oceans, Environment and Science. I did this kind of environmental policy work in no small part because of their influence, the ethic of conservation and value of public service that they quietly bestowed.

Their habits of the heart have become engrained in me. Thinking of my grandparents, and influences becoming engrained, I recall Gandhi's quote which starts with the importance of a positive attitude—something my grandma had in droves—which leads to positive habits and eventually to positive values which become our destiny! Let's draw upon our ancestors, from at least one relative hopefully, or from someone special in the greater community alternatively, who influence and guide us in the direction of integrity and revival.

Someone special in the world who already has influenced so many including me—and hopefully will continue to influence all of us to renewed action—is Nelson Mandela. One of the most inspiring stories I have read is his autobiography called the *Long Walk to Freedom* (Reference). In it, he writes, "there is a saying: 'Ndiwelimilambo enamagama' (I have crossed rivers). It means that one has traveled a great distance, that one has had wide experience and gained some wisdom from it." (p. 74). Nelson Mandela journeyed far, starting as a child in a traditional Thembu village and coming of age in South Africa as a lawyer, a leader of the African National Congress and a freedom fighter battling against apartheid, the harsh and inhumane system in support of white supremacy, which alarmingly is rearing its ugly head in our country. Mandela's powerful opposition landed him a life sentence in Robben Island prison which lasted him from the age of 44 to when he was 71 years old. The uplifting culmination of his journey was his subsequent release and extraordinary election as the president of South Africa.

From all his life experience there are some takeaways, pillars that we can draw on in our current movement(s) for racial and climate justice. A wisdom, he initially gained from his father and deepened from his participation in the struggle, is to never tolerate unfairness and ardently rebel against crimes against humanity (p. 6). His ultimate wisdom was that the journey doesn't stop with the attainment of liberty but begins anew in the quest for responsibility in freedom, which the United States and other democracies should take to heart. Another lesson from Mandela, that we could likewise benefit from today, was his optimism in the face of adversity. As he writes: "I always knew that I would once again feel the grass under my feet and walk in the sunshine as a free man. I am fundamentally an optimist....Part of being an optimist is keeping our head pointed toward the sun, one's feet moving forward. There were many dark moments when my faith in humanity was sorely tested, but I would not and could not give myself up to despair" (p. 341).

Nelson Mandela was upbeat about the gathering forces of liberation including the power of widespread education, which he calls "the enemy of prejudice" (p. 439) and the antidote of ignorance. Another such force is humanity itself whereby even in the depths of oppression you see, as Mandela describes, "the heights of character" (p. 542) exhibited by the brave and unselfish sacrifices of so many extraordinary as well as ordinary people over the course of this transformational history.

The then newly elected President Nelson Mandela congratulating the Afrikaner rugby player Francois Pienaar after the South African team won the World Cup. This picture is emblematic of the teamwork and unity we direly need to solve our intractable challenges. Incidentally and humorously, Mandela writes in his biography that he played sports for the love of the game, "not for the glory, for I received none." (Illustration by AuPalette)

Nelson Mandela displayed utmost humanity by talking with the enemy, the white ruling class that imprisoned him and tortured so many of the African people, and working out together a democratic governing solution that was unifying. The Truth and Reconciliation to follow made sure not to forget the devastation that was caused by apartheid, so it could heal and not happen again. All the while, thanks to Mandela and so many other dedicated people, the ideals of forgiveness and empowerment were co-planted deep in the heart of South Africa which created opportunities for restoration. Mandela espoused the important understanding that "the oppressor must be liberated just as surely as the oppressed" (p. 544). This understanding—and all the other lessons of his life story which he began writing about to inspire young people—are true gifts, heritage values, that we can draw upon if we wish to unify, to heal and overcome pressing challenges and divisions that we face today.

September 21st, 2021 was serendipitously sandwiched between the Harvest Moon and the autumn equinox. The term harvest moon came from the notion of farmers being able to extend harvesting with the help of the full moon that continued offering sufficient light after sunset. The fall equinox is special because it is precisely the middle point between summer and winter, between the period of the longest daylight and the period of most darkness. Possibilities arise when we intersect the seeming stark contrasts of this world.

I love fall. For me it's the most compelling of the seasons. The transition of colors: green to yellow, yellow to orange, orange to red. The refreshing temperature (not too hot, not too cold). A sense of purpose and busy-ness in the air. Fall, October 18-22 in particular, is when I will be taking the longest walk of this four direction journey. I will depart from my home in Santa Fe and journey westward some 160 miles to Chaco Canyon, home of the Ancient Puebloans and a major center of ancestral culture between 850 and 1250 A.D. It's no fluke that I am going there. It is a stellar embodiment of culture, environment and heritage, I'm told. Indeed it is one of the few World Heritage sites designated in the US by the United Nations Educational, Scientific and Culture Organization (UNESCO). I am going there to pay tribute to the traditional ancestors as well as the Tribes and Pueblos who are all together essential to flourishing on earth and to the regeneration of life in our greater culture.

It is essential to our collective healing, to our survival and to our utter well-being as humankind that we consider and heed the perspectives, the lessons, and the heritage values of Indigenous communities.

One lesson that Indigenous communities have exemplified is that we are all deeply interconnected. Not just human beings, although that lesson needs to be known now as ever, but all of life is interconnected. "The well being of one is linked to the well being of all." Robin Wall Kimmerer knows this all too well and focuses much of her works on the promise of such relationship. In her traditional language she sacredly uses the phrase "Kee" or the more widely known "kin" (plural) to describe our natural ancestors (Reference). A parallel in New Mexico is how the Pueblo and Tribal communities refer to corn, beans and squash as the "three sisters" because this vital trio of foods has an origin and special history here of providing sustenance, nurturing and teaching kinship.

Plants are considered our original ancestors and teachers. In Robin's original book, *Gathering Moss: A Natural and Cultural History* (Reference) she delves into the remarkable heritage of moss, which she calls our original "kee." As a stark comparison: modern man is only 200,000 years old; Ardipithecus, the first human like primate group, the first to begin standing upright and walking outright, is just six million years old; Moss is 350 million years old! "What is it that has enabled them to persist…through every kind of catastrophe, every climate change that's ever happened on this planet, and what might we learn from that?" she asks. The answer is they collaborate, rather than compete. They interact well with rocks and water, hard and soft. They are closely intertwined in symbiosis with a cross-section of life including salmon, humming birds and redwood trees. And so they thrive in bio-diversity. According to Robin's research, one small handful of moss from the forest floor contains 150,000 protozoa, 132,000 tardigrades, 3,000 springtails , 800 rotifers, 500 nematodes and 200 fly larvae. Mosses are exemplars of survival. They endure and flourish because they are nimble, they give to the ecosystem more than they take from it, and they stick together (there are 22,000 species of mosses).

We can and must learn from both our ancient as well as our more current ancestors—including plants (who have lapped our time on earth a thousand times over), animals and old school humans, and Indigenous communities alike—if we care to likewise survive and thrive on earth. In her epilogue *Braiding Sweetgrass*, she concludes with images of dancing, the sound of drum beats and a refrain: "our elders say that ceremony is the way we can remember to remember." I take this message to heart. I again thank my son Fisher for encouraging me to read Robin Wall Kimmerer's deeply stirring and insightful books, and I remember that Fisher also wisely recommended I read another enchanting book called *Ceremony* (Reference) that's also directly relevant to the journey for regeneration.

The exquisite writer of *Ceremony* is Leslie Marmon Silko, who is from the Laguna Pueblo in New Mexico. She has mixed ancestry (Laguna, White and Mexican) and the story she tells is about a young man named Tayo, also of mixed race (White and Laguna) who returns to the Pueblo after serving in World War II. His war experience was totally devastating emotionally and psychologically. He struggles to overcome post traumatic stress disorder (PTSD) and he has a deep longing to find a sense of belonging in his community. He is also encircling a broader life or death quest for healing in a drought ridden society, not too different from ours today. After further traumatizing bouts with alcohol and violence, and a sentenced treatment at a military hospital in Los Angeles, which only brought him closer to the brink, Tayo eventually turns to the storied wisdom of the elders, to a Pueblo and Diné medicine man, and to the soothing rituals of ceremony for his and earth's rejuvenation.

Before I read the book when he was telling me about it I asked Fisher if he thought it was safe to have the references to traditional knowledge and life force wisdom shared so openly, and he said, that "readers who are respectful may have a doorway to understanding and those who are not will not." Once I finished reading the heart wrenching story I agreed with Fisher and I found Fisher's point very insightful. The truth of it is very cool, the notion that the sacred is protected by a force field, a living shield which can be penetrated by a reader's tenderness and open mindedness. Is it possible in real life that only those who are humble can pass through the gauntlet and enter the realm?

Then the question percolated: did I have the respectfulness and mindset necessary, not only to understand but to share the heritage being passed on in this sacred story? I took a walk on an early fall morning to ponder this. I returned to the place we call Little Pequeno. My dogs led the way. They were bounding along—happier than normal. One thing that I couldn't help notice was the bear scat at several different spots along the way. It tells me to be careful and tread lightly in any re-telling of the story that I do. At the end of the trail, after going under the canopy for a while, there is an opening, a meadow, and just as we made it to that point, the sun peaked over Picacho Peak and shined on us. A ritual I learned long ago, is to greet the sun in the early morning when I first witness it. So I paused, closed my eyes and, with my face angled up toward the warm light, I said "good morning Sun!"

Ceremony begins and ends with the beautiful life giving force of "Sunrise." We are encouraged to accept Sunrise as an "offering" not only for the life giving properties in the present day but also potentially for the wholesale restoration of the world.

I learned during the walk at Little Pequeo—beyond highlighting the Sunrise as it was highlighted to me—that I was not going to retell this extraordinary story. I would only do it an injustice. Everyone, who hasn't done so already, should read the story for their well being, for the common good, as well as for the remarkable writing, and for the sense of place—in this case the Land of Enchantment—that comes alive. So while I am going to remember and cherish the story, I was not going to re-tell it mainly because Leslie Marmon Silko does such a truly magnificent job of telling the story to begin with. What I was going to do—and this was what also and mainly occurred to me on the walk that morning—is share what the story means to me and what it could mean for us.

For one thing the story means anguish to me. Just writing the word anguish in connection with the book brings tears of heartache to my eyes. I want to cry for Tayo who feels such personal guilt and crippling grief from losing his "brother" Rocky in the war with whom he enlisted and for whom he feels responsible. Tayo can't stop crying and shriveling up inside because of the utter inhumanity of war that he participated in—in his case in the Pacific during World War II featuring the Bataan Death March and ultimately the dropping of the atom bomb on the Japanese by the United States. Of course it is better than not that the Axis powers were forced to unconditional surrender, but the devastation from and prospect of nuclear war is horrifying for the human race. I want to weep for New Mexico's role in this form of destruction: the nuclear bomb development that took place here; all the uranium mined so indiscriminately from sacred Pueblo lands; the Cochiti Pueblo land that was taken so unjustly to build Los Alamos; and how the atom bomb was tested at the Trinity site near Alamogordo with widespread ramifications; and the Waste Isolation Pilot Plant (WIPP) that houses radioactive waste which remains life threatening for tens of thousands of years.

It's anguishing to witness the United States investing so much of our national wealth and brain power in nuclear armament and military misadventure when we could be using Los Alamos and Sandia Labs as well as Departments of Defense and Energy to focus on solving climate change, the world's most pivotal challenge which by far is causing the most worldwide insecurity. One relevant civilian use of the atom research instead of nuclear fission could be nuclear fusion, which some experts think is "a solution [to the climate crisis] at the scale of the problem" given that, as Steven Cowley of Princeton's Plasma Physics Laboratory says, "we have to learn how to leave [oil and gas] in the ground in order to survive, to save civilization. It's that simple" (Reference).

The anguish I feel after reading Ceremony is also from our role, as citizens of the United States, in the loss of innocent life—perversely called "collateral damage"—from both our wars of necessity like Word War II and the Civil War and even more so from our wars of choice like Vietnam and Iraq. And then there are the wars allegedly coached in between choice and necessity like the US War in Afghanistan which became a 20 year misadventure. Withdrawing our troops from Afghanistan was the right choice because militarily we were not winning the hearts and minds. A major diplomatic, educational and humanitarian investment could have led and still can to a different and brighter outcome. But in the rural parts of the county where over 70 percent of the Afghan people reside, our military intervention was failing miserably according to the reporting of Anand Gopal in "The Other Afghan Women" (Reference). After our troops and allies departed hastily and haphazardly, and then there were terrible casualties from an egregious terrorist attack, there was an ill advised retaliatory drone strike by the US that wound up killing an entire innocent family. The Afghan father was mistaken as a terrorist, his jugs of water in the car were mistaken as bombs. He had a tradition of letting his kids drive his car into his driveway when he got home, and just as they were playing this game the drone strike exploded killing all seven children and the other family members inside and outside the car. I grieve this loss of innocent life and know it is a metaphor of the broader tragedy and human cost of war.

But the anguish runs deeper than the loss of innocent lives. As Ceremony so poetically illustrates, warfare so brutally reveals, and the present day climate crisis so sadly reaffirms, the anguish stems from witnessing and being part of an underlining disregard for the sacredness of life.

The point of telling this is, and the heritage value may be, we have to feel anguish and walk in Tayo's shoes or else we may become feelingless. Without feeling pain and compassion, we may not take the commensurate remedy, and we could let crumble the world that is only held together so delicately. As the story goes: "Tayo rolled over on his belly...He pressed his face into the pillow and pushed his head hard against the bed frame. He cried trying to release the great pressure that was swelling inside his chest, but he got no relief from crying any more. The pain was solid and constant as the beating of his own heart. The old man made him certain of something he had feared all along, something in the old stories. It took only one person to tear away the delicate strands of the web, spilling the rays of sun into the sand, and the fragile world would be injured" (p. 35).

On the flip side, *Ceremony* evokes—and makes us feel a necessary part of—the great possibility of redemption, which is so sorely needed in our society. One illustration is how Tayo felt despair that he contributed to the death of his uncle Josiah because he promised he would help him tend to the drought resistant cattle Josiah got from Mexico, but the cattle wound up being stolen and despairingly Josiah passed away while Tayo was still away at war. Near the end of the story, after receiving council from a medicine man, Tayo adventures north toward "pa'to'ch" which was colonized and renamed Mount Taylor by White people, even though the medicine man says: "They only fool themselves when they think it is theirs. The deeds and papers don't mean anything. It is the people who belong to the mountain." In spiritually stirring, life threatening but life affirming fashion, Tayo reclaims the heard from a private ranch way up north and eventually shepherds them home, finding a new sense of purpose in caring for them back at the Laguna Pueblo. Tayo plays out what he heard in the chanting from the ceremony: "Following my footprints, walk home, following my footprints, Come home...I'm walking home, I'm walking back to belonging."

The thing about redemption, in the story and as it now pertains to the climate crisis, which we all have contributed to, some more than others, is that we all need to find our way toward redemption. It is truly a journey that needs to be taken by some farther than others but ultimately by one and all alike. "Old Betoni (the medicine man) might explain it this way—Tayo didn't know for sure: there were transitions that had to be made in order to become whole again, in order to be the people our Mother would remember" (p. 157).

I have been thinking a lot while reading this story, wouldn't it be nice if our whole society had a medicine man—or woman—to set us on a transformational path. It is easy to get disillusioned. And think our on-going and exorbitant emissions will irrevocably bury our transitional pathway to wholeness and that we won't be able to find it again. But as Leslie Marmon Silko writes based on her tradition, nothing can be lost, all is retained between the sky and the earth, and within ourselves. People despoil the land but the land outlasts their destruction just as love outlasts death (p. 204). We all can make transition from sickness to health, from death to life, and from grieving to healing.

What is striking about the author is that she was in a massive state of depression, suffering from severe migraine headaches, and it was only by writing *Ceremony* and story-telling, the manifestation of her regenerative pathway, that she felt better. As I acknowledge the author's renewal, on this day September 27th, 2021, I will also acknowledge something stirring in me as a reader: this is my late father's 80th birthday. I am reminded of the painful loss but uplifted by the continuous flow of energy extending from him, through me and my brothers and to our children. I can feel how sacred life is. I realize the importance of *Ceremony* is not only the main character Tayo's transition from excruciating hurt to well being, and the author's own healing through her cathartic telling, but it also sets the readers on a journey from brokenness to redemption as well. Like the Sun itself, the story shines light on and gives life force to our widespread renewal by opening pathways for our collective resurgence and honoring renewed traditional ways of keeping earth in balance amidst a constantly changing universe.

My wife told me—with my upcoming walk to Chaco in the forefront (the "Walk About" as she was calling it)—that our friends were joking I may be going through a mid life crisis. At my then ripe age of 50 and my unconventional mindset, this was perhaps true. And if it were true, it would not be the worst thing to be walking varying distances and in different directions as my principal symptom, considering that other people in mid life crises have been known to have affairs, gain weight, drink heavily, experience aggravated anger or depression...or grow a mullet even. If I grew a mullet it would be long hair from my neck down and bald on top, and then people would really think I were crazy. But, again, it may not be such a bad thing to be a little crazy. I think of the Waylon Jennings' song "I've Always Been Crazy" (Appendix 2) which goes:

"I've always been different with one foot over the line,
Winding up somewhere one step ahead or behind
It ain't been so easy but I shouldn't complain
I've Always Been Crazy
but it keeps me from going insane."

We all may need to break from the conventional norm if it keeps us from driving off a cliff. James Skeet, from the Diné/Navajo Tribe along with his wife Joyce who has Dutch background have taken a different path from conventional agriculture. They live way out west in Vanderwagen, New Mexico, and run Spirit Farm, which is dedicated to "indigenous regenerative pathways" honoring native and natural principles. They practice microbiological composting, traditional farming, land stewardship, and spiritual resiliency in a water sparse landscape where it is difficult to grow anything. They persevere by relying on their heritage and notions like "hidden bugs," medicinal plants, sacred stones and "the living sponge" which is the soil. They are endeavoring to strike the right balance between fungi and bacteria, and facilitate an exchange of reciprocity among the insects, the microorganisms (the nematodes, the protozoa...), pollinators and plants. They know the importance of microbes and they care to protect the mycorrhizae. They do this by planting vegetative cover and mulching which have the multiplier benefits of infiltration and holding the limited water in the ground, as well as moderating the temperature (lessening the runaway warming effects of climate change) and drawing down carbon into the earth through photosynthesis.

In contrast to mono cropping, they seek to maximize biodiversity—by growing a plethora of cover crops and integrating sheep on the farm and pastures. The outcomes are promising. For example, the corn, beans, squash, and green chili that they grow have greater nutrient density and better taste. But the purpose runs deeper than this. There is a corrupt, deeply unhealthy food system throughout our westernized world which has grave ramifications including obesity and diabetes. James and Joyce are striving to replace industrialized agriculture and the colonialist "commoditized economy" with a "kinship economy" rooted in native cosmology and working in partnership with nature.

James says, "Our vision is to emulate ancient rhythms and patters which connect us to the past, present and future. We are going back to our heart's message. Journeying back to our own center and indigenous mindset…upholding key pillars of coexistence…and honoring the sacredness of life" (Reference). I am thankful to say James and Joyce are my friends. I have the honor and privilege of knowing them, learning from them as well as working together as allies in the greater quest for restoration.

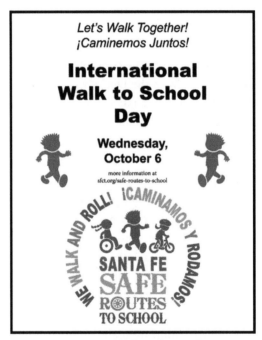

International Walk to School Day.

I woke up early on October 6th 2021 because it was International Walk to School Day and I wanted to walk to school with Holden for the occasion. Communities in over 40 countries and all 50 states and hundreds of thousands of children in all participate. It's held every year on the first Wednesday of October. The purpose is to promote health and physical activity. Since the event started in 1997 it has led to a movement for generating safe walking and biking routes to school. It also of course benefits the environment by fostering less vehicle use which means less pollution. So on the morning of the event (featured in the flyer shown here) I woke up early to get Holden's lunch and breakfast ready and I went into his room to wake him up, hoping he would be up for it. He grumbled at me waking him because it was still dark out but after I explained the reason he responded, "I guess we can do it." What a guy! I thought. Most people in his half sleep state would come up with reasons not to do it. He had no negativity. His only concern was getting to school on time, so we got ready quickly, fed the dogs and we all headed out.

It was lovely being outside early in the morning before the hustle and bustle. In the clouds and over the mountains in the west there was a soft pink light from the sunrise and there was a little rainbow in the horizon. I had never seen a rainbow that early in the day.

The dogs walked with us which was fun. They always want to be part of the action, and just like Holden they were in good spirits, embracing the moment. We ventured down an arroyo for the downhill section. For a while I carried Holden's backpack so he could play frisbee along the way. We walked past the baseball field and then by the post office. We saw a mailman carrying his delivery pouch; he told us he does a walking mail delivery route which is old school. We passed the bus depot. Heading through downtown Santa Fe Holden continued playing frisbee which was fine because there were so few cars on the roads.

Holden playing frisbee through historic downtown Santa Fe.

There was something special, a certain camaraderie, about being out and about just as the day was getting going. When we got closer to his school we saw some other kids with their parents walking or biking. At that point Holden took back his back pack, and put away the frisbee. There we parted ways because dogs were not allowed on school campus (what a travesty). I wanted to hug Holden because I loved him always and I loved his attitude that morning, but I didn't want to embarrass him in front of his classmates so I just said "have a great day" which it already was for me thanks to being with him and the dogs and thanks to International Walk to School Day.

The dogs and I had to make the return trip home on our own. But I didn't mind because I needed the practice. I needed to get my legs in shape. I needed to be ready for a 160 mile walking journey that was coming up in two week's time. On the way back I passed a statue of a man with a shovel—a dedication to the Civilian Conservation Corps (CCC) which included over 55,000 New Mexicans who served in President Roosevelt's nationwide "Tree Army." This civilian army planted forests, prevented erosion, enhanced parks and revitalized the land. All in all the CCC left a legacy that would inspire future generations including mine and now Holden's.

A tribute to the Civilian Conservation Corps.

The heritage value of this historic program is very relevant today as efforts were underway to create a Civilian Climate Corps (a new CCC), putting young Americans to work addressing climate change. This time the focus was on environmental restoration, clean energy, resiliency and carbon sequestration. It was part of Biden's Build Back Better legislation, which was being touted as our era's equivalent to the New Deal. The problem was how the financing kept shrinking inversely to the degree of our society's equity, health and environmental challenges. The progressive leaders started at a more fitting price tag of over six trillion, properly paid for by higher taxes on corporations and the wealthiest Americans. Biden compromised to 3.5 trillion. But with a razor slim majority in Congress, hold out Democrats like Senator Joe Manchin of West Virginia, who is backed by coal and other fossil fuel lobbies, only allegedly supported a price tag of 1.5 trillion which—although better than nothing—would inevitably eliminate the scale of investment (in the new CCC and otherwise) needed to begin solving the climate crisis.

We didn't have the time to haggle over and keep minimizing our commitment level. We needed to get a move on. Just in the first week of October more warning signs were upon us. This time an oil spill, a massive one, happened along the southern coast of California, despoiling the state's iconic beaches. Their governor responded by vowing to vehemently oppose any new drilling in federal waters near the coastline saying "we need to grow up, grow out of this dependency, this mindset that we can't do more [to solve the problem]." Doing less now will cost so much more in the future. Doing more now would mean at minimum adhering to September's study in Nature which found that 60 percent of earth's oil and fossil methane gas and 90 percent of coal reserves must remain in the ground for the world to have a chance of limiting warming to 1.5 degrees Celsius (2.7 degrees Fahrenheit)—the threshold that scientists say would spare humanity.

The dogs and I paused at the Santa Fe River where they refreshed themselves. I love watching Coaster drink and play in the water. She puts her whole snout in as she slurps it up and she lies down in the middle of the stream to cool off her body. Perhaps sensing the widespread need for rejuvenation, the rain came, which is always a relief here in New Mexico. As we headed up the last uphill portion home, all of us damp from the rain, more and more cars sped past us and I longed for the early morning relative quiet and calm with Holden.

As I said, I need to be physically ready to walk 160 miles, over mountain ranges and across Pueblos and tribal reservation lands. But physical fitness would only carry me so far. I also needed to be mentally and spiritually fit for this journey. But over the last few weeks some doubts crept into my mind and apprehension entered my thinking, which is new for me. People who care about me were cautioning me. And instead of ignoring these cautions or being stubborn in response I realized it was worth trying to listen to and learn from them. I knew I needed to be clearly committed to my purpose but I also needed to be smart—which meant taking cautionary signs seriously and making adjustments.

One adjustment I made was to have mapping ready and available on my phone—in addition to my hand held map of the route. I got some training on Google Maps from an expert named Dave Dean who taught me how to pre-save an "offline map" of the area so that the GPS would work even without cell service (there will be a lot of areas without cell service along the way). He also suggested to keep the phone in airplane mode a good amount of the time to preserve the battery power for the phone. Which brings up another thing which was to bring sufficient manual phone re-charging capability, considering that I will be trekking for four and a half days mostly without any available power outlets. I made some adjustments to my route, opting for safety over directness. And I decided, instead of camping every single night, that once I passed the half way point I would stay overnight at a motel to recharge my batteries literally and physically speaking.

Another adjustment I made was with my shoes. When I walked to Chimayo and part way back I got blisters and rocks in the soles of the shoes. I was determined not to allow that to happen again. So I ditched the "On" running shoes and I went with Holden and picked out a brand called "Altra" instead. I also got some pairs of "smart wool" socks that are really good for long distance hiking because they wick away sweat and moisture (a leading cause of irritation) and they comfortably hold your feet. I ordered something called WURU wool for my feet. Another thing on the gear front was choosing to bring a glow in the dark jacket and cover for my back pack, as well as head lamps so that if I were ever walking in the dark, either after twilight or early in the morning, cars would be able to clearly see me along the shoulder.

Then I came in for lunch and I was apparently shaking a little bit and shivering from wearing only a t-shirt and being cold up in my office. Numi got upset at me for not having the judgment to be wearing a jacket. She said I darn well better bring a good jacket for my walkabout. Even though I was planning to bring different layers, I wasn't planning to bring a jacket but now that she mentioned it I got on board. I decided to bring a jacket and use it as a pillow at night in my bivy sack. I knew just the one: my soft down Patagonia, which is bright orange and features on the left shoulder a World War II Air Force patch I got from my paternal grandfather, the fellow walker, who served in the war as a weather man but, like many of that generation, never wanted to talk about it.

One good friend of ours suggested I bring a gun with me. That was too much precaution for my blood. She was concerned that I would be overly trusting of all the people I would meet along the way. I wondered about that. While I believe all have the capacity for humanity and decency, not everyone has our best interests at heart, and some, if they are in a bad way, could try to inflict harm. This kind of thinking, even though it was rational, produced anxiety in me and contributed to a bad dream I had ten days or so before embarking. I dreamt that I was around a camp fire visiting with a medicine man, like Tayo did in the story Ceremony, but unlike the genuine healer man Tayo visited with, the person visiting with me turned out to be a trickster who was weaving deception and doubt in me. I woke up feeling not only sleep deprived but more deeply concerned and uneasy.

I started having some second thoughts and doubts about taking the trip, which again is unusual for me. But just then I received a text message from a good friend named Chris who said: "I heard about your walkabout to Chaco. One of the coolest things I have heard of. It will definitely be a memorable birthday." What Chris and I share in common, we realized serendipitously some years ago, is that our maternal grandparents were best friends in life. We share heritage—the heritage of good spirited and humorous grandparents. And having levity in life, like having good friends, helps keep us going.

The birthday Chris referenced in his text to me was mine and the reason he referenced my birthday was because Numi and I planned to host a birthday gathering at Chaco with some close friends the night I arrived. The "gathering" was going to include a special dinner, a night camping out under the stars as well as some tours of this sacred place provided by Heritage Tours. I was going to do something like this for my 50th birthday which was last year but that was cancelled because of COVID. I figured this year, even though it was just my 51st birthday, why not still celebrate friendship and do it at this remarkable place in conjunction with the third leg of my four direction walk. A dozen couples RSVP-ed they wanted to join in and so they would take the tour vans to the park and assuming I made it, we would all meet out there on Friday on my birthday. Some of the friends coming said that I would be in no condition to celebrate with them after walking so long. They were possibly right, but I was going to put by best foot forward.

The text message from my buddy Chris gave me encouragement when I was hesitant and it made me feel confident that I was on the right path.

Together, the uneasy dream coupled with this encouraging text, and a lot of other feedback pro and con, all brought up in me not a fight or flight reaction, not simply whether to go on the journey or not to go, but rather the inclination to reconcile my journey with my dream and any lingering concerns that were festering. Essentially I have chosen—not to sweep concerns under the rug, but rather—to process concerns as they arise, and then move on. In terms of the reconciliation to go forth on this journey more mindfully, I felt the notion that the walking quest itself, this long walkabout, would be good medicine, or at least it may help spur the potential for good medicine, and so I was excited to see what was in store.

On the second Monday of October, one week out from the departure date of the westward journey, we commemorated Indigenous People Day in place of Columbus Day. Columbus Day evokes the painful history of colonialism, whereas Indigenous Peoples Day celebrates the resilience and the respectful values of Native American communities. New Mexico has already changed the holidays (along with 13 other states to date) and there is a movement underway to make Indigenous Peoples Day a federal holiday. The United States has a long history of violence against Native Americans. We have a long road ahead to repair the harm that was done. Making this a federal holiday would be a first small step.

Of course there were much bigger steps needed. For example, a Truth and Healing Commission to investigate the US government's hurtful policy of taking Native American children from their families and sending them to abusive boarding schools. Protecting and returning lands and waterways that are sacred to Native Americans is another example, as well as preventing pipelines from crossing tribal lands and more broadly pressing for an end to fossil fuel production which causes so much harm. Protesting in Washington DC this week along with the People vs. Fossil Fuels campaign, Joyce Braun, a member of the Cheyenne River Sioux Tribe and organizer with the Indigenous Environmental Network said to the US government and society: "How can you say that we are in this climate emergency...and at the same time be giving away land for additional oil and gas infrastructure?" Likewise from New Mexico, a delegation was sent to the White House by the Pueblo Action Alliance, the Greater Chaco Coalition and Diné C.A.R.E. to stop fossil fuel projects like fracking operations occurring within the Greater Chaco Region. This was being done in coordination with a larger national mobilization being coordinated by Build Back Fossil Free, a coalition of hundreds of indigenous, BIPOC, youth, environmental and social justice organizations and other front-line communities.

A message by the Pueblo Action Alliance brings home the local significance of this national movement against fossil fuels (Reference): "New Mexico has been deemed an energy sacrifice zone and has a history of extraction, testing, implementation of federal policies and no consultation with local Tribal nations. The Greater Chaco region is a living and ancient cultural landscape. A thousand years ago, Chaco Canyon in northern New Mexico was the ceremonial and economic center of the Chaco Cultural Landscape, an area encompassing more than 75,000 square miles of the Southwest in NM, AZ, CO and UT and sacred to Indigenous Peoples. Today, Chaco Canyon in northwestern New Mexico is a National Park and UNESCO World Heritage Site, considered one of the most important archaeological sites in the 'Americas,' yet the vast majority of the area is leased to oil and gas activities. Indigenous People, primarily Pueblo and Navajo (Diné) peoples, sacred cultural sites, precious water resources, and the area's biodiversity are under grave and growing threats from fracking.

In approving wide-scale fracking on public and Tribal lands, the Department of Interior has failed to consider: The health, wealth, and wellness of impacted communities, especially that of local Navajo communities, Chapter Houses, and Allotment Land Owners.

The Greater Chaco Landscape expands far beyond the Chaco Culture National Historic Park and immediate vicinity and holds spiritual and cultural significance to all Indigenous peoples who are rooted in Chaco culture, not limited to the Navajo Nation. The long term, cumulative impacts of fracking on health, land, water, air and climate."

I of course support all of these sensitive demands and favor the kinds of steps mentioned for reconciliation and remediation, and I believe in taking many more steps. It is why I am taking my walking journey to Chaco Canyon to honor and uphold the land ethic, life embracing spirit and heritage values of Native American Tribes and Pueblos as well as of Indigenous communities beyond.

But I was not on my way and out of the (dog) house just yet. As the day of embarking got closer, the domestic entanglements ramped up. I was appreciating that my wife was acting calmer this time around but that turned out not to be the whole story. On day six before departure I told her, mistakenly in hindsight, that I had already got the food and power bars I needed so she wouldn't need to get anything for me. She asked how many power bars did I purchase and I said enough for two per day at which point she went ballistic saying: "You're out of your mind, total hubris! You need a lot more calories!" I tried to explain that the power bars were in addition to turkey jerky packs, bananas, almonds and peanut butter snacks but she wanted none of it. She screamed "Who do you think you are? You're not 27 like when you did the 'Climate Ride' and even then you wisely ate tons of food and drank tons of liquids every day." I tried to explain that every day there will be a stop and convenience store along the way where I can and will replenish my water and get more food and power bars. "You're going to need them and you should know that!" I was up against a brick wall. There was no reasonable talking it out that night; just high temperatures and fuming—all the while our boys were in the kitchen listening to us carry on so antagonistically.

Later that night as I went to bed, after I told her to please turn off the light and didn't speak another word to her—as if that was effective retaliation—I struggled to go back to sleep and so I pondered what she said earlier. Of course I didn't want to act with hubris; in fact "hubris" is a word I use. She only used it to get at me, and it worked. Hubris is the antithesis of what I am after in this quest. Hubris is the way our society is acting in terms of how we caused and are now exacerbating, not addressing, the climate crisis. I thought about my "Climate Ride" that she brought up. It was a 6000 mile bike journey through 30 states encouraging the US to lead on climate change and like I said it culminated with me meeting her at NYC's Bar 13. It is no wonder I fell for her because she was so beautiful, alluring and there was this longing about her that gravitated me. It is no wonder she fell for me too because—after peddling 100 miles per day for two and half months time—I was pretty damn strong, and somewhat sensitive too, wearing a New Zealand jade neck piece which appealed to her. I think I better bring that back out of storage.

Anyways, the reason I reflected back on this, as I was struggling to fall back asleep was to recall that time in my life in contrast to my older self now. Back then I lived up to my favorite Bob Seger song "Like a Rock" (Appendix 2). I was unwavering, bold, decisive and true to my convictions. I didn't give embarking on the climate ride a second thought, even though people questioned and doubted it when I conceived the idea. I just had a small purple back bungie corded to my mountain bike (not even a road bike). I wore old Converse high tops (not even strap-in bike shoes). Not so much anymore. Now I have twice as much gear for a five day walk as I had for a two and half month bike journey. Now I bring gear including ordering something called WURU wool to prevent blisters and a recently borrowed Garmin GPS unit that can send an SOS signal if I need to. I am not even close to as tough as I was, as Numi aptly pointed out and doesn't hesitate to remind me, so I thought I better make up in nimbleness and spiritual will what I lack in physical capability. These days I act more like water than rock: bending around banks; flowing more gently; sometimes changing course; weaving around obstacles. I actually can be receptive, to the point where, even though it would make my pack heavier and even though I could replenish them each day, I decided not to be stubborn to a fault but to heed Numi's urging to take more bars on my trip. To drive it home, Holden, before going to bed that night, whispered "bring more power bars to make mama happy." Now how could I refuse or resist that?

The thing was, at this stage of my life, I didn't wand to be completely compromising like the criticism water gets or unbending like the problem with granite. What I wanted, it occurred to me the next morning, was to be more like Moss: dwelling in equanimity between the enduring sureness of rock and the flowing gracefulness of water.

Just before seven, when Holden gets up and gets ready for school and I get up to feed and walk the dogs, I turned to Numi, the best sleeper of all time, and told her "I'd like to speak with you now or right after Holden goes to school. Whichever you prefer." She chose the present and I paused for a moment to collect my thoughts and then said, "I definitely make mistakes in my life, I hopefully will learn from those mistakes. I am listening to feedback (your's and others') and I hear you when out of concern you say for God sakes bring more protein rich food and be more prepared! I am going to do that. I appreciate the feedback. I really do care as you do to be safe and smart about this. And what I need from you, irrespective of all this, is to speak calmly and with common courtesy. Especially in front of our kids, for whom we should show our true affection as much as possible." And then she responded, "I will make an effort to do that. I appreciate what you are saying. And what I need from you is common sense." Touché.

Fisher and I on his college trip getting some sound advice from a Boston Terrier.

Before the walk on Monday, we spent the long weekend back East. Numi was with Holden visiting our daughter for parents weekend and I was with Fisher taking him around to look at colleges. His favorite it turned out was Wesleyan which is where my father and maternal grandfather went to school. Fisher liked the campus, the people were friendly, and he appreciated the film program as well as the sports offerings (including golf and fly fishing in the vicinity). I told Fisher I am proud of him and of course love him whatever he ultimately chooses to do. I just wanted him to do his thing and follow his heart. Before our return flight, after checking out colleges in the region, we had a few hours to spare and visited my brother Scott and my sister in law Melissa in the City. They hosted us and treated us to gluten free pizza, soup and other nice treats.

While we ate they told us about a memorial service they had been to earlier that day on Roosevelt Island for Bill Van-den Heuvel. Among many uplifting endeavors, he helped integrate public schools in the South and advised Robert F. Kennedy's '68 campaign for president which stood up for alleviating poverty and healing race relations. Bill also established the Roosevelt Institute (my brother served on the board), which carries on the legacy of Franklin Roosevelt's Four

Freedoms which were articulated in his state of the union in 1941. The reason I mention all of this is that there are heritage values in our country that have to do with public service and bettering the lives of all Americans, which BVH, RFK and FDR all exemplified (Reference). We need this spirit of public service to take shape anew today.

We returned to our home in New Mexico late Sunday night and my plan was to leave on my journey early Monday morning. Good thing I had already packed my back pack beforehand. I showered (knowing that wouldn't happen much over the coming days), I got some shut eye and I woke up in time to have a freshly made breakfast sandwich which Numi kindly made for me. I gave Numi a big kiss. Then I gave Holden a big hug. He was brushing his teeth and wanted to make sure I brought my tooth brush with me which I had so I passed the first test! I was prepared, I hoped, and I was off to the races!

Holden sending me off, saying "Make sure to brush your teeth!"

11
JOURNEY 3
DAY 1: LAGUNA

I descend from my home onto the dirt roads called Stagecoach and Hillcrest and soon head across Fort Marcy Park, over the bridge, through the outskirts of downtown and over to Alameda street which parallels the Santa Fe River. I take in the city walking because I know I won't have many more densely populated areas on my journey west. I relish the sidewalks, and cross walk buttons that stop the traffic. I hear church bells sound and can't help but notice the fall colors of the trees growing beside the river. The sound of running water initially drowns out the sound of vehicles going by. I pass the Boys and Girls Club where I ran a program called Young Peacemakers for the kids when I first moved to town working with Americorps. My Dad had visited nearly 25 years ago from then and I remember him joining me as I was playing with the kids in the park I'm passing by right now. As I follow the river trail more recreation areas come into sight including the Alto Street baseball fields where I coached Little League that both Fisher and Holden participated in. I admire the street art on the bridge walls. I acknowledge the dog walkers and a woman with a walking stick. I appreciate the concept of a green belt, which I'm moving though, making cities more livable.

A few miles from home I turn around and greet the morning sun and with my eyes closed briefly I remember that I forgot something: the bag of WURU Wool that came in the mail which is supposed to be helpful for foot care and blister prevention. I debate in my head whether to just leave it alone or call Numi and ask if she will bring it to me. I decide to call and she is so easy going about helping me, understanding that by vehicle she is just a skip and a jump from my location. In the meantime I continue on, departing the green belt at Siler Road, joining the side walk of Agua Fria Street where I soon come to a welcome sign to the Historic Village of Agua Fria featuring a classic picture of two Burros seemingly from the neighborhood a century ago. I reflect on how donkeys/ burros are animal walking heroes (Appendix 1) and I aspire to be like them, not for their name "Jack Ass" which my grandfather Chet used to say disparagingly, but rather for their incredible stamina which I will need in my five day trek and we will need in our greater quest.

At the Village of Agua Fria, paying tribute to Burros who are resilient walkers.

It is not a good sign that a disheveled looking guy drinking a can of beer and smoking a cigarette walks (I should say zooms) right past me, soon to the point where I can't see him ahead of me anymore. Right as my self esteem is deflated, Numi pulls up alongside me to give me the New Zealand wool I had ordered and forgotten. I thank her, and smile as we wave good bye. She takes a picture (or social media video for all I know) as I stoically walk off in the westerly direction. She turns around and drives off in the opposite direction. I want to say more to her. I want to thank her for now supporting my journey and holding down the home and work front while I am away. I want to hug her for being my true love. Why I don't is my shortcoming, but I trust she knows how I feel about her. How I feel is: I can't imagine this world without her; she's a star; and no matter the journey I set myself on, at the end of the day, I return home to her bright allure and encompassing affection.

On Airport road where the sidewalk ends.

I find myself all alone on Aiport road and once I cross Highway 599, the sidewalk ends, in the spirit of Shell Silverstein. Things become more industrial at first and then more wide open at last. Not only is the city portion of the trip on its last legs, so is my bladder. I have been drinking more water than I expected I would. I relieve myself under the shade of a tree and have that "ahhhhh" feeling. I finally make it to a dirt road, 56 C, and intuitively you would think traffic would ebb and nature would flow but not so fast. For the first portion a series of semis and cement trucks drive by one after the other heading up La Bajada. Dust particles fly into the air, and I wonder where on earth are they going. Seemingly nowhere.

When I finally make it to the top of La Bajada Hill I hear off to the right a gun shooting range and it is the same turn off that the trucks are all taking to pick up cement or something. The good news is I am heading left away from all that noise. Now, when I am not swallowing the dust, I am appreciating the dirt road. I feel at home on them probably because I grew up on them. The wind picks up in my face, I think I am tough heading into it but then I look south and I realize that I don't really know what tough is as I see the sturdy Sandia peaks in the background and in the foreground I see cactus plants which are truly tough. They are true survivors. I laugh at the vulnerability of myself in comparison. The cactus plant is adapted to absorb, store and use water most efficiently over a prolonged period. They have potent water storage cells in their stem and sometimes in their roots. Plus they have a protective layer that prevents water loss. As I take another sip of water from my Camel Back I marvel at how long a cactus can survive before having new water. They can last for as long as two years whereas humans can survive without water for only a few days.

Sandia Peak in the distance and cactus plants in the foreground.
They can teach us a thing or two about endurance.

Soon I am wondering about being able to survive today. First I'm thinking if I don't develop a way to walk gently on the tough dirt road, on the hardened land, and if my body doesn't bend and absorb with every impact, but rather stiffly resists or repels the impacts, the land will soon break me like a stick. Second I'm thinking, I've already almost gone through my whole water rations for the day and I have over 10 miles left before I get to the lone convenience store in the vicinity—assuming I can even get to it in time before it closes at seven o'clock. Panic doesn't set in yet, but concern does and a question forms in my consciousness: how am I going to do this?

There is a whole (puzzling) world in a tile size section of dirt.

I start going down a rabbit hole in my mind and then a cricket jumps into my face, seemingly karate kicking me between the nose and my right upper cheek, and thankfully the cricket wakes me up from my slumber. I notice the light blue sky all around with barely a cloud in any direction. I also notice the indentations in the road, which appear like a puzzle and I think we are all interdependent pieces which fit into a greater pattern.

I reach the end of the expansive mesa top and look down into the valley below. I take a rocky zig zag road down. I am very alert and vigilant, not wanting to sprain an ankle or encounter a rattle snake. It's hot enough out for them and I can imagine them dwelling in some of the crevices. I make it down unscathed and now have a choosing moment. Either I go right, directly toward the west, which is a less known, more natural, slightly longer route or I go left, toward the southwest, which looks to connect to the main road to Cochiti.

The zig zag rocky road
down into the valley.

An oasis with hospitable people
and hospitable dogs.

I choose the latter and as it turns out I choose wisely because there is a home (among a handful of homes in a tiny community that I have never known existed) that I come to on my way which has a car parked in the driveway and three dogs who are the friendliest. I would think if they saw a stranger walking up to their home they would get startled and bark at me. But they don't bark at all. They just wag their tales and say hello, casually and care-freely. I am emboldened by their hospitality to knock on the door and when I do a kind woman answers with her little boy in her arms. I explain that I am walking on a long journey and ask if there is any way I could have some drinking water. Without hesitating she fully opens the door, invites me in and tells me to sit down on her couch while she gets me some water. I tell her how thankful I am—how the water couldn't have come at a better time, how I didn't know how much to ration as this is the first day on my long walk but now I know I will carry more water in the days ahead.

She not only comes over with a refill for my camel back but also with three water bottles along with an apple and an orange. I am over the moon with appreciation. As I fill up the camel back (some of which spills on the floor, and she doesn't let me get up to help but just gracefully gets some paper towels and wipes it up while still holding her little boy in her right arm) and as I tend to my aching feet, we talk a while and introduce ourselves. She tells me she is from the Laguna Pueblo, she tells me her name and I tell her she looks familiar and we realize we have together been on several zoom meetings focused on the subject of regenerative agriculture.

I am kind of blown away. Just before I head off, I give her my name and number after she gives me hers and I let her know that if she ever needs anything in Santa Fe to please let me know. As I walk off on my way she sends me off with heartfelt blessings for the journey ahead.

Looking back in gratitude to the flat top hill called La Bajada.

I'm thinking, what a kind world. What a small world! And as I head back onto the road a song just starts playing on my phone without me doing anything (I wasn't listening to music at all so it's a bit strange that it just popped up). It's John Melloncamp's song called "Small Town" (Appendix 2): "I was born in a small town...and I can breath in a small town!" It's so cool how New Mexico has long lasting iterations of a small town community. I think about my caring host being from the Laguna Pueblo, which is what the *Ceremony* book is centered on, and I think about the meaning of Laguna which is little lake, lagoon, or, as I am starting to realize, oasis. I just stumbled upon an oasis of kindness, life nourishment (water and fruit) and hospitality just when I was out of water and needed it most. The location too is an oasis with dozens of trees and fresh water flowing in an otherwise dry and rough landscape.

A single lane highway, Route 16, heading west
toward Cochiti Pueblo.

I make it to Highway 16 with now about eight miles to go to get to Cochiti. There is not much of a shoulder on Route 16 but the light from the afternoon sun illuminates me clearly for anyone passing by to see. An hour later, with about five miles left, a pick up truck pulls over next to me and the man driving introduces himself and asks if I want a ride into Cochiti. I say how much that means to me but I am determined to walk the rest of the way, and even take the Cochiti Lake damn passageway which prohibits vehicles, which he confirms is open to foot traffic only. Before he heads off he tells me he is a former Governor of the Cochiti Pueblo and that when he was sworn in he said: "I promise to not just take care of my people but to take care of all people!" We give each other a fist pump, and with our hands touch our hearts twice in solidarity. I am touched. This is the exact kind of humanity that we need more of in the world. It's what I am looking for.

Another hour later and three miles further down the road, I make it to the first sighting of Cochiti Lake, and soon it's magic hour no less. My legs are getting more tired by the minute but my spirits are soaring from the previous encounters, and from what seem to be supernatural occurrences happening.

Magic hour at Cochiti Lake.

Near full moon rising at dusk.

As twilight falls, the almost full moon rises. I get a second wind that carries me through the final push. I am in awe, not only from the people I'm meeting here but also from the high dessert southwest. Night falls and I walk up to the Cochiti gas station and convenience store ten minutes ahead of seven o'clock. I have just the right amount of time to restock my water and purchase back up batteries for my headlamp as well as a nail clipper. My left toe nail has been digging into my toe and causing pain.

When I leave the store I don't feel like back tracking to the lakeside campsites so I look for a spot off the beaten path. I find a couple of trees just up from the station and I set up my little camp under them.

My first night accommodations next to Cochiti Mini Mart.

My little camp consists of a sleeping pad, a bivy sack and sleeping bag that fits inside. I organize my things. I hang up my bag of food from one of the trees in case of bears. I take off my shoes and socks. Then I preform my nail clipping surgery but it goes woefully wrong. The piercing nail is so engrained into my toe that when I try to clip it off I puncture the skin and a stream of puss and blood flows from my toe. I realize at this moment that my planned journey to Chaco could be in serious jeopardy. I clean the area with antiseptic, I apply Neosporin for soothing and, after debating whether to let it breathe or not I decide to cover the wound with a bandage. However when I finally get in the sleeping bag I experience sharp pain simply by my toe touching the top of the sleeping bag.

My doubts increase about being able to continue my walk in the morning. In fact with the sore legs and feet and this nail problem my doubts are stronger than anytime before the trip started. It's already arduous as hell, but the exponential issue is whether or not I can maintain wound and blister free feet to be able to handle the arduousness.

To make matters worse, right before I tuck under my sleeping bag, a night watchman drives around the vicinity presumably looking for me or people like me illegally camping on semi private land. The white van weaves all around my location and even parks a stones' throw away. I lie down staying as still as can be, and thankfully he doesn't see me and then heads off out of sight. Trying to sleep seems futile. I toss and turn hoping to find a comfortable position for my toe, not to mention the sore rest of my body. Finally, thanks to all the walking I did that day, I drift off.

Day 1 Steps: 72,400

12
JOURNEY 3
DAY 2: COCHITI

I wake up at 6:30 and immediately go to work on my toe. I apply some more Neosporin and then a patch of Second Skin. Then I take out the WURU Wool that Numi thankfully delivered to me when I was still in Santa Fe. It's raw, un-processed New Zealand lambs wool and I simply peal off a piece and place it on the areas of my feet that are sensitive, especially of course above and around my left toe. I carefully put on a new pair of Injinji Smart Wool socks, which cover the toes like mittens so they don't rub against each other and, as I said, the smart wool wicks moisture preventing blisters, a word I refuse to say any longer during this trip, and one that I rarely even let seep into my brain as a thought. I put on my shoes, pack up, and I am on the road just before seven.

I stop at the gas station to throw out a few little items of trash I accumulated and while at the station a woman who is filling up her car with gas, says that she would like to buy me breakfast and coffee since I have been camping out. I thank her profusely but I refuse. We talk for a while longer and she tells me she is from the Cochiti Pueblo. After we say goodbye I am thinking: what a way to start the trip and start a new day, with the generosity of strangers. I feel their kindness as if they were relatives! How we need to treat one another is how I've been treated by the folks from Cochiti and Laguna these two days.

The horizon in the west stirs me. To myself I am singing the song from the Secret Life of Walter Mitty called "Stay Alive" (Appendix 2): "There is a truth and it is on our side. Dawn is coming, open your eyes. Look into the sun as a new days rise!"

Renewal.

To add to the momentum, my toe doesn't bother me at all. The WURU wool is working! I think "if my foot can be restored so can the way we treat the earth and each other. I am so moved by all of the confluence of events—the sunrise, the show of humanity, the song, the hope of healing—that tears are streaming down my face. To top it off, when I check my phone for the directions, I see a text from Tabatha that says "I am thinking of you all the time and I am so proud of you." I feel from the magnitude of support and good fortune I am receiving and the depth of emotions that I am experiencing that this is what I'm supposed to be doing right now in my life. I get extra confirmation from a pack of ducks flying in a v pattern right over me. I am so thankful not only for not having to be sidelined because of my toe, but also for all the forces carrying me and enabling me.

The Pueblo of Cochiti welcomed me to take the enchanting way toward Dome Trail.

I arrive at the Pueblo of Cochiti Golf Course just before it opens. I have been talking about the route I am about to be taking with Sedrick, another former Governor of the Pueblo who now works at the course. I thought I would stop in to say good morning and thank him for his help. Back out on the road I come to a gate which says "closed to vehicle and pedestrian travel" but I had permission so I am good. I head north on "forest road 289," which is what both the local ranger and Sedrick each recommended. A sign says Dome Road is nine miles away and NM4, the road I wanted, is 17 miles away. What the sign didn't say is how the sandy dirt road is perfect for walking, how the wilderness and mesa lands span for as far as my eyes can see, and nothing about the elevation changes in store.

As I set out on this old trail (new for me), I am still feeling good, my toe and legs and feet and otherwise. It occurs to me to enjoy the times when I am feeling good because they may be few and far between. It also occurs to me as I am walking north for the first several miles that sometimes you have to go north in order to go west. Not unlike the saying one step backward, two steps forward. There was another way shown on my Google maps which looked to be more direct but there were dangerous uncertainties going that way that I didn't want to take chances with. Again, I was content going north, going a little ways out of the way, if I could safely and reliably get to Highway 4.

No place I'd rather walk: Route 289.

What I soon came to realize is how utterly amazing this Road 289 way of going is. For one thing the walking conditions are ideal: soft ground, nature noises, vehicles prohibited, great views...For another thing it smacks of adventure, especially being in the lands of the Cochiti Pueblo. Also the weather is perfect: fall colors and blue sky abound and refreshing temperatures keep me cool even as I ascend the foothills of the Jemez Mountains. Immediately ahead of me, a black beetle marches by. I pause to let it pass and I am in awe of its speed and size. There are about 2,500 types of beetles and they all can high tail it. Not only that, many beetles can carry as much as 850 times their body weight. And here I am complaining about carrying a 35-pound back back. These are just a few reasons why beetles are being highlighted here as insect walking heroes of mine (Appendix 1). They put me to shame, give me something to aspire to and help me to stay positive during this long and increasingly uphill journey.

Boulder Land.

The vertical climb is getting serious. It's not as steep as a staircase (yet?) but it's relentless. The on-going climbing starts to shape my brain's thought patterns, as if I'm becoming the environment that surrounds me; it's absorbing. I'm thinking about discomfort and what the lesson of feeling uncomfortable is. As I am ruminating in slow motion I come to a new environment. Massive rocks are all around. I call it: Boulder Land! The boulders are speaking to me or they are testing me. Do I chose physical power or another kind of power? My heart and old age say another kind of power. If I approach this journey as an endeavor of physical conquest I will surely fail. My capabilities are not sufficient in the raw strength department. But if I approach this as a quest of spiritual fortitude, I have some capacities here that have evolved over the years, and most importantly I have so much room to grow in this department! My sense is that the spiritual realm can handle discomfort and potentially help overcome it.

This mind over matter internal conversation I am having carries me to the next milestone which is, as I step over a cattle guard, the transition from Pueblo of Cochiti land to National Forest. I have profound gratitude to the Pueblo of Cochiti for letting me take this prohibited and extraordinary route, for treating me with such kindness and for protecting me while I have been here. I've said this in other words and I say it again: I'm doing this walk to Chaco to honor all Indigenous people and communities, to honor their whole hearted love of the land and love for those who dwell on it.

Departing the Cochiti Pueblo.

As I enter the National Forest land starting at Dome Wilderness, I spontaneously begin singing Woody Guthrie's iconic song "This Land is Your Land" (Appendix 2):

"...As I went walking that ribbon of highway, I saw above me
that endless skyway,
Saw below me that golden valley, this land was made for you and me;
I roamed and rambled and I have followed my footsteps,
To the sparking sands of her diamond deserts,
All around me the voice was sounding,
This land was made for you and me..."

One way besides singing that I am coping with the discomfort of the journey is experimentation. The long distance walking with my back pack on makes my shoulders feel strained. So I realized that by lifting up the shoulder straps into the sky, as if I am doing a shoulder press, helps alleviate the stress and soreness. And I have other tricks up my sleeve like for example lifting up and tightening the main waist belt of the back pack. This helps a lot because it takes the pressure off the shoulders and my spine and onto the strongest body parts: the hips and core. Another thing that helps is crossing my arm to the opposite shoulder strap and pulling the side of the back pack toward the center of my body. I am getting ready for trick or treating in a few weeks with all the tricks I am learning out here.

I see birds darting about on either side of the trail. I imagine they know I am coming and they are getting ready to tip off other birds around the bend and so on so that it becomes an endless greeting party. Stiff winds are blowing, more at me when I am going due west and more with me when I am going due north which seems to be half of the time. I pass a red, seemingly abandoned, motorcycle. This is the first indication of human life I have had except for sparsely scattered signs and odds and ends—like an old key, bottle cap, a spent triple A battery. I think of the land ethic: Leave no trace. And the more ambitious one: Leave it better than we find it. I consider occasionally picking up something but I decide against it. The act of simply stopping, bending over and picking some trash up from the ground and then resuming walking raises the intensity of my body's aches and pains exponentially.

Steady and relentless incline.

Every time I get to a seeming high point in the trail there is another after it, and another and another. I realize that this could be torture if it wasn't so stunningly beautiful. Another good thing is that I didn't know the extent of vertical incline and elevation I would be climbing when I woke up this morning. If I had, at the start of the day, I may never have started. If I had, it could have sapped with dread the magical and emotionally uplifting feeling I experienced all morning.

A look out point back to the east from where I have journeyed.

After another steep climb, I come to a fork in the road and I think of Yogi Berra's great line "When you come to a fork in the road take it!" Thinking of a fork makes me hungry, so I seize the opportunity to take a break and eat a snack right at the spot where the two paths diverge. And right at that spot is a suitable sitting area from where I can rest and look back on the breathtaking vistas and all the sheer distance I have come. I take out the granola that my thoughtful friend Bart sent to me recently and with a smile on my face, and relief penetrating my legs, I wolf it down!

I resume my walk heading left at the fork toward Highway 4. I feel a sudden burst of hope that I have reached the summit with a plateau to follow. But I soon find out that that is magical thinking or even worse: hubris. Of course I spoke (in my head) too soon and I should have known better. The only thing I have going for me, besides everything I have mentioned, is that the few times I have descended briefly after high points have been painful on the legs and knees. So if I had to choose either to walk up or walk down, I might—believe it or not—choose to go up to spare my aching knee bones. What I really desire is flatness, but that seems so damn elusive. And every time I dream of arriving to and walking on a plateau, I jinx it just by thinking about it.

What I desire is flatness.

Well, flatness is where I find myself right now, thank goodness, and I wisely don't make any forecasts that it will be that way for long. I just appreciate it in the moment—and that seems like a lesson this journey is teaching me, among others. Speaking of appreciation and wisdom, I am so lucky I have listened to the wisdom of Sedrick from Cochiti as well as from the park ranger encouraging me to go on this path. If I had followed the Google maps seemingly more direct route it could have gotten me lost in mesa lands and steep canyons that I have no business being in. It could have gotten me in some dangerous trouble.

The impassable terrain I avoided thanks to the guidance of folks
from the Pueblo of Cochiti and the parkland.

A pick up truck heading in the opposite direction stops beside me and asks a) if I lost a dog and b) if I have seen any elk on my way up here. The reason for the second question is self evident because the people inside are decked out in hunting attire, camouflage and orange vests. I answer both their questions in the negative and after they ask and hear how long I have come today, the hunter in the backseat who happens to be a beautiful woman smiles at me. I am not sure if she is smiling because she thinks I am crazy walking so far or if she thinks I look silly in my brimmed hat or if she kind of likes me. I have never hunted before and I only have eyes for Numi but if Numi and I weren't married and I had to go hunting I would like to hunt with this woman in the lead.

After we part ways I think of their first question and how cool it would be to have the faithful companionship of a dog by my side on this journey. Far from home I think of Wombat. Closer to home I think of Coaster but she has arthritis. Then I think of Gary and how when he gets tired or sore he just stops in his tracks and doesn't budge. I would have to carry him. I stop imagining because it makes me too fatigued to think about. I pass a sign featuring an old fashion mother and child as if I were in the 1950s in a sophisticated urban area with pedestrians all around instead of a place where I have seen three cars and three people in the past three hours.

1950s style entrance to Bandelier National Monument.

I enter Bandelier National Monument lands and marvel at the spectacular scenery and history: the park spans 33,000 acres of rugged canyon and mesa country as well as evidence of Native Americans dating back over 11,000 years. I am not seeing the dwellings as I am in the southeastern part of the park and I don't have time to walk further north but I have been there before to see the remarkable cliff dwellings and learned a bit about the petroglyphs, carvings and standing masonry walls, all together paying homage to the enduring culture then and now in the surrounding pueblo communities along the Rio Grande. It has been said that the people of the Cochiti Pueblo are the most direct descendants of the Ancestral Pueblo people who built homes in the Frijoles Canyon near here.

I finally make it to Highway 4 in the mid to late afternoon. I use the occasion to take another break, this time taking my shoes and socks off to let them and my feet air out. I could sit here for ages I feel but I know time is not on my side. I need to make it to Amanda's convenience store before it closes at eight o'clock. I need to refill my water supply. But I've got about 17 miles left and I realize, if I'm traveling at about three mph, the math doesn't add up. One thing's for sure, I can't sit here on break worrying about it. I need to get up and keep moving my body and stimulating my mind and perhaps a solution will arise.

Valles Caldera.

What arises first is the Valle Grande, also known as the Valles Caldera. This magnificent and iconic valley was formed about a million years ago after a series of extremely powerful volcanic eruptions (500 times greater than the eruption in 1980 at Mount Saint Helens) caused a widespread collapse of land. The valley, spanning about 1,500 square miles, is breathtaking to view. I have the wonderful pleasure of spending this late afternoon walking beside it for many miles. It takes my mind off where I need to be and by when and onto the landscape immediately before me. It also could not be a better time to visit with mild temperature and beautiful light. I make it from one end to the other as time passes quickly.

And now I am entering the Jemez National Recreation Area and Forest. It is fitting after spending all morning hiking the base of these bad boys to finally officially be in the Jemez Mountains. What strikes me besides their might, is their accessibility—a perfect combination if you are going to be walking over and across them as I am doing. What also strikes me is the hang over that's still here from the Cerro Grande Fire that happened in 2000. It started as a controlled burn but then disastrously spread due to high winds and drought conditions. In the end it burned up an area 43,000 acres in size including parts of Los Alamos and many of the national park lands I have been walking through today. Ironically, from the Smokey Bear sign that says "Fire Danger HIGH," you can't avoid seeing in the hills beyond the remnants of the last major wildfire.

Irony.

The good news is that the Pueblo of Jemez, due south from where I am walking, has a steeped heritage of wildfire prevention. The Pueblo has proactively introduced small purposeful burns before the peak natural fire season. They have a tradition of using fire preemptively in dozens of small patches. Trees immediately near the pueblo homes have been harvested for heating fuel and thinning has reduced the landscape's combustibility and created defensible zones. Also they have used fire on the landscape during safe weather conditions to lessen the likelihood of burns during dangerous weather conditions. Their wildfire approach merits greater co-management opportunities with the federal government, especially in surrounding lands that the Pueblo has a traditional claim to including lands that I am walking through now.

Las Conchas trailhead.

South of the Valle Grande I walk past Las Conchas trailhead replete with a flowing creek, an iconic rock landmark, high grasses and sprawling forests. What a place! And then I discover a sign that shows cross country skiing is welcome here in the winter. I think of my mom who loved the sport. She gave me and my kids our first cross country skis. Now we all enjoy doing it when we get the chance. It's like walking on snow, connecting with the splendid outdoors, meditative to the mind, and a full body work out all at once.

Trudging along into the evening, my Google map shows that I am near a camp spot, but the problem is that it remains ten miles away from Amanda's convenience store, which closes at seven and opens at 8:30 tomorrow morning which is too late if I intend to make it to Cuba the next day by nightfall. Ultimately I have a lot of work to do to have any chance at making it to Chaco by Friday midday. In the midst of mulling over this predicament, an old sedan pulls over and the woman driving asks if I need a ride. I ask her if she could bring me to Amanda's before it closes; she says she's going right past there and tells me to hop in. After I get in she warns me she has no problem driving into a tree if I try to pull a fast one on her. Then, disarmingly, she tell me that her name is Miracle and that she's from Española. She says she isn't vaccinated and has had COVID three times. I quietly put on my face mask, for both courtesy and prevention sake. I ask her why she would pick up a man like me hiking along the road. She tells me that she is an "instinct person" and that she trusts me. I tell her a little about my long walk to Chaco. She perks up and tells me how she recently met up—and walked for a few miles—with a man who calls himself Bear Son who was walking coast to coast for health awareness (mental health, autism and cancer awareness). The kicker is, she says, he wears a 70 pound bear suit which includes all his gear and so you never can see his face. She tells me, as she is dropping me off, to watch out for mountain lions and to have a safe journey.

I thank her a lot, and I'm thinking she and the others who have shown such fearless friendliness are one of the main reasons I am indeed having such a worthwhile journey. I rationalize and justify that I took a ten mile car ride on the fact that my path from Cochiti took me six or so many miles further north than the alternative more direct Google map route showed but worth it for safety sake just like getting this ride was worth it in order to replenish my water and make it to my ultimate destination alive and in time. Amanda's is a classic establishment and I am so glad I made it there with Miracle's help. I spent basically a half an hour before it closed stocking up on water, sitting on a chair at the back of the store, resting my feet, eating fruit, drinking a Kombucha, and organizing my gear for the night walking that I planned to do.

Amanda's Country Store.

I have my glow in the dark jacket on (and one for my backpack), my forward and backward facing headlamps are shining away. I head off uphill into the dark but soon it's not nearly as dark anymore because the nearly full moon rises. As it does an RV pulls over and the young hippies inside tell me they are bound for the Jemez hot springs and invite me to join them. I pass on their gracious offer, letting them know I am content walking and, after Amanda's, I have no where in a hurry to get to. What is super nice is that the southwest wind that was blowing pretty hard earlier has completely died down. What's also nice is that there are hardly any cars on Road 126.

Brace ourselves for Shenanigans.

Hours pass and as I almost reach the top of the hill, I come to a most peculiar sign that says "shenanigans" up ahead. Well sure enough a little ways further a man pulls over his beaten up red car right ahead of me and asks me if he can give me a ride. I thank him, politely declining, but he's not done talking. He carries on saying kind things but in a rambling way. He tells me his name is Francis. He tells me he has some goats and horses and other animals in the woods nearby. He says, and I agree, that "we are all brothers and sisters." He mentions that "we are supposed to return the favor." He says he is on a spiritual quest but that everyone he encounters is so independent (referring to me presumably). He's concerned about tomorrow night. He says something's "going down" and he'll have to go gather his animals. I'm wondering if that something is Noah's Arc. I also see now he is drinking beer and I encourage him to go home and stop driving. He tells me his car is his home and so I say please go to a safe place nearby and as soon as possible stop driving so he doesn't hurt himself or others. Minutes later, after I steadfastly refuse to get a ride, he finally catches on and heads off, hopefully to a safe place.

Speaking of which I need to find a safe place myself to camp, and not far ahead is a dirt road off the main road with a sign for dispersed camping and I walk aways through the trees to a place where I find a relatively secluded flat location to set up my pad and bivy sack. It takes me a while longer to organize but when I do, and after hanging my food bag on a barbed wire fence a ways away, I nestle in for a good night's sleep. Even though that's the intention, the reality is a cold night sleep. Temperatures drop below freezing and I am shivering but when I close up the top of my sleeping bag under the bivy sack I get some relief to the point where it is warm enough to fade off to sleep.

—Day 2 Steps: 75,239

13
JOURNEY 3
DAY 3: JEMEZ

I wake up when it's still dark out at about five am. No bears or mountain lions found me or ate my food that's hanging on the fence so I got that going for me. It takes me a half an hour to get organized, after brushing my teeth (Holden would be happy), taking care of my feet, packing up my sleeping bag, getting out my day snacks and loading them in my mini pack so I can easily access them there (along with my lip balm and sun screen).

I'm in the dark, but with some help from a lingering near full moon. Light is starting to appear in the horizon. I'm sailing along, energized in what I term "dawn walking." As I said, it's early and late in the day when my body functions best. Middle of the day not so much. Anguish comes to mind just thinking about it. But it's day three on my journey and I am really happy. I don't take it for granted that I have made it this far. There are many things that could have halted me in my tracks or knocked me off course and there are many things to remain vigilant about. Cars are one primary concern. Thankfully on this Route 126, or yesterday's forest Road 289, there are not many, or yesterday not any, cars to contend with. My footing is another concern. Yesterday I looked up to take a picture and I stepped down on a loose impediment that made me trip and I nearly sprained my ankle which could have sidelined me.

A habitat and time of day
conducive to wildlife.

I have to watch my step. Then of course there are animals in the wild—bears, mountain lions, rattle snakes and the like—which have so far been kind to me (knock on wood). Just as I am thinking about wildlife I hear a noise in the forest to my left and there I see two mighty elk making their way up the ridge. I think of the hunters from yesterday and I surmise that if they asked me if I had an elk sighting today I would tell them no I haven't. They are majestic creatures who are doing no harm, certainly not harming us, so why harm them unless we have to hunt them for food to survive or for ceremonial reasons.

Another thing that could have hampered this trip is the weather. But it's been remarkable out, in the low sixties for the highs and lows in the mid thirties except last night which got below freezing. I know it froze because when I try to take a sip of water from the nozzle of my camel back nothing comes out. It's frozen solid. Imagine if high temperatures this week were in the forties or even fifties, how the lows could have been in the twenties or with wind chill, even lower, and how that could have precluded me from camping out unless I brought much heavier gear which I would have struggled to shlep around. Again, I am happy to make it to day three. I feel really lucky to be at this point. And as the light penetrates the darkness I can see more of my surroundings. I feel lucky to be here in the Jemez Mountains.

Fenton Lake.

I make it to Fenton Lake State Park, which is apparently used for several recreational activities including—as the sign says—"dog sledding!" I never knew there was dog sledding up here and I never knew that Fenton Lake even existed before now. There is a lot of new country in New Mexico that I am exploring for the first time. It definitely makes it more interesting. I never know what is coming around the bend. It keeps me guessing. This time what comes around the bend is a steady incline and then a sign that says "summit 7,940 feet." I am not fooled into thinking it's all down hill from here. In fact I believe in my head that the ups and downs and further ups, even higher ups, are a certainty. I am not going to get tricked like I did yesterday.

What we tell ourselves in our brains is very potent, it can be used like ammunition to harm us and hold us back from our true potential. Or it can be a source of well being and inspiration to exceed what we think we are capable of. If I say internally, "I have reached the summit, it's smooth sailing from here on," my body lets down and gets weak when that's not the case. If alternatively I say, "I don't know what is going to happen but I can handle it no matter what," my body follows my mind and becomes more resilient to anything that comes its way. As you can see, I have some time on my hands to brainstorm all of this. Yes I could be going a bit crazy having on-going conversations with myself like this, or I am already crazy to do something like this to begin with (but like Waylon Jennings sang, it keeps me from going insane or from walking into a dead end).

Jemez Mountains.

So a better sign than the summit, as far as positive self talk and mindfulness go, is the one I am now passing that reads "Pavement Ends." Like I said I feel at ease when I'm walking on dirt roads. And, as I take a picture of the dirt below my feet, I want to give a shout out not only to the ground but also to my shoes, the blue Altras, which are keeping me in good stead. As I follow along this dirt road (which I was told from the store clerk at Amanda's would last eight miles), I am blown away by how pleasant it is and I am thinking what a road it is for walking! Sandy, sunny, shady, steady.

A gateway through the towering trees.

But not all is beautiful nor hunky-dory. I have been quiet about the pain and anguish I am feeling hoping that if I give it less attention I won't feel it as much. But I am feeling it, and if it is not one thing it is another. The top of my right foot (nearer to the ankle than the toes) is killing me, but if I don't dwell on that then I can dwell on my left knee, which is particularly painful when I travel downhill and put too much weight on it by doing so. And if it isn't my knee, I could always mention the unrelenting discomfort of my shoulders from carrying the back pack so long. There is something compelling about being wounded in that I learn to empathize. More on that later I presume but now, having reached the top of the hill I need to take a break, and hopefully let any negative energy in my body be released and blow away with the wind. I feel like I have never enjoyed eating power bars, drinking water and resting my feet as I do now.

I am restored mentally and physically to the point when, as I walk in the full sunlight, I realize joyfully that the phrase 'if it isn't one thing, it's another' can be said in the reciprocal positive sense. i.e., if it's not the occasional moments of shade from walking under trees that leaves me delighted in cool air, it could be the blue sky for as far as the eye can see—leaving me with the feeling of vast potential—or it could just as easily be the oxygen from the mountainous forests, spurring me to breath deeply and think clearly (I couldn't imagine doing this epic walk in vast urban areas as it would be too draining of the life essentials needed to go on which are so abundant here)!

Approaching the end of the dirt road stretch.

I come to a wide open meadow and I see a lone horse who is quite interested in me. The lone horse is staring at me as I walk past. Maybe she has never seen a middle aged man hiking from Santa Fe to Chaco before. More fall colors come into view and I reflect on the autumn season. It seems, more than any other season I can think of, to be about changing (color changing, temperature changing, life changing). We need to change. Maybe we can learn how to do so from the Fall. We need to learn how to transition ourselves and overcome challenges that are seemingly intractable. Maybe the way it will play out is like the old adage says: when—as plain as day—the pain of staying the same becomes greater than the pain of transforming then we will step out of our comfort zone and into the solution zone.

The half way mark.

Maybe the hot sun is wearing me down or maybe the dust particles are seeping into my brain from the pick-up truck that just flew by leaving a cloud in it's wake. The good news is I just passed the half way mark for today's distance and almost for the whole journey. Being less than half way there feels grueling like there is no end in sight while being over the proverbial hump makes every step feel like progress. A biker with no helmet and no gear, just wearing the clothes on his back, cruises past me. I marvel at his simplicity. It makes me day dream about my friend Charles' recommendation that I bike rather than walk to Chaco. If I did that, I am thinking, I would already be there with time to spare. A half hour later I see the biker sitting on the rail beside the road. He asks me where I am heading and I tell him Chaco via Cuba, and he says he is doing the same. I say "Get out of town, you're biking to Chaco!?" He says no, he is waiting for his parents who have a pick up truck. They are going to pick him up and head there later. He was just out for a few hour midday cruise. Well that explains him not having more gear than just the clothes on his back.

Across the creek to the cleanest public restroom.

Stopping even for a few seconds, just to bend down and itch my foot, requires will power and discretion. It is dangerous because the body, once you stop, however briefly, immediately realizes how it feels, which in my case is miserable. But my misery is abated by the sound of a babbling brook called Clear Creek. It puts me in the mood to…go to the bathroom and not the easy kind. Luckily just over the bridge less than a football field away is a little camp site area featuring a public restroom facility (one of the very few I've seen). I enter the men's room and to my surprise not only does the bathroom smell better than any camping bathroom I can recall, it is also cleaner than any bathroom I have been to. It's truly remarkable. Maybe no one ever goes here or maybe the park ranger is a fastidious, first rate germaphobe. Regardless, I spend extra time in there and I appreciate every minute.

I have also been appreciating the Jemez Mountains all day long (and last evening). They are gorgeous in an understated kind of way. They seem not pretentious in any way but inviting to all. I didn't have the privilege of visiting the Jemez Pueblo on this trip. I understand that a majority of the 3,500 or so total Jemez Pueblo members reside in their village known as Walatowa—which means this is the place! And what a meaning that is. It's a very enviable attitude that the Jemez Pueblo people have wrapped up in that expression. I can understand having been through this country that this is an extraordinary place. But even if it weren't physically beautiful, I love the idea that wherever you are or wherever you find yourself, is the place to be. That is a secret to life that I also subscribe to. Meaning, the grass is greenest right where we are, instead of always envying or yearning for something better somewhere else. Even though I didn't go inside the boundary of the current Jemez Pueblo lands in this journey, I still recognize that I have been walking much of the time through lands that have traditional significance for the Jemez Pueblo people and therefore I consider these lands to be sacred too, knowing I am just a visitor and knowing the importance of having respect.

Putting one foot in front of the other.

I cross the Rio de Las Vacas and I am perplexed by the name considering that cows and rivers don't typically go well together. Thinking about pollution in vital riparian areas, and experiencing the sensation of my whole body aching every step I take, I get some relief thinking how nice it might be to get run over right now. I know that sounds morbid but it would put me out of my misery. Instead of dwelling in morbidity I instead think of my grandmother Pixie and what she told me the one time I asked how on earth she coped when her oldest son passed away at a relatively young age. She simply said, "I just put one foot in front of the other." What an attitude and approach to have in response to such a deeply painful situation! I fully understand that my pain is just temporary whereas her grief was a million times more lasting and poignant but her wise and positive frame of mind is a keystone heritage value that I learn from and aspire to. And so I do, put one foot in front of the other and it gets me up and over the mountain. And now I can see in the horizon, way down on the other side, the vicinity of my day's destination point: Cuba, New Mexico. So I know this one time at least that it's all down hill from here to there.

Intellectually I understand the concept that it is not the arriving that counts, it's the on-going journey, but selfishly and metaphysically I would sure like to arrive right now. Instead, I arrive at a mile marker that I planned to take a break at, and let me say that this is the place! This is the best break of all breaks (they all feel that way). I once again take off my shoes and socks, as is the ritual, but different this time was that I eat un-salted almonds, a lot of them, and I feel in this moment that they are the best snack food of all time. I am grateful as can be to taste them, so many of them, one after the other. The other unique thing I do on this break is take a little cat nap—which puts my body and soul at ease and in confluence. Lastly, right before I start again, I apply a hefty amount of WURU Lambs Wool around the sore places of my feet to cushion the bottom most parts of my body for the significant downhill portion that remains.

Descent

I have hardly used my phone except to take pictures and occasionally to check distances on Google maps. Most of the day I keep my phone on airplane mode to preserve my battery power and to preserve some semblance of presence and peace of mind. But on one or two occasions per day, especially at a high point where there is sometimes cell reception I take my phone off airplane mode and I'll contact Numi to let her know I am all right. She ordered a temporary subscription of Life360 so the few times I come off airplane mode she can figure out my whereabouts. Anyhow, after checking in with her on my way down the mountain, I forgot to resume airplane mode and sure enough I get a phone call. It's Stampa calling to get my brother Scott's cell phone number which he somehow misplaced. He isn't calling to check in on my journey—because he doesn't know I am doing it at this moment until I remind him. He was really excited and encouraging about my trip when I first told him about it, but right now he is preoccupied. But then he does ask "how's it going?" And I tell him that the journey is exhilaratingly joyful and excruciatingly painful all at once. He wonders aloud—in endeavoring on this expedition—if I have bitten off more than I can chew? It's a fair question.

Have I? I don't know the answer. The question stays in my mind, especially as the experience gets more difficult.

In the last several hours, a road biker (well outfitted with helmet and clip in shoes, wearing a professional bike racing jersey) comes sailing passed me for what seems like the third or forth time (I can't keep track). He is repeatedly going up and down this ten miles stretch of the mountain I am descending. Each time he laps me my self esteem, which is already in the dumps, ticks down a notch. I feel like I did the one time I ran the New York City Marathon, when at first you get excited by the massive crowd support but at the end you cannot handle even looking at, not to mention acknowledging the cheering spectators lined along either side. All you want to be is anonymous, and whatever you do you don't want to expend any additional energy than necessary to get to the finish line because when you are worn down it feels like you barely have enough to get there.

Like with running I suppose, breathing helps, in through the nose out from the mouth. What also helps is the intake of a power bar, turkey jerky and energy gummies. I don't hold back. Sadly, I probably look like I went to the bathroom in my pants because I am hobbling down the road, desperately compensating for my extreme feet and leg soreness. I pass another falling rock sign and think how much it would suck to expend all this effort only to be wiped out and crushed on the roadside by a falling boulder. But then I think about being put out of my misery again and it kind of feels appealing.

Late afternoon sunshine.

At least there is not a stiff wind in my face. But there is steady heat and direct late afternoon sunshine. I see cows on the side of the roadway. They don't see me until I'm right up next to them and then they run away startled. I pass a sign, as I am leaving the national forest lands, that says "Land of Many Uses" which now I guess includes cattle grazing and long distance walking. I'm enamored with my silhouette, and I have been walking long enough to the point where I am delirious enough that I am tempted to have a conversation with my shadow. I haven't been around people these days so it's understandable to entertain self companionship. Instead I get a few moments of the best kind of companionship, and that is of course being with dogs. Two Great Pyrenees (big white long haired dogs) come up to me on the road and walk alongside me for a while. I am honored but I am also concerned for their well being and happy that no cars are passing by. I look across to the house and pasture where they came from and I see what looks to be a colony of Great Pyrenees but as I get closer I realize it's a sheep colony which makes sense because Great Pyrenees are bred to protect sheep by deterring wolves, coyotes and other predators. The dogs make it back to their property and I make it back to a healthier state of mind, no longer yearning to have a conversation with my shadow.

Making friends with others beyond just my silhouette.

As the sun sinks below the horizon an important concept rises into focus. I realize that I need help and that I can't do this alone. Moments after this revelation a red pick up pulls up beside me and a man who appears to be Native American asks if I would like a ride into the town of Cuba. I let the man know that I have come this far and that I can walk the little way that is still left but I let him know it means a lot to me him stopping to help. Less than a mile further I pass another man, who appears to be Mexican American, working on his fence. He sees me passing and he says hello. He asks if I would like some water. Then he asks if I have a place to stay the night; if I would like to stay over he says he would be happy to host me. I let him know that I have a reservation at the Cuban Lodge and he says, "Oh, living fancy are we." We both smile (knowing that the Cuban lodge is a bare bones motel) and then we say farewell but not before my heart is warmed by the show of affection from people I do not know just as I was putting out in the universe a call for help. I realize in fact that I am not at all doing this alone. There are people like these two gentlemen who are waiting in the wings to assist. There are my wife and kids who are thinking about me every step of the way. There are countless friends providing emotional encouragement and support. Unbeknownst to me Numi posted a picture and description of my walk on instagram and she said she received hundreds of likes and uplifting messages: statements like "Go Robb!", "We're rooting for you", "Walk tall", "Be strong", "We are cheering you on", and on and on and on. I can feel their support and solidarity. It keeps me going in discomfort. And there is something greater too, a deeper dynamic that is out there and on my side. I can feel it looking out for me, soothing me, guiding me. Almost as if every step I take is energized and guided by a gently compelling force field.

Half of the last mile into Cuba goes alongside the St. Francis de Assisi Park and I take the dedicated pathway that parallels the main road. I am struck by the generosity I am receiving from all walks of life, both from the closest people in my life and perfect strangers. The bottom line is: I am not alone on this journey and the reason why I can do this at all is that I am walking together with forces greater than myself.

Once I get to 550 I have to walk a mile in the opposite direction of my final destination to get to the motel. I go into the Dollar Store at eight o'clock to get some water and rations. Next door I check into the Cuban Lodge and the owner named Flo is a fire ball, giving me a hard time, saying "walking here from Santa Fe is no big whoop." But she warms up to me when I speak with her in Spanish (however incorrectly), and she gives me the room key which I cherish. I am not blowing smoke when I say that this is the best hotel accommodations

I have experienced. There is not one flashy thing about the room. It's small and very simple, no frills. But it is clean and it is heavenly. I lay out and re-organize all my gear. I decide to leave behind a bag with stuff I don't need (like overly used clothes, unnecessary food, extraneous battery packs, etc) to shed a few pounds. I take a hot shower, which is truly magnificent. I turn on the portable heater next to the bed, and hang my socks on it. I fill up the plastic trash receptacle with cold water and soak my feet and knees in it. I turn on the lamp and lie in the bed, what a joyful feeling that is. Then I talk with my daughter on the phone, and tell her stories from my trip. She says she has been thinking of me all the time, and I tell her I know. She tells me that Nama and Grandpa Gerry, my mom and dad, would be proud of me and are with me too. I let her know how all of this support moves me and I reiterate that I couldn't do it alone. She tells me about the book she is reading about how "doing nothing"—doing things we take for granted like walking or listening to birds (the author can identify what kind of bird it is from the sound it makes; Saint Francis would surely appreciate that!)— "is doing something truly meaningful." Now it's time for me to do the nothing that's really something: aka sleeping. I say goodnight. I turn out the light and I fall right to sleep feeling comforted by the wonderful accommodation and camaraderie going on.

—Day 3 Steps: 79,255

14
JOURNEY 3
DAY 4: APACHE

I wake up earlier than any other morning on the trip so far. I get my night walking gear on, leave my drop off bag on the desk like Flo told me to do and I head out the door at 4:30. I stop at a convenience store and purchase a little container of Advil, something that I have not used up until this point but I know it's something that could help me carry on without being so hamstrung by my right foot pain in particular.

Waking up ready to go after a glorious night's rest
in the best motel I've ever stayed at.

Something strange happened last night. At some point the power went off, the heater stopped working and when I rolled over and switched the light on nothing happened, but at about three in the morning the power resumed because the light came on. Anyhow the woman at the convenience store says that someone drove into a utility pole by the McDonalds. My first thought is that I hope it wasn't Francis the man with the animals who had been drinking and stopped to talk with me saying something was going to go down tonight. Whoever it was, the incident instills in me a heightened sense of caution about drunk drivers in particular and about safety in general. Today I would be walking along the busiest road of the trip, Highway 550, that goes from Bernallio (south of Albuquerque) to Farmington, so there are a lot of trucks and cars that will be cruising by at high speeds. I did some reconnaissance before the trip, knowing there were a few different ways I could get to Chaco but I settled on this route— not only because of the awesomeness of where I have been already but also— because of the safety and clarity of this section which I confirmed had significant shoulder space on the side of the road.

After hearing about the car accident I want more assurance than the people I interviewed by phone beforehand. I pray for a big shoulder and for getting to Chaco in one piece. Sure enough, the shoulder, at least on this section of 550, turns out to be fantastic. There is room for a car to park there it is so wide, and there are also rumble strips (sleeper lines or alert strips) beside the white line of the two lane highway.

As I walk out of Cuba in the pre-dawn time I start to find a rhythm with my body, but my brain is not fully awake yet. I know this because my thoughts are not complete, or at least not in complete sentences. Roosters rousing. Dogs barking. Dogs perceptive. Semi's loud! Now I know how good I have had it the last three days in terms of quietude and the abundance of nature. But there is something mechanical and industrial now that helps me in the sense of putting one foot after the other like a machine that just pumps out product without thinking. This factory like way of walking helps me climb the huge hill heading northwest out of Cuba. But there's a minute when no cars or trucks are coming from either direction and it becomes quiet for a moment to the point that it feels like it's just me and the moon going along.

I see big white writing on the side of the road that reads "First Drum!" I contemplate drum beats, and concentrate on putting each foot on the ground to match the beating of my heart. That feels and works much better than a machine in terms of keeping me going. This kind of drumbeat walking enables me to make it to the top of the hill, which is a bear of a hill. And I am grateful for this "First Drum" message that helps me walk on the earth in a more harmonious way. I have to close my eyes to really get into the natural rhythm but I can't risk tripping and spraining an ankle so I have to close my eyes without closing my eyes if that makes sense. With my eyes metaphorically closed I meditate on the First Drum beating creation—the whole vast universe and our little world in it—into existence. I reflect on the Sky Father, who is tied to the west where I am heading and who is tied to the weather, to the sun and to the rain. I ponder the situation of drought aggravated like never before by our climate crisis and I understand that we need to do a ceremony like never before to overcome the spiritual crisis that we find ourselves in or dug ourselves in. My mind and soul are now waking up, transitioning from the dark-light of night behind to the purple light of morning ahead.

Drumbeat Walking.

In this dawn transition I'm compelled to dedicate my four direction walk. I say aloud that it is "Dedicated to my parents and ancestors past and to my children and young people forward who have the courage we've thus far lacked to stand up for a livable climate; may we have the wisdom to walk in their shoes and be likewise inspired so that all together we heal the world."

I start sobbing. The idea of the young generation with the spirit of the ancestors on their side standing up with the bravery that we have been missing; and then us being moved by them to the point when all as one we rise to the occasion makes tears flow down my face: tears of inadequacy, tears of admiration, tears of hope. It doesn't stop for a while, but it's okay. It feels good to cry and it feels right to cry in this dire moment.

With all the mechanization, the drum beats and the moving emotions, I have climbed the summit (I have come to hate that word), and the beautiful thing I am realizing now, and I say this carefully and respectfully, is I have reached the point of the journey where there are no extreme elevation changes left. I started at about 7,500 feet in Santa Fe, descended to about 5,000 feet in Cochiti, climbed about 5,000 feet to 10,000 feet at the Valles Caldera, and then scaled up and down from 7,000 to 9,000 feet through the Jemez Mountains, and now the elevation of Cuba New Mexico of 6,906 feet is almost the same as Nageezi where I will turn off toward Chaco Canyon which of course is ultimately a bit lower. Confirmation comes with road side information, a sign the header of which says "Welcome to the San Juan Basin!" Welcome to 20,000 square miles of flattened land and 1,000 feet of sedimentary strata.

Beginning
of the San Juan Basin.

All I can think about is the oil, gas and coal industry making this region one of the world's hot spots for fossil fuel energy development and pollution despoiling our civilization. It may have started out with a benevolent intention to fuel our modern civilization. But with what we have come to know—at least over the past 30+ years—about the greenhouse effect, about CO2 and methane emissions, and coal ash contamination (the list goes on and on) fossil fuel extraction is unmistakably destroying us. Plus any responsible business/ industrial endeavor and government regulatory framework together, in the name of civilization, needs to assess the ramifications of the product and pay for/ account for the remediation required beforehand and all throughout the process instead of treating it all as an externality and kicking the pollution response and payment can down the road for others to deal with later.

View from the shoulder of Highway 550.

I make it the next few miles by pretending to use a walking stick. Just the act of pretending and the adjusted gait that comes with it, eases the pain in my right foot and helps me carry on. The warm glow from the sunrise behind me warms my back and I'm thankful to the sun. I turn around and walk backwards for a while so I can properly say good morning. When I turn forward again I am struck by the relative flatness for as far as my eyes can see and I am thrilled, as well as rethinking my choice of residence. Maybe I should live in the Midwest somewhere or in Holland, my imagination wanders and wonders. I think of our home in Santa Fe, New Mexico. I take my phone out of airplane mode to check in with my wife. I tell her I'm safe and sound, that despite the pain in my foot I'm hanging in there and that I know I am on the right track because I'm having stirring emotions. She responds, "so you like limping along the side of the highway crying to yourself?" What a hilarious statement! It should make me question my sanity but it only winds up making me laugh. And I think "yeah, I do enjoy walking down the road laughing and crying. It makes me feel alive." Numi suggested I take some Advil which I just picked up at the convenience store early this morning (in addition to a big Gatorade which I downed in three and half seconds). I say my body is not used to Advil and that I should pace myself because it makes me a little out of it. But she researches it and says I can be reasonable and have as much as 400 milligrams every four hours and the capsules are only 200 milligrams so I can have two tablets every four hours if I like. I will start with one tablet every four hours and see how that goes.

Before Numi gets off the phone with me she expresses concern that I've only been eating power bars and snacks the whole time and she worries when I get to Chaco for the celebration that will include real meals like Buffalo Steak and Turkey sandwiches for lunch that I might throw up. I'm glad she's thinking I'm making it to Chaco because I'm just taking it one mile at a time at this point. I am also finding this throw up concept very funny and so without realizing it she has cheered me up. And to be cheered up further, I next have the wonderful opportunity to have a phone conversation with Fisher, who has been really busy lately with school, college applications, sports and filming. He tells me he wasn't too busy to not think about me on the walking quest—he tells me he's been thinking about me a lot (and I feel that). He offers some thoughtful and wise advice: "wherever the journey takes me that's where I want to be;" he says "no worries;" and finally he says "seek discomfort" which is profound. In fact there is a recent book that my buddy Lee just told me about called *The Comfort Crisis* by Michael Easter (Reference) about embracing discomfort in order to reclaim our wild, happy and healthy selves. It's true, we have to get out of our comfort zone to grow and restore as a people and yes to solve the climate crisis.

Before resuming airplane mode I check in with another good buddy of mine Bart, who is a fellow journeyman, who gave me the granola that I ate on Day 2 and who presently provides some uplifting humor and then reads to me the thought of the day from Al-Anon. He shares, "The choices I make are not as important as the fact that I make them." I like the idea that we have agency, we have choices, and making them is a healthy thing—versus throwing up our hands in despair or paralysis.

It's nice to check in with my wife, my son and my close friend. It's also nice to get back in airplane mode and into the present place and state of mind, aided now by Advil. It sets in soon and I am thinking what have I been waiting for: it helps my foot feel tolerable and it helps reduce the swelling. But I'm happy because I got here without it and now I get to use it sparingly when I need it the most.

I pass the Continental Divide, 7,380 feet elevation. Another milestone.

The Continental Divide.

I can't get my mind off the Advil topic. The problem with pain pills, I'm diagnosing, is that the true problem ceases to be healed. In other words, the wound is still there whether we want to see it or feel it or not. The pain pills don't ultimately work to heal our wound but rather just to make us numb to it. I wonder, as I move along, what is our deepest wound, what is at the core of our spiritual crisis? My knee jerk response is "Our way of life." But instead of hastily jumping to that or other conclusions, I decide not to answer definitively right now but rather to ponder the question and walk on it for a while. And so I do.

A while has gone by, the pain at the top of my right foot returns. I hobble along and soon I enter the Jicarilla Apache Reservation. On the land, in the air, from the people here there is ample food for thought about the unanswered question of what is at the source of our modern society's illness. What has crystallized for me here over the several hours pondering is that at our core we have been lacking backbone. Backbone literally means our spine, and the mainstay or chief support of a system or organization. In slang it means bravery and strength of character or will. It's hard to stand up for ourselves, for the dignity of one another and our earth, without one. How can we have allowed thieves to rape and pillage the land and pollute our atmosphere so indiscriminately? We haven't shown the backbone to stop it. Rather we have been numb to it. The theft of the commons has taken place right under our noses yet we have failed to have the righteous indignation you would think we should have. We have not had a backbone or else we would never let this happen. I don't care how many pills we take, there is no way to resolve our spiritual crisis, the climate crisis (not to mention walking to a place of healing and restoration) without backbone. There is no way to stand with any semblance of integrity before our children, who are watching and counting on us, without backbone.

Jicarilla Apache Reservation.

There are people who came before us who had, and still have, backbone. The bands of the Apache tribes throughout the history of the west, for example, were brave in countless kinds of ways including wilderness survival and defense of their territory. The Apache Nation fiercely resisted encroachment on their lands. There are different communities of Apache that responded differently of course, but there was an overarching character trait of standing up for the land as a people. The Jicarilla Apache have a more nomadic heritage, which includes reliance on buffalo, residence in teepees (made from buffalo hide) and basket making, which is what "Jicarilla" means. Mescalero Apache, also New Mexico based, have similarities and contrasts. They were known to be expert guerrilla fighters and horsemen who steadfastly defended their homelands and wreaked havoc on Spanish, American and Mexican aggressors. It is known that Geronimo's descendants reside on the Mescalero Apache Reservation which is located in south central New Mexico. Geronimo (1829–1909), who was born in present day New Mexico and became Chief of the Chiricahua Apaches, proudly stood up against the egregious intrusion by the US Government and refused to compromise. He was a great spiritual leader and medicine man who was said to have supernatural powers. It was told that he could see the future and he could walk without creating footprints. It should go without saying that Geronimo is a walking hero of mine and an inspiration for all who stand up boldly for justice (Appendix 1).

Walking along the Jicarilla Apache Reservation helps me understand the central and vital importance of courageously standing up for the land, for one another and for the sacredness of life that enable our existence. We all like so many of the Apache tribes need to have or grow a backbone in order to stand up against the colonialism that continues to this day, not only in the form of fossil fuel extraction but also in the wider excessive forms of industrialism and capitalism. We must stand up to any ways that our economy is despoiling the environment and harming humanity and wildlife alike. We must not tolerate destruction in the name of greed. The anecdote that comes to mind, as I trudge along the highway, is Star Wars. In the Last Hope, if Luke, Leah, Yoda, Obi Wan Kenobi and Hans Solo were all spineless, the dark side would have prevailed and what a sad universe that would be. The same goes for our planetary system and us.

There are some things that I have got going in my favor on this fourth day of walking. I'm not only aided by concentrating on the resistance and pride of the Apache people, I'm also aided by the relative flatness of the terrain, and by the relative lightness of my back pack having shed some weight at the Cuban lodge. Numi was right to underscore the magnitude of this trek at my age, and to be maximally prepared for it but she was wrong to insist I carry much more food which I could have replenished at the convenience store(s) each day. The extra weight of the backpack from shlepping extra food over the first three days probably took a year off my life!

Being a little lighter on my feet from a lighter back pack, having wounded swollen feet that cringe every time I step clumsily, and being inspired by Geronimo not leaving any footprints behind, all together make me want to step lightly on the ground. Touching the ground gently is an art which I haven't learned fully enough. It not only can enable my feet and knees to endure but like the "First Drum" it can teach us how to treat the Earth. With my head up but thankfully my eyes on the ground, I see a Tarantula spider walk right by my foot steps and I marvel at how gently they walk without impact, without leaving footprints. I'm grateful that I'm paying attention and didn't step on this marvelous creature, which is another animal walking hero (Appendix 1).

With spontaneous inclination, perhaps inspired by the Tarantula, I start playing a game of chanting to drown out the noise every time a vehicle passes me in either direction. My chanting needs a lot of work but it beats the sound of cars and semi trucks going by. In fact the more I do it, the more I get into the idea of chanting loudly to rail against the fossil fuel culture. I don't yell my chant at EVs because of the greener alternative they provide nor do I chant at RVs because of their adventurous spirit. But the rest of the vehicles zooming by receive my loud drum beat chanting expressions. The nice thing about this exercise is not only drowning out the noise of the gas engine vehicles but also the fact that it kills time. One hour or so later (I'm losing track of time), when my loud chants are reduced to a lackluster, one syllable murmur, I know the time has come to stop playing the chanting game. What fitting timing because moments later I arrive at the exit for the Jicarilla Apache Casino (closed) and gas station (open). It's just after high noon and it's high time I take a break, especially given that this is the only convenience store in over a dozen miles in either direction (specifically it is 20 miles back to Cuba and 13 miles ahead to Counselor).

I purchase a few waters and Gatorades and then I visit the Subway sandwich shop thinking that I may as well get used to some "real food" like Numi suggested so I don't throw up the meals that are planned at Chaco courtesy of Heritage Tours. I order a full size multigrain submarine sandwich with turkey, pepper jack cheese, extra shredded lettuce, red onions, olive oil and mayonnaise. I didn't care that it wasn't gluten free. I was determined to treat myself. I sit down outside on a bench, take off my shoes, lay out my things and then dig into the sandwich. And I am not just saying this for affect. But it is hands down the best sandwich I have ever eaten. Not just the best Subway sandwich. The best sandwich period. I try to extend the sheer delight by not wolfing it down so quickly. I try to savor it. But I have trouble controlling myself. I wind up wolfing down the first half and somewhat savoring the second.

An officer from the Jicarilla Apache walks by and stops to say hello. He gives me a welcome greeting and I tell him how much I appreciate the lands and the landscape here. We soon go our own ways, but not without my appreciation of this brief visit. If I were thinking better, more clearly, I would have asked questions about his community but I was at a loss for words. And sometimes spoken words are over rated anyhow.

I've been thinking that time is my friend on this journey; the day or so that's left will go quickly even though it feels like forever remains. But time is my friend only when I am walking. When I'm taking a break, like I'm doing now, time is my enemy. A 40 minute break is over doing it I realize but I love every minute of it, plus it takes me a while to get organized (sunscreen, filling up my camel back, changing from baseball cap to my wide brim sun hat, switching socks, applying Second Skin and WURU wool, taking off a layer).

Back on the road, I'm initially very sore and seemingly very slow but I pick up some pace after having my second Advil of the trip. Another pick me up comes from speaking briefly with my good friend Charles who tells me two things. First, that he fully expects me to be lying down waiting for everyone in a lounge chair having a cocktail at the Visitor Center when they all arrive tomorrow (and there is little chance of that given how far I have to go. I'd be lucky to make it to the outer park - greater Chaco area at this rate but the image he shares makes me smile). The other thing he says is that "the gods are shining down" on me because he says I'm "atoning" for my sins. I respond that I would have to walk a hell of a lot longer, probably months on end or years even, to atone for all the mistakes I have made and to make up for all my shortcomings. But as I get off airplane mode and put by phone away I do believe that the weather gods have been extraordinarily kind to me. Besides all the good fortune of the weather that I've experienced every day including low winds and mild temperatures every day, this afternoon the sky is almost completely covered in clouds which is a minor miracle and so unusual for New Mexico which boasts of over 300 days per year of direct sunshine. What the cloud cover means to me is that the sun is not beating down on me and the temperature remains cool when I most need it. And so, no joke, I am grateful to the gods and feel like they are truly looking out for me.

Just then a trucker comes by in the opposite direction and gives me a supportive honk as if to acknowledge the gratitude that I am feeling. And moments later another trucker going in my same direction honks in solidarity. The force is with me, and what is also with me this afternoon is the mindset that this trip is helping reinforce of how awesome the simple things in life are: a sandwich, a bed, a drink of water, an unsalted almond, bare feet in the breeze (the list goes on…). This grueling—exhilarating walk is teaching me to appreciate the very basics of life's pleasures and not to take them for granted.

My attention shifts back to my foot and leg aggravation. To ameliorate the situation my college lacrosse buddy Chad comes to mind, how he always referred to his thick leg muscles, his quads in particular, as "dogs!" He would always be talking to and looking out for his dogs, cause he knew they were fundamental to success. So right now I am channeling Chad and his loving attention on his dogs. I would like to extend the reference beyond the quads, to my whole legs, my feet and knees in particular, and say "come on dogs, you can do it! Don't fail me now but rather carry me home!" Dogs are such a good reference because they are faithful, loyal and would do anything for us. We only have to feed them and yet they take care of us and sooth us in so many ways. So I'm determined to feed my dogs, my legs, with nutrition, with hydration, with electrolytes, proteins and carbohydrates and think by doing so and by honoring and calling on them they will come though for me like sled dogs crossing the Arctic.

I wonder what my dogs, Coaster and Gary, are up to and if they think of me or miss me as I miss them. I sure need their spiritual comfort and support right about now. In their honor I sneak in a leak off the side of the road just before any cars come cruising by which is a feat on Highway 550.

For some reason, probably exhaustion and yearning something stable in my teetering faith, I start singing "...Glory, Glory hallelujah, Glory Glory hallelujah, Glory Glory hallelujah, His truth is marching on. He has sounded from the trumpet that shall never call retreat, He is sifting out the hearts of men before his judgment seat, Oh, be swift, my soul to answer, oh, be jubilant, my feet, His truth is marching on..." (Appendix 2). As I finish singing the lyrics and walk on down the road, I blurt out "this is a moment of truth" and just from saying that, thinking about the song and feeling it resonate, I almost shed a tear.

Holding it back, I witness the embodiment of toughness in the form of native grasses and plants growing and surviving only through slivers and cracks in the cement on the highway's shoulder. Talk about tough! I am nothing in comparison. I'm a little delirious, I am not going to lie, and I am sure that readers have known this for some time already.

Another song comes to mind, a Bill Haley & His Comets song, which I change to say "I'm going to walk, walk, walk around the clock tonight" (Appendix 2). I wonder if it is prophetic regarding the night to come, or if it's just a catchy song to keep a semblance of rhythm going as I hobble along.

Quick roadside break.

I take a quick roadside break, on a little wall right beside the highway. I lay out my things, discreetly take another quick leak on the other side of the wall, I put on my night gear (glow in the dark jacket, headlamps, etc) for later, and I down another liter of Gatorade. When I resume my journey I soon pass a sign that I'm entering the San Juan Soil and Water Conservation District, which is another healthy legacy from the New Deal, part of Franklin Roosevelt administration's wise response to the Dust Bowl.

Now, with a concept of drought and degraded lands, I start thinking about nothingness, a Buddhist aspiration, which helps carry me on step after step. What also seems to help my stepping forward is walking backwards. It instills balance, it loosens my stiff aching legs and I gain a new perspective, a beautiful view from where I have come. It's quite possible that my whole sensibility is being shaped from this experience. Certainly my present state of mind is being cultivated by journeying through this landscape. The brilliant light and changing sky dynamics prompt me to feel magical. No joke. As I have already commented, the latest part of the day and the earliest part of the morning have been my favorite times for walking, it's when I am connected the most and thus feeling my best.

As darkness sets in I am about two miles from a place called Counselor which is on the map and I am looking forward to restocking my water there. But presently I pass a convenience store, above the road, off to the right. There is no gas station affiliated with it and hardly any cars so it seems not so central but the lights are on and there is a person who just pulls up and is seemingly about to go in. I almost walk right by figuring there will be better stops in a few miles but I decide to ask the man in the car if there are other places soon up ahead or if this is the only place in the vicinity. I knock on his passenger side window and understandably he is a bit startled because he didn't see me coming. Instead of rolling down the window he gets out of the car and answers my question—there aren't any other places except for a Sinclair station 16 or so miles ahead. I'm relieved I asked. He's still a little spooked by me because I am following him into the store. We get inside and each go about our business. I get another liter of Gatorade and large container of water. I ask the store clerk guy if I can borrow a map and if it's okay to sit down on the floor somewhere to refill my water and gear up. He says no problem and suggests I sit in the back of the store where there are some steps to sit on.

As I organize my stuff, enjoying being off my feet, the man from the car comes over to where I am and starts talking with me. He introduces himself as Rafay. He tells me he wanted to visit with me for a moment because as he ascertains and explains, "we both seem to be on a spiritual journey." He continues: "the journey involves dismantling our egos and understanding that we are not perfect; we're just human beings." He goes on to say that he works for an oil and gas company, that he just came from Bloomfield and he is on the way to Albuquerque to catch the red eye flight to New York City. He says he doesn't agree with the people he works with politically—many are Trump supporters he frowns, but he says that he has a greater purpose in the works and that is to interact with people from all walks of life. He tells me he is a Muslim and he invites me to his mosque in Albuquerque if I am ever in the vicinity. He says ultimately we're here to serve our Creator and creation, which includes helping people who may be down and out and who need a lift in life. He tells me before he leaves that I am going to find what I'm searching for and that I'm going to the right place by going to Chaco.

As we shake hands, I reflect on the importance of understanding different walks of life. I'm a bit blown away by the serendipity unfolding. The man's wearing a tee shirt featuring the Millennium Falcon, Hans Solo's ship in Star Wars which is exactly what I was just thinking about earlier today with regards to the urgent need to have backbone and coming to the aid of the land and humankind alike. As we head off in opposite directions I call out "I love your shirt" and—thankfully—he says "you're not the only one to say that."

After walking a few miles in the dark, the wondrous circle of life continues to spiral around me this time in the form of a pickup truck that had pulled over ahead of me and was waiting there seemingly to assist me. The passenger side window is rolled down and the woman driving introduces herself as a Navajo woman named Moleta along with her grandmother who is in the passenger seat who is the most darling old woman I have seen in some time. Moleta says "hop in the back of the pickup and just knock on the window when you want me to let you off." I am speechless in uncertainty thinking I should just huff it on my own but also so appreciative of their kindness and bravery (to stop in the dark to help a strange looking backpacker). I decide to reach out to the hand that is extended to me, as Gandhi advised, and instead of saying no or saying yes for the duration I decide to take a third approach and thankfully accept a brief ride up the hill. After about three miles I knock on the back window and Moleta, true to her word of course, pulls over to let me get out and offers her "blessings" for my journey.

I thank my lucky stars for all the demonstrations of human generosity I'm experiencing on this trip. And speaking of stars, they are out in full force tonight. The full moon hasn't risen yet. Right in front of me I see the Big Dipper and I begin singing another one of my favorite songs, "Ripple" by Grateful Dead (Appendix 2): "...Ripple in still water, When there is no pebble tossed, Nor wind to blow, Reach out your hand if your cup be empty, If your cup is full, may it be again, Let it be known there is a fountain, That was not made by the hands of men, There is a road, no simple highway, Between the dawn and dark of night, And if you go, no one may follow, That path is for your steps alone."

I realize that another benefit to it being so dark, besides the opportunity to see the constellations is that I am shielded from all the oil and gas developments and storage tanks that I am passing by. When the full moon comes out I am passed most of it for the time being. I am thinking of my grandfather Chet who used to say the quote: "There is no rest for the weary." But I am going to try to find a place to rest anyway. Someplace not far from 550 (I can only walk so far) and some place hidden from view. The first dirt road I come to leads up to a look out spot where there is a cross and rosaries. Staying there doesn't seem right, so I pass by that road. But the next little turn off seems promising. It goes enough away from the highway that you can't hear the loud semis going by as much and it's out of view like I want. There is a sign that reads, "Christian Fellowship Center" and I am thinking this might be safe and welcoming for a lonely pilgrim.

I come to a gate and I see a car and a house with the lights on and I consider going over and knocking on the door to ask if it would be okay to stay outside here. But then their dogs catch wind of me and start barking in my direction. I start backing up along the dirt road toward the highway but the dogs don't stop barking. I find a good camping place under a tree and before getting everything out I sit and wait to see if the dogs lose interest. Fifteen minutes or so go by and the dogs are still barking but then finally they quiet down.

So I take out my sleeping stuff and after all the various preparations I finally get snug enough to where I can drift off for the night.

—Day 4 Steps: 84,936

15
JOURNEY 3
DAY 5: CHACO

I wake up certain that one of the big dogs is right beside me checking me out or possibly worse about to pounce on me. The problem is I am so snug in my sleeping bag and bivy that I can't move my arms and my face is exposed to the night through the little opening. I am as vulnerable as can be but—I remember what Holden says that—"Dogs are better than humans are" and so—I don't panic. I just slowly get my hands to the point where they can quietly unzip the sleeping gear and I carefully sit up. No dog pounces on me and no dog is in sight, but the dogs are now barking again from over by the house. At this point I decide to vacate the premises. Not only do I not want to be attacked by a frightened dog but even more so I don't want to get their owners startled to the point where they come out in hyper caution mode perhaps even with a gun to see what all the fuss is about. It takes me at least 20 minutes to organize myself but when I finally do I happily get back on 550 and resume walking. I check my phone which says two am. It feels like two am. Total quiet except for the premature early morning sound of a rooster and the semi regular stark sound of semis going by. The good news is that it's arrival day, and not only that, it's my birthday! I recall from the birth certificate that I was born in the mid morning and so I have a little more than a handful of hours left of my fiftieth year. What better way to end my fiftieth than to walk from Santa Fe to Chaco (I can think of a lot more enjoyable options but none as soul stirring as this). And what better way to celebrate my fifty-first birthday than to be awake for most of the whole 24 hour day (except sleeping the whole day actually doesn't sound bad as an alternative scenario).

The now full moon is directly overhead. I feel like I am being ushered in to sacred lands by the moon. I am very thankful for the escort and for the moonlight so I can see and, more importantly, so drivers can see me! At this pre-dawn hour, every time I exhale I can see my breath rise up above my headlight.

I think about the Bill Haley & His Comets song and wonder how I knew that I would indeed be walking around the clock tonight and this morning. Coyotes are yelping in the distance, and I remember or realize how these are another amazing animal walking hero of mine (Appendix 1). They have resiliently walked their way all across North America, and now reside in every state except Hawaii, in urban and rural areas alike. They roam territories as large as 36 square miles. They are heroes because they have managed to survive and thrive for centuries beside humans, which regrettably not a lot of other wild animals can say. They are also integral to epic story telling, and I am delighted to say, they have made a mockery of human attempts to destroy them and human attempts to tame the wild natural world (Reference).

Coyotes are mythical and resilient walking heroes.

I'm not going to lie. This is painful. I kind of wish I were as resilient as a coyote right about now. My right foot really hurts. I feel like I can barely walk. But who knows? If I keep just putting one foot in front of the other maybe I'll get there, either that or get my foot amputated. I try something different. I try sticking my butt out in a more pronounced way behind me, but that only helps for so long. I decide to take my fourth Advil of the trip. I don't want to be miserable on my birthday, but the Advil only does so much good, and believe me I take and appreciate the little good it does. I'm so close I can taste it but Chaco feels so elusive, so far away still. Itches in my shoe(s) drive me crazy. I certainly don't want to take off my shoes and socks and re-start nor do I want to bend down and itch because, like I said, stopping even for a mili-second brings up the hurt. So I just let the itching sensation hopefully fade away, which sometimes it does, if I train my mind to pay attention to other things. Now I pay attention to the mile markers. I play a new game. Every mile marker I pass, without daring to stop, I eat something new and drink some water. This mile marker I choose electrolyte gummies. Next mile marker I am thinking blueberry crumble Cliff Bar.

It would be cool if I could put myself on auto-pilot, stay on the far right side of the shoulder and for a while just sleep walk, which is something that Fisher has been known to do occasionally. It's cool to look up and see the stars and full moon shining at once. The moon is glowing on Orion's Belt. I think about Native American cosmology, something Chaco Culture is known for. There's a special kind of integrity of a people who can be so native to a place, so locally rooted, while at the same time so in tune with the heavens. In my quest to assemble ingredients to restore our humanity and to solve the climate crisis, this sixth sense of integrity—integrating the universe with our little place in it—certainly seems like it qualifies.

The sign I have been yearning for in my mind, body, heart and soul.

Out of nowhere it seems, maybe from the heavens above, the sign I've been longing for comes into view: Chaco Culture National Historic Park - Exit 1 Mile. There is a God (and gods)! I have to temper myself because this is just the turn off to the park, not the entrance to the park. There are many miles left but nonetheless, it's getting real people!

There is a confluence of excitement building up in and around me: a mile up ahead is the Sinclair gas station (I can't wait for a breakfast burrito!) and on my left, to the south side of the highway, is the Bisti Badlands in the heart of Navajo country. This landscape inspired Georgia O'Keeffe's compelling painting called "A Mile of Elephants" because it is grey and dark and abounding with mounds like the body of an elephant. Elephants are the largest land animal and another walking animal hero (Appendix 1) for many reasons including: they support those in need, they can hear through their feet, they need and honor their ancestors, and unlike us they never forget. By the way, the painter Georgia O'Keeffe was married to the photographer Alfred Stieglitz who my dad's side of the family happens to be related to. But the creativity passed over me. It was evident in my father who loved to paint and it's now evident in my kids: Tabatha who loves making songs, Fisher who loves filming videos and Holden who loves painting fish.

I get to the Sinclair station at 5:15 am, and I see on the door that it doesn't open until six. No worries (like Fisher encouraged me to think), I just go to the picnic table and dose off to sleep. When I awake the store is open. I go to the bathroom and wash my face, I replenish my water and then I wolf down a Chorizo burrito. I don't eat pork in the real world but I've thrown aside my food restrictions on this trip (the thought occurs to me that if I don't ever stop walking across the land I could keep eating whatever I want). As I head back on the road and take the exit for Chaco, I am happy to have made it safely through the extensive Highway 550 stretch and happy now again to explore a road that I've never been on before.

I contact Numi by text letting her know my general whereabouts and that I am safe. Quickly understanding how far I have gotten this morning she wants to know what time I woke up. I dodge the question until she persists to the point where I can't dodge it anymore. She is upset that I left at two am, thinking—probably correctly—that I will be a mess for this evening with our friends for the celebration. I tell her not to worry, I tell her—besides my feet—that I'm feeling good and I use my birthday card: "aren't you going to stop giving me grief and wish me a happy birthday for goodness sakes?!" She, as someone who actively appreciates her, my and everyone's birthdays, immediately changes her tune and becomes supportive. I know I am out of the doghouse when I receive this text from her: "I will start over—happy birthday, Robby!!! So grateful you were born. It is something to celebrate (she knows that will irk me because I want to celebrate all of life, not my birth). Can't wait to see you! Be safe!! Love u (with star and heart emojis)."

After turning off Highway 550, making my last pit stop at Sinclair station and resolving my domestic matters, I'm foot loose and fancy free on the road to Chaco.

I'm heading south now and as I do I sing the Crosby, Stills, Nash & Young classic Southern Cross (Appendix 2) in particular the part that goes "…Think about how many times I have fallen, Spirits are moving me larger voices calling, What heaven brought you and me, Cannot be forgotten, I have been around the world, Looking for that woman-girl, Who knows love can endure, And you know it will…" Transitioning, my mind wonders from the love I feel for my woman to the respect I have for the traditional culture of this place, as well as for the endurance of a people.

A woman in a pickup truck is waiting at the top of the hill at the fork in the road, she asks if I am all right. I give her a big thumbs up and I head right at the fork. This is the last turn off of the trip. As I follow the road heading west, southwest I know Chaco park is straight ahead. It's maybe 15 miles or so to the visitor center but I'm already on the national park road and already in the greater Chaco area. I've effectively made it but I keep walking until I meet up with the caravan that's coming with Numi and our many friends which is only a few hours from now.

Wild horses are grazing in the pasture. I make it onto the gravel section of the road. It's the first time since crossing the Jemez Mountains that I have been walking on a dirt road and it contributes to my overall upbeat-ness. Another thing that is making me happy is talking to friends and family who are calling because of my birthday. Surprisingly I have cell reception and so I decide to take my phone out of airplane mode. My best buddy from college Rob Santos calls and humorously compares my walking expedition to the movie scene when Rocky Balboa is training, running through the outskirts of Philadelphia and all the kids are chasing him, cheering him on. I say the problem with this analogy is that I am hardly going through any towns and seeing any people at all. "Well," he responds, "it can be gophers, mountain lions, jack rabbits and such following you, pushing you forward!" We laugh at the spectacle of it and shoot the breeze some more. Before we end the call he asks if I could send him a picture of me walking and it occurs to me I don't have any pictures of me walking. Just then a man drives up from behind and asks if I need any assistance and I say "actually, would you mind taking a picture of me?" And he says no problem, he gets out and takes this shot. He departs with these words about Chaco where he is heading for the 5th time in his life: "it's going to be the treat of your life; it's the most special, spiritual place in the world!"

I don't have any pictures of me walking until now.

I proceed to have a long conversation with my brother Scott and sister in law Melissa and their daughter Marilla who are driving to see their older daughter Holliss at college so they have some time on their hands. Little do they know I am going to take advantage of it. They ask such nice questions about my walk and we talk for what seems to be about an hour or more. This morning it seems so fluid to be walking and talking at once. Maybe it's because I have been up since two am and my mind is strangely lucid, or maybe it's because it's my birthday. Whatever the reason, it takes my mind off the lingering foot pain and gets me further down the road toward the enchanted canyon. When I ask Melissa if she ever had the idea to do something like this off the beaten path, before she mentions biking the pacific coast highway, she gives Mark Twain's hysterical refrain: "Whenever I get the urge to exercise I lie down until the feeling goes away!" If only I took this advice five days ago.

The ever elusive finish line.

As I approach Chaco, it's time to resume airplane mode and reflect on the experience getting here. In addition to appreciating the simple things in life, another thing that has been reaffirmed day after day is the unequivocal kindness of strangers. It's especially noteworthy in this day and age with the alleged high level of divisiveness in our society. So many people along the way have stopped to check on me, honked their support, offered a helping hand, invited me to stay at their house, given me fruit and water, given me a lift at a time of need, and so on. It happened to be that a disproportionate amount of these kind offerings came from Native Americans and other people of color, but of course just as I am noting this a nice anglo couple stops beside me asking if I need anything. And so indeed the humanity shown to me has been universal, from every direction. And I experienced no ill will of any kind which says a lot about the character of people in this region of the world.

I also take away from this experience how extraordinary the Land of Enchantment is. This is such wild and beautiful country replete with vast lands, blue skies, enticing mesas, meandering meadows, mysterious arroyos, flowing forests, majestic mountains and the list goes on. And on top of that there is a trustworthy, small town vibe to go with all the wide openness and wonder.

I gotta say, it's been a genuine pleasure to step away completely from the hustle and bustle, from the cynical and conflictual media culture of our society. I haven't checked the news once (and I am better off for it). Rather I've stayed present. Presently, another stranger, this time a ranger, pulls over to assist me. I don't ask for anything except a question which is what impresses him most about this place we're heading to, and he answers without much hesitation, "how the original people here were so in tune with finding their place in the world."

This quest—stepping across the land for hours upon hours each day—has not only bound me closer to the Land of Enchantment, it has taught me about perseverance in adversity. From my minor battle, dealing with foot pain and such, I have gained a greater admiration for people struggling with and overcoming adversity. Many peoples struggles have lasted for centuries, not just over a measly five day period. The Native American people have endured incredible hardships including surviving in this arid land and, not least, surviving the destructive impact of colonization which has been so devastating. Yet they have somehow persevered over millennia. How? I think theirs is more than physical and mental capability: it is sheer soul force, brave backbone and spiritual fortitude. Deep determination. A sense of the wider cosmology. An epic connection with the place where they reside. Like the Jemez Pueblo meaning "This is the Place!"—

they are greatly in tune with, drawn to and appreciative of their place of belonging in the world.

I'm singing in my head Pearl Jam's song "Alive" (Appendix 2). It's high noon and I am still walking to this sacred place where I am gleefully in the immediate surroundings. I have a natural high, not Advil induced, although my feet are still crying out for help. They get some in the form of Heritage Tours taking my back pack for the final stretch since they were passing by anyway to set up camp in advance. I realize firsthand how walking without carrying 35 pounds on my back can be oh so enjoyable.

The caravan has arrived!

The next thing I know there is honking behind me. The caravan has arrived! I hug my wife for more than a moment and embrace our friends who get out to greet me. I can assure anyone interested that I'm not for one second too stubborn to join them in the vans for the remaining miles to the Visitor Center. I'm on cloud nine, but my wife and our friends might say I'm incomprehensible. It's to be expected after going off the grid for five days. But I feel clear and alert and just so damn happy to be alive and to be here with everyone.

Celebration at the park entrance.

We stop at the official welcome sign for a team picture. As we travel on into the park we get a briefing from Bobby, the amazing and so knowledgeable guide. He tells us we are at the epicenter of the ancient Puebloan cultural home, as significant as Machu Picchu. He tells us while this place is extraordinary, at the same time it is fitting to know that there were approximately 250 other villages throughout this region where Puebloan and ancient tribal people including the Hopi dwelled. He tells us there was hardly any water here and no wood, in fact the people here would have to hike to the Chuskas, 75 miles away and back to haul tree trunks to use for wood for their buildings. Not with oxen or wagons or horses (there were none of those), but rather just with their own two feet! And I think I had it rough carrying 35 pounds 35 miles a day. No joke though, I am blown away in amazement by their incredible dedication to settling here. Bobby says it was something much deeper than any convenience (because there was none) that made them come here in the first place. He believes it was a spiritual purpose that led the people here, manifested by the transcendental lure of Fajada Butte which is the centerpiece of Chaco Canyon. This place, and sites that were settled thereafter in this wider region, have the distinction of a mystical connection where the earth meets the heavens.

Fajada Butte.

So how did the Chacoans survive without hardly any water and few of the resources we have grown to expect? Bobby says, they developed prescient ways to store and manage the limited water that they did have; they practiced high dessert farming; they developed a far reaching network of commerce and trading (exchanging sea shells, macaws, copper bells and cacao); they built an elaborate system of roads and buildings oriented carefully in alignment with the sun, moon, stars and seasons; and they performed special ceremonies, among other life affirming rituals which still take place to this day.

We stop at the visitor center and have a sweet ritual of our own, featuring lunch under portals looking out over Fajada Butte. Joking around with our friends is one of the highlights. Another is the homemade turkey sandwiches which taste so good, I have two of them. But I have to admit—and don't tell this to Heritage Tours or to Numi—the Subway sandwich I had yesterday was superior. Nonetheless, I don't throw up and I haven't collapsed yet. Instead I do more walking and sight seeing. You would think I would be passed out already but I feel ethereal and honestly honored to walk in this setting, on these hollowed grounds, with my wife and our friends. It's like a cake walk and the cake is this place and the people, present and past.

Pueblo Bonito con mi Esposa Bonita.

We visit Pueblo Bonito, one of the most incredible buildings in the complex. It is an excellent example of ingenuity and why the people survived here for nearly 400 years, and thrived some of that time. The place is elegant and massive, built in a half moon semi circle. In its heyday there were 600 rooms with only one door in and one door out, but it was also evolving and not ever finished because they kept making improvements to the grand structure. It's made of stone and mortar, with rubble cores, added stone veneers and internal wooden supports. In its semi completed stage there were five levels, four above and one below the level we are walking through today. What strikes me more than anything is how wonderfully cool the rooms are inside even though it is a hot afternoon outside. They invented natural air conditioning and ways to retain the cool air and warmth when you need it most. The part of the tour that I struggle with the most is bending over and getting through the little openings between each room. My legs (aka dogs) are like "what the hell are you doing to us!"

Brilliant architecture.

A little help from my friends.

After a few hours touring, and marveling at, this place, I welcome some help from my friends. With my arms over their shoulders, we make it back to our vans to then go to base camp. Only about one thousand people lived here at Chaco back in the day from 850–1250. They must have shown some major collaboration to pull all of this off, kind of like the way I feel about this journey's culmination. Heritage Tours, officially called Heritage Inspirations, with an awesome assist from my wife, organized a great event, and it's evident when we pull into camp how much teamwork goes into it. While all of us brought and set up our own tents, one for each couple, the tour guides, who couldn't be nicer and more respectful of the place, set up social tents, an enchanting fire circle, an amazing drink station, a beautiful dinner area, and all kinds of other thoughtful gestures (sparkles, personalized water containers, greeting signs, hand made hummus appetizers, and on and on...). In between vitamin c waters I enjoy a mescal margarita while hunkered down in one of the social tents, icing my feet and being treated on by Angelisa the head of the touring company. She is really an angel and our friends too couldn't be kinder, coming in to check in on me. I feel unworthy but then again I am not refusing any of the love.

Receiving world class care from Heritage Inspirations, including icing my "cankle."

Angelisa tells me some of the special lore and orientation of Chaco. She informs me that the sense of equanimity that we as visitors may be feeling (I am certainly tapping into it) is no fluke. She explains that the Chacoans were very centered here, deliberately so as Chaco was created and is located at the epicenter of four sacred mountain ranges: the San Juans (to the north), Mount Taylor (to the south), the Jemez (to the east) and Chukkas (to the west).

Honoring friendship.

The night comes with bells and whistles in the form of a beautiful sunset, spectacular moon rise, and a truly magnificent meal featuring buffalo steak prepared by the Heritage chef and cooking team. Fun and partying is enjoyed by all, some more than others. While I partake and share in the laughter, I feel a little bit on the outside looking in. What I mean is I have been on a wild spiritual journey to the point where social interaction and partying feel a little bit foreign to me. I am in a different mindset, but nonetheless my gratitude runs deep and my spirits run high. After the meal, which included toasts that Numi and I give to the group celebrating friendship and the sacredness of life, and after a lot and long amount of revelry by the camp fire, we finally retire to our tent just before midnight. The noise and enjoyment outside carries on into the am hours and we probably don't wind up falling asleep until after two am; so it becomes official that I stayed up for 24 hours on my birthday for a magical time visiting Chaco Canyon.

—Day 5 Steps: 52,538

Total Steps for the whole journey: 364,368

16
AFTERMATH

Sunrise: honoring the sacredness of life.

The next morning I woke up at dawn and met with Bobby, who Angelisa said is fourteenth generation Pojoaque Puebloan. We sip some hot tea while waiting to see if anyone else will join for the sunrise hike to the mesa that stands above the campground. For a while, given all the fun that was had into the late night last night, I think it might just be me ironically, but then our friends Justin and Jenny show up and, to our delight, Numi shows up right at the deadline of 6:30. We walked up the switchback trail and once on the mesa, especially at the western end, we raved about the beautiful light in the sky and the sunrise. Bobby elaborated on the orientation of the place, how everything was designed to capture the sun at the perfect angles especially during the equinox and the solstices. I was feeling moved in that moment, and I enjoyed the moments that followed that morning, which included blue corn pancakes by the fire and a later morning hike above the dwellings.

I can't believe I participated in all the walks and my feet didn't rebel and not budge like Gary my dog when he isn't feeling well. By the way, I earned the nickname "Cankle" because of how swollen my right foot was. I enjoyed the company of our people, teasing and all, and I enjoyed the chicken salad sandwich we had right at the time of departure, but once out of the park heading home by van I became increasingly down and disoriented.

It was so strange driving back, retracing many of my steps in the reverse direction. I was blown away how relatively quickly it took to get home, only three and a half hours compared to five long days. When we got home, I teared up when my kids greeted me in our driveway. In their embrace I felt the release and emotion of alas making it home safely after the uncertain journey. Numi worried I was crying out of sadness but I was crying from the love I felt for my children. I cry more often from uplifting feelings than from being down. But she was perceptive. I was also sad, tender and vulnerable. In the week that followed I was as raw in my emotions as any other sensitive time in my life. I didn't really know what was going on in me. At night before going to sleep I held Numi, and with the feeling of breaking down welling up, I told her that I wasn't doing well inside. She held me close and was steadfastly there for me during this emotional period. I love her dearly and deeply, and I expressed my feelings to her. She calmly and completely reciprocated, so assuringly. And like the night we met at Bar 13, she stayed by my side helping me cope with the material world that I had become alienated from.

I wasn't somber. Just full of a spectrum of feelings like the colors in a rainbow. Often I would smile and even laugh at the strange predicament I found myself in. My brother kidded me that I should be sleeping outside in the courtyard in my bivy sack instead of in my bed. But it wasn't fully a laughing matter. Getting back into the rhythms and social interactions of society wasn't at all easy. I preferred the quieter pace. When I took the car out, either to pick up

Holden from school or do errands I couldn't listen to the news. I only listened to the Bridge, which plays easy listening rock songs from the 1970s. The song that stirred me up the most was Rocky Mountain High by John Denver (Appendix 2), my mom's favorite song that goes like this: "...Now he walks in quiet solitude, the forests and the streams, Seeking grace with every step he takes... Rocky Mountain High...talk to God and listen to the casual reply, Now his life is full of wonder but his heart still knows some fear of a simple thing he just can't comprehend why they try to tear the mountains down to bring in a couple more, More people more scars upon the land...Rocky Mountain High, I know he'd be a poorer man if he never saw an eagle fly..." Needless to say, I related to the song.

When we did go out and see friends, I wouldn't stray far from Numi's comforting side. I would give friends long embraces, which normally makes people on the receiving end uncomfortable, but they kindly went along with it. My right foot still felt like it was broken, especially when I moved the toe end of my foot toward my shin; but the swelling eventually, gradually went down and the mobility went up, especially after swimming laps which I decided to do again, instead of only walking for exercise. I started wondering if what Numi said was true that I may not want to walk again, but the truth was I was happy and inclined to walk once my foot healed.

But I realized that it wasn't just my foot that needed healing. The core of me needed healing as well and that's one of the reasons I think I was so raw during this period. I didn't just want to get back to normal or as quickly as possible to get over these tender feelings I was experiencing. I didn't want to have these feelings for no good reason. Perhaps I was having these feelings in order to shake out the brokenness and spur on wholeness in me or at least in order to prompt a clear change in me in that direction. Perhaps I yearned to better synthesize being a deep and decisive person in confluence with being a humorous and light hearted person. Maybe what was going on was that I was in the process of growing a backbone, one that fit for a 51 year old instead of the Energizer Bunny version I molded as a 27 year old. And in order to mold a new backbone most fittingly and fruitfully, perhaps I needed to be weak in order to become strong. I needed to suffer in order to surge. I needed to be gentle in order to be larger than life or to at least stand up for life. Whatever was going on in me, I knew it would help to draw on inspiration from time immemorial.

I reflected on the Land of Enchantment and those to whom I dedicated the now completed west direction of my journey: Indigenous communities broadly, and more specifically the Chacoans and Pueblos as well the descending and original Native American Tribes and Pueblos who subsequently settled at many vital places along the Rio Grande, not only for more accessible water but also for renewed connection to their native homelands. Drought had been overtaken by colonization as the major threat to their communities, to their cultures and to the sacredness of life which held it all together. Spanish conquistadors ruthlessly colonized the Pueblo people and systematically sought to destroy their language, way of life, customs, beliefs and lands. This assimilation and devastation grew more vicious throughout the seventeenth century, but in 1680 there was a major counter movement underway that came to the forefront. There was a powerful Pueblo alliance formed led by one Native American in particular who broke the mold.

Po'Pay.

Po' Pay from the Tewa-speaking San Juan Pueblo (known today as the Ohkay Owingeh nation) was a Pueblo leader, medicine man, shaman and farmer who had been wrongly imprisoned. When he finally secured his release he hid at the Taos Pueblo where he planned a revolution with the guidance and inspiration of tribal ancestral spirits (kachinas) calling for a restoration of the life force of the native people and regeneration of their cultural heritage. Po' Pay secretly orchestrated a team of foot soldiers, long distance runners, and presumably walkers, to bring messages to all of the Pueblo communities. The Pueblos heeded the call and rose up in unison. On August 10th, 1680, Po' Pay in concert with the Pueblo communities led a united revolt against the Spanish colonial rulers who had flogged and mistreated the Pueblo people for so long. All the Pueblos participated in the revolt at the Spanish capital of Santa Fe and demanded a return of the homelands. The revolution did not last but the unified Pueblo action secured lasting impacts including this powerful legacy of resistance.

Po' Pay along with the all collaborators deserve a high place in the pantheon of stellar walking heroes (Appendix 1). They are heroes for many reasons. They stood up for their vital heritage, for their culture, for their way of honoring life and for the land itself. They exhibited amazing teamwork and kinship. They dedicated themselves to a common cause, not only by risking their very lives in the revolt but also by running and walking hundreds of miles to all the dispersed Pueblos to coordinate the revolt to begin with. I have such admiration and a deep appreciation for how hard it is to walk across this land and these brave foot soldiers ran across the state carrying enormous consequence on their shoulders. More over, Po' Pay and the Pueblo Alliance did not succumb to the oppressive regime, which in this case was the Spanish conquistadors but could as easily have been the colonialism of the United States that followed. Not succumbing was their brilliance. Resistance was their stardom. Revolting from the dark forces threatening their well being is the brave example that they set. And their example is a form of heritage values that is not only passed down to their people but to all caring people. Hopefully we will heed the call of Po' Pay and the Pueblo people. Hopefully we are inspired to lead a massive resistance against the present day oppression threatening our world, the present day colonialism of the fossil fuel industry and the fossil fuel culture. Hopefully we rise to the occasion as they did and embrace the "fierce urgency of now" by re-creating the Beloved Community.

SECTION V
SOUTH, BELOVED COMMUNITY

"We are living in an historic moment. We are each called to take part in a great transformation. Our survival as a species is threatened by global warming… and an ever increasing gap between rich and poor. Yet these threats offer an opportunity to awaken as an interconnected and beloved community."
—Archbishop Desmond Tutu

17
BUILDING COMMUNITY

It's time we awaken as a beloved community and stand up as one against the forces perpetrating the climate and human crisis. In order to do that successfully it is important to understand what the beloved community means, how we journey there and why it is so important in this present and urgent struggle. In other words, what makes it so foundational to the solution that we need and how come I dedicate the last of the four directions, the keystone pillars of restoration, to the manifestation of this paradigm?

Philosopher and theologian Josiah Royce, who founded the Fellowship of Reconciliation, coined the phrase "Beloved Community" early in the twentieth century. Martin Luther King Jr., who was a later member, popularized the phrase, imbued it with more meaning and casted it out widely. According to the King Center, the notion of the Beloved Community is a global vision, by which all people can share in the wealth of the earth, and the planet is a hospitable place where vital standards of justice and humanity prevail. In terms of how to get there, MLK Jr. said, "our goal is to create a beloved community, and this will require a qualitative change in our souls as well as a quantitative change in our lives." This offers a compelling clue about what we need to do to arrive to this meaningful place in our collective lives, and personally we all may want to reflect on this in our own way. When I reflected on this statement, I thought about the rawness I felt after my long walk to Chaco, harkening a change in my soul, that could lead to a transformation in my behavior. The change in me could manifest by way of boycotting fossil fuels and treating other beings, both near and far, with more humanity as I had been treated in my journey.

MLK Jr. also said, "The end is reconciliation; the end is redemption; the end is the creation of the Beloved Community. It is this type of spirit and this type of love that can transform opponents into friends. It is this type of understanding goodwill that will transform the deep gloom of the old age into exuberant gladness of the new age. It is this love which will bring about miracles in the hearts of men" (Reference). There is something so jubilant here in the transformative process he is describing; it is enticing on a deep level. The gloom of the human caused climate change situation is so overwhelming that it sucks the life out of us and that's because it stems from our paralysis in the face of great challenge; but when there is bold movement—engagement, action, embracing of solutions, endeavoring, concerted human effort, mounting a response in the magnitude of a central organizing principle—there is real hope, the potential for lasting gladness and even greatness. Martin Luther King Jr.'s final remarks come to mind, the remarks he gave the very night before his assassination. That could have been a grave and somber occasion. It took place during the later stage of the civil rights movement for economic justice which wasn't panning out, which is why he and his team were in Memphis, Tennessee to begin with, there to support striking sanitation workers. MLK Jr. in his talk revealed that he may not live much longer given that he was aware of threats to his life. But instead of this being a downcast occasion, it was one of the most stirring, uplifting, telling and rejuvenating sermons he ever gave. Perhaps this was because his soul had already journeyed so far and gave him clear command, deep confidence and poignant intuition.

He said that fateful night: "…Somewhere I read of the freedom of assembly, somewhere I read of the freedom of speech, somewhere I read of the freedom of the press, and somewhere I read that the greatness of America is the right to protest!…We aren't going to let any dogs or water hoses or any injunction turn us around…Well I don't know what will happen now, we have some difficult days ahead but it really doesn't matter to me now because I have been to the mountaintop…and I have seen the promised land! I may not get there with you but I want you to know tonight that we as a people will get to the promised land! So I am happy tonight. I'm not worried about anything, I am not fearing any man…"

MLK Jr. verbalized and exemplified the idea of human transformation and collective action that's integral to reaching and securing a Beloved Community. He also emphasized that there is an essential precursor or prerequisite to arriving there. "The aftermath of non-violence" he said "is the creation of the beloved community." In other words, non-violence is the essential first step. And the man who taught MLK Jr. and the world the power of non-violence was none other than Mahatma Gandhi, who like MLK Jr. is a great walking hero and a great teacher of humankind (Appendix 1). First on the walking front, Gandhi walked about 25 miles everyday; it was his principal way of getting around. Including all his campaigns for independence and non-violence he walked about

50,000 miles over the course of his lifetime which is enough to circle the globe twice. As a young lawyer in training in London, his walking spurred on good health and saved him money in avoided transportation costs. As an activist in South Africa he led organized walks including strikes to demonstrate unjust conditions of Indian mine workers. The most famous walk he led was the Salt March to the sea in 1931 which spanned 240 miles and took 24 days all for the purpose of both protesting against the colonialist salt laws of the British Empire and demonstrating self determination. He stood up to physical and economic oppression in countless ways, and he distinguished himself by not taking on the flawed mindset of the oppressor, saying "I will not let anyone walk through my mind with dirty feet."

Mahatma Gandhi.
(Illustration by AuPalette)

But it was as a teacher of humankind, inspiring masses of people to rise up through empowering principles and leadership by example, that he truly shined. He said "if we want to put this body in the service of truth and humanity, we must first raise our soul by developing virtues like satyagraha." Raising up our soul by understanding and practicing satyagraha is key if we care to arrive at and live up to the Beloved Community. Satyagraha means brave non-violence. It does not mean passivity. It is nonviolent active resistance powered by "soul-force" and ahimsa, "the power of love," which is "the only force of universal application." Gandhi said "we are alive solely because of love" and he said "all people—big or small, men and women—can become satyagrahis." Also he said "the sword of the satyagraha is love and the unshakable firmness that comes from it" (Reference). Wielding this method and aim of powerful and loving non-violence in a disciplined and collective fashion enables effective non-cooperation and constructive boycotting of the oppressive regime. At once satyagraha is disarming because opponents are always treated humanely not as the ultimate enemy—the enemy in this case is the act and mentality of colonialism and pollution—and satyagraha is invigorating because proponents (everyday activists) have the power through collective action (boycotting, building a movement, etc) to reverse their downtrodden condition and change the condition of the world.

This is powerful stuff. A combination of heady universal principles and grassroots grounded work, civil disobedience type work, that builds the character and caliber of a community, society and civilization—one that stands up for itself and for the planet where we all reside.

Here in the Land of Enchantment we have a symbol that represents to me the idea and ideals of the Beloved Community. The symbol is known as the Zia Sun Symbol. It originated from the Zia Pueblo and it now exists on our state flag, and exists in the state pledge that all public school students say in conjunction with the Pledge of Allegiance every morning. It goes: "I salute the flag of the state of New Mexico, the Zia symbol of perfect friendship among united cultures." Obviously this statement is aspirational because we don't have perfect friendship and we are not altogether united cultures, but there is a genuine spirit of and potential for teamwork and multiculturalism expressed here. The potential not for assimilation, but for respect for different cultures who reside in a common place and share some overlapping common purpose. Bell Hooks said "Beloved Community is formed not by the eradication of difference but by its affirmation, by each of us claiming the identities and cultural legacies that shape who we are and how we live in the world;" and she also said that "if we want a beloved community, we must stand for justice"—underscoring in both statements the power of our diversity and the opportunity to unite as a society around the achievement of widespread justice. The Sun Zia symbol represents this hope.

The Sun Zia is compelling in further ways, for example in the fact that featured front and center is the sun which gives life. Then there are the four directions symbolized in the symbol which of course have different meanings in different contexts and traditions. Robin Kimmerer's view based on her traditions is summarized as follows: the East—being the direction of learning, starting anew; the West—being the direction of turbulence (both the power to create and the power to destroy) and the humbleness that comes with that; the South—representing birth and growth; and the North—representing compassion, kindness and healing (Reference).

Wally, a Navajo teacher of traditions (Reference) says that "everything is based on the sacred number four." He says it is no surprise that the word Diné is four letters, like the Sun Zia has four rays, and he says people often mistake the Diné term to be the Navajo word for 'the people' but he explains that "Di" means up where there is no surface, aka Sky Father, and "Né" means down where we reside on the surface, aka Mother Earth. Together: a no surface to a surface being. "Diné tells us where we come from...and so we always introduce ourselves by our four clans," by the origin story of the four grandparents, followed by the statement "that is what makes us Diné!"

As far as broader humanity goes, the Zia Sun symbol provides imagery which can be viewed as many becoming one (more illustrative than "E pluribus unum") and/or it can be viewed as one becoming many. Within this imagery there is both the sense that we are bound together at our core, and at the same time that we proudly shine light on different cultures and multiple life sustaining pathways, all crucial in our shared journey.

New Mexico can become a leader in providing cross cultural solutions to the world's most intractable problems like climate change and disunity, and that is one of the compelling reasons why many of us live here. However, New Mexico is hesitant and even lagging in leadership not only because of unresolved cultural divides but also because we are a major oil and gas producing state, and the revenues from fossil fuel development provide much of the funding for critical state services. We are in a catch 22, "insisting on [some] regulations [on methane emissions] while benefitting from oil and gas" (Reference). This contradiction was evident in a climate conference at the Roundhouse that was hosted late that fall by the Speaker of the House. While it is always good to focus on this subject, there was not much interaction with the community that went on in earnest. It was more like talking heads speaking at us. The big news was the Governor proposing to achieve net zero carbon emissions by 2050, but that is an easy commitment to make politically because she won't be in office in a decade or more from now when the heavy lifting to meet that goal happens. We're great at setting goals for the future, not so great at taking responsibility in the present when we need to most. At least the New Mexico oil and industry grumbled at her announcement which was better than completely appeasing them which is what we normally have done. But now we need to stand up to them courageously. We cannot just tip toe around.

We need to put our foot down and make major binding commitments along with regulations and enforcement that all take effect immediately—not only of course here in New Mexico, but throughout our nation and worldwide. Tragically that is not happening. In November of 2021 the United Nations held the Conference of Parties (COP) twenty sixth international meeting since 1995 on climate change held this time in Glasgow, Scotland. COP 26, as it was called, represented such a poignant opportunity to lead on the world stage. The UN General Secretary wisely said, "the world will either succeed or fail on the climate as one." More delegates and world leaders than ever were there, notably however the leaders of China, Russia and Brazil were absent which is so weak given how much they contribute to the problem. Mary Robinson the former Irish President said it right when she said "we need to be on an emergency footing for the planet." Former President Barack Obama, speaking as a private citizen talked about the "steps we need to take" because as he clearly put it "time is running out" and "collectively and individually we are falling short." He noted some positive signs: that over 100 countries agreed to cut methane emissions 30% by 2030; that three million people and growing currently work in clean energy, which is already more than the number of people employed in the fossil fuel industry; and he could have mentioned a tentative but important agreement to curtail deforestation. Ultimately though, as the number one historical and per capita emitter of greenhouse gas emissions, he said the US has "enormous responsibilities to lead," but powers that be haven't stepped up as they must and so "we are going to have to muster the will and the passion and the activism of citizens, pushing governments, companies, and everyone else to meet this challenge." His two closing statements were: "To all the young people out there, as well as those who consider yourselves young at heart…gird yourself for a marathon" and finally quoting Shakespeare, "what wound did ever heal but by degrees."

A core issue is about degrees: limiting warming to under 1.5 degrees Celsius as we must do to preserve balance and life itself. But on the basis of the overall lack of US and worldwide commitment, we are fast approaching and likely to exceed two degrees Celsius which would be catastrophic. The problem is not only not enough forward progress, but also that we are going backward. The forces of the status quo and for a continuation of fossil fuels are still prevailing. There were over 500 delegates at COP 26 representing the oil and gas industry, greater than any other of the largest countries or benign lobbies. Because of this undue influence, the parties could not agree on language to halt or even phase out fossil fuel use, the principal cause of the climate crisis. The undue influence of the fossil fuels and special interests directly relates to why the US and President Biden wasn't able to announce commanding progress or formidable policy on climate change. Biden's Build Back Better (BBB) was still being held up by two Democratic senators, Manchin and Sinema, plus all 50 Republican senators, all 52 were on the take. Thanks to them and others doing the bidding of the dark lobbies, the US outcomes thus far were bleak: still no present day sacrifice; greed prevailing; appeasement to the principal industry causing the climate crisis continuing. This was epitomized a week after the COP 26 conference, when the US offered up in the Gulf of Mexico the largest oil and gas lease sale in history. I think the Biden administration in all kinds of slippery ways was tip toeing around the fossil fuel industry to appease Manchin and try to win his support for BBB, but at that bleak point I thought such appeasement was just getting us burned.

Special interests have been prevailing at the expense of the common good, holding us back from the Beloved Community. The power of the corporate and monied interests over the last half century has been waxing while inversely the power of 'we the people' has been waning. Yet not everyone has rolled over as this dangerous trend has been happening in America. One person who did not roll over is Casey Harrell even though it would be understandable if he rested because he sadly was diagnosed with ALS, also known as Lou Gehrig's Disease, and even though it debilitated him, he courageously continued his vital work to hold Wall Street and corporations accountable. BlackRock's Big Problem (BBP), the campaign Harrell co-created with a team of NGOs, has had a momentous impact in beginning to balance the climate—board room playing field. BlackRock is one of the largest shareholders in the most major US corporations, and Casey Harrell along with countless colleagues held the CEO founder Larry Fink's feet to the fire in his promises to make the businesses he invests in more sustainable and climate worthy. It worked and delivered powerful results including on May 26 of 2021—a day termed by the oil and gas industry "Black Wednesday"— when BlackRock expelled two Exxon Mobil board members in favor of ones more responsive to the climate crisis; and on the same day 60% of Chevron's board members voted in favor of stronger company wide climate policies.

Even though he was in a wheelchair, Casey was hard at work saying: "This is an all-hands-on-deck moment in human history. Everyone that can should be fighting for a livable climate and a healthy biosphere...My ALS diagnosis has not changed that at all, it has only reinforced within me [the need] to do the work with urgency because my ALS clock may mean that I do not live as long as I had hoped I would." He was still pushing BlackRock to push companies forward but he was also pivoting to Vanguard, another huge investor, as well as mobilizing a range of influencers—not just shareholders, CEOs and boards but also customers, employees and every day citizens. Harrells's wife Levana, who knew first hand the pain at home and globally, said, "As much as it hurts, I also care about the planet" and " I want to see him win." At the same time she knew that true change stems from teamwork: "it takes mass mobilization and mass mobilization takes intense effort." His wife and their young daughter inspired Casey to give extraordinary effort and be effective at once which was why along side him there was a beloved community at work (Reference).

Another person who did not roll over to the special interests and corporate donors, who remains a bright example of resistance like Casey, is Doris Haddock, a New Hampshire native otherwise known as "Granny D." She at the ripe young age of 90 walked 3,200 miles, across the continental united states, from Pasadena, California to the steps of our nation's capitol to advocate for campaign finance reform and to draw attention to the utter corruption that comes from lavish money in politics. Encouraging alternatives she said, "let us choose life...and use ourselves in loving service to one another...and to protect the condition of our earth." She said ours should be "a government of, by and for the people, not the special interests." She went on: "Our first priority today, then, is to defeat utterly those forces of greed and corruption that have come between us and our self governance." She lived to be 100 years old, just in time, sadly to say, to witness the Supreme Court's bitterly divided ruling in favor of Citizens United enabling corporate and wealthy donors to spend unlimited money on elections. She did not remain silent in the face of this atrocity. Rather she issued this statement: "The Supreme Court, representing a radical fringe that does not share the despair of the grand majority of Americans, has today made things considerably worse by undoing the modest reforms I walked for and went to jail for and that tens of thousand of other Americans fought very hard to see enacted. The Supreme Court now opens the floodgates to usher in a new tsunami of corporate money into politics."

We should all be so incensed. We should not remain silent either. We should do like Granny D did—go to jail, run for office, start a community based organization and walk thousands of miles to save our democracy (or like Casey Harrell exemplified, we should start and build better businesses and collaborate to hold corporations accountable). We should all be adamantly protesting that our democratic republic has been and is being hijacked by the perverse influence of money in politics. Granny D is of course another walking hero of mine (Appendix 1), and should be a hero to all of us who care for the basic integrity of our government. She reminds us never to become apathetic. Apathy and cynicism among voters and the public at large is what the corporate and big donors want because their agenda prevails the more we tune out, the more we give up, and the more we—from being understandably disgusted—do nothing.

On the other hand, the Apache as well as Po' Pay and the Pueblo Alliance did something in the face of grave oppression and the degradation of human and natural rights. Rosa Parks and the Montgomery bus boycotters who walked and car pooled to work did something by sacrificing their livelihood for the greater good. Churchill and Roosevelt and other leaders along with all the brave men and women who served in combat against the rise of Nazi Germany did something for the sake of preserving freedom and human rights in the world. Rachel Carson when she published Silent Spring did something to stand up to the dangerous, cancer causing use of pesticides. Greta Thunberg and all the young people joining her in not equivocating in our response to the climate crisis are doing something. A beloved community does something to defend itself!

A beloved community is the antithesis of apathy, paralysis and appeasement, and here in New Mexico we had some confirmation of its healthy existence and its promising potential. Just after the disappointing news from COP 26, there was some encouraging news in the form of an announcement from President Joe Biden and Interior Secretary Deb Haaland that the United States will ban new fossil fuel extraction within ten miles out from Chaco Canyon. This didn't just happen from thin air. There were at least a dozen years of requests and activism from well over a dozen tribal groups diligently practicing staunch direct action. Tribal entities such as the National Congress of American Indians, All Pueblo Council of Governors, Navajo Nation and the Greater Chaco Coalition Members including the Pueblo Action Alliance and Diné Citizens Against Ruining Our Environment (Diné Care) have tirelessly been organizing for environmental justice and advocating against using this region as a "sacrifice zone" for fossil fuels. More than 91% of available lands in the region in the San Juan Basin are already leased for oil and gas extraction fueling the recent boom of industrialized fracking which has led to ungodly pollution, exorbitant and irresponsible use of fresh water and one of the largest methane plumes in the world. And the leaking is much worse than we thought (Reference). The oil and gas industry in this region not only perpetrated these environmental abuses but committed abuses in the form of racism, cultural degradation and crimes against humanity to the Tribes, Pueblos and other Indigenous communities that call this region home or whom have ancestral grounds there.

So it was heart warming to see this good news about a ban on new oil and gas leasing in a portion of the greater Chaco region. This could be a beginning of a turning of the tide. The hard fought democratic work of so many was starting to pay off to the point where we can witness a glimpse of the beloved community prevailing—like the top of the sun rising over the mountaintops. It was also heartwarming to see the strong pushback from industry groups after this announcement; listening to their indignant bluster made me smile. It seems they are at their angriest when they are most insecure and vulnerable: when communities assert themselves; when the common interest prevails over their special interest; when dozens of groups team up and hundreds of people work together successfully exemplifying bold, consistent and clear resistance from the fossil fuel culture.

The American Bison. (Illustration by Mike Beaumont - Unsplash)

The Buffalo or more aptly called the American Bison is another ray of sun peaking over the mountaintop, and another valiant animal walking hero of mine (Appendix 1). Buffalos tell us a lot about the Beloved Community because not only do they roam together in herds and not only are they native to the land of our nation but they also are instrumental to the restoration of the landscape. Their vitality and population grew to as strong as 60 million in the late 18th century—they then spanned the continent and the prairie grasses they roamed on were as vibrant and healthy as ever. But due to violent colonialism and systematic eradication, as well as the introduction of bovine diseases from domestic cattle, over the course of only about one hundred years by 1887 they numbered only 541 animals and nearly went extinct. What a great tragedy that would have been. Thankfully they are making a resurgence to currently then over 500,000 spanning over 6,000 locations of public, private and Native American lands. And with this resurgence researchers are gaining deeper knowledge about their very significant ecological value. The findings are revealing that as the bison are restored, the land and people are being restored with them.

Bison eat primarily grasses, and by doing so they contribute to the biodiversity of the pasture because other vegetation, like forbs (non grass flowering plants), normally dominated by grasses, have a chance to "coexist." Bison "create a diverse mosaic of habitats" by grazing intensely on burnt zones and leaving other areas virtually untouched. Also "they like to move" which spreads their beneficial impact over vast areas. Impacts include spreading nutrients across the landscape through their digestion of vegetation and excretion of waste. Another reason why they are emblematic of the Beloved Community is their presence has been shown to benefit other animals making the whole ecosystem stronger and more resilient; for example their way of grazing and moving has been shown to increase the proliferation of birds and beneficial insects. They also help their environment around them by "wallowing"—rolling on the ground incessantly to shed fur and repel bugs—which enhances the life in depression zones left in their wake. All told, the American bison is a keystone species and the way they walk over and interact with the land is helping to infiltrate water, sequester carbon, make the land more resilient to extreme weather events, and restore native grasses and other vegetation critical for the health of the soil which in turn is critical for our health. It's notable too that if you eat bison meat—which I do instead of beef while offering a prayer of gratitude beforehand—it is leaner and tastes great. Researcher Matthew Moran, who makes these points, concludes saying "as their comeback continues, I believe they can teach us how to be better stewards of the land and provide a future where ecosystems and human cultures thrive" (Reference).

The highly acclaimed recent Netflix film called "Gather," co-produced by the First Nations Development Institute, features stories of Native Americans restoring and reclaiming their traditional "foodways." One of the stories is about Elsie DuBray, a young Lakota woman of the Cheyenne River Sioux Tribe and her father Fred who started the Intertribal Buffalo Council (ITBC), which is all about revitalizing the American Bison as a source of spiritual and physical nourishment. The ITBC is a collection of 69 Tribes from 19 different states with the collective mission to restore the buffalo on Tribal lands "in order to preserve our historical, cultural, traditional and spiritual relationship for future generations." It is that sense of relationship that is so integral to the Beloved Community, to the mending of our spiritual crisis and therefore to the restoration of our world. As the ITBC says, "returning the buffalo…will help heal the land, the animal and the spirit of the…people."

When I was twenty-five years old I attended a Lakota Sioux Sun Dance and volunteered to help support this momentous community custom. The dancing ceremony took place over four days. Beforehand there was a traditional hunt for a buffalo the meet from which would be eaten at the end of the Sun Dance, and its hide and other parts would be used in full. But on the day of the hunt everyone including me ate a piece of the buffalo's liver as a way to be connected with the land and the animal's spirit. During the Sun Dance ceremony the next morning, the dancers through a skin piercing attached themselves with a line to poles that were erected in the center of the arena and they danced all day as a form of sacrifice and faced the sun as it crossed the sky. Not being a member of the Tribe I was of course not allowed to dance. My job during the ceremony was to keep the sweat lodge going strong throughout the event. To keep solidarity with the dancers though, who were dedicating themselves so, I ran just over six miles every morning at dawn which I thought could equate to the amount of steps the dancers would take each day. By the end of the four days I ran the equivalent of a marathon. I fasted the whole time. And I perspired a lot in the sweat lodge I was tending. Besides learning the best way ever to lose a lot of weight (I went from about 200 pounds to 170 pounds in those four days), I learned that the Sun Dance was all about giving oneself to the greater good, giving thanks to the sacred life force of the sun. It was a celebration of renewal for the Tribe and the renewal of the Earth. I was grateful to be involved and I see now how relevant this ceremony is to the Beloved Community—because it is not railing against anything but rather standing up bravely for life.

It is important to actively and commemoratively embrace life and shine light in addition to resisting the dark forces that harm life. Many Black Lives Matter activists have emphasized the Block, Build, Be (3B) framework as an integral way of not just fighting oppression but of honoring creative solutions and having an empowering mindset at the same time. Leaders of the movement speak to the principles and the power of this framework (Reference), especially when the 3B tenets are integrated in confluence. Katie Loncke and her colleagues for instance talk about "balancing" the three—applying all at once a combination of "throwing a monkey wrench in the status quo" (Block), spearheading "uplifting alternatives" (Build) and spiritually connecting to the "deep wisdom well" (Be). A fitting example of the integration of all three methods is relayed by Rahil Rojiani, a queer/trans, BIPOC person who has since participated in the BLM/ M4BL protests and served as a medic during these events. While Rahil was at Yale Med School in 2018, they along with "fellow culture workers" occupied the Yale Investment Office to encourage divestment in fossil fuels ("block"). During the sit in there were contemplative actions ("Be") including praying for Mother Earth and the ancestors as well as writing poetry and singing inspiring songs while they held down the building for several hours. Rahil recounts, "there were also 'Build' elements both in the inherent vision of the world we were trying to create" (i.e. distributed renewable energy, clean transportation, conservation and community led sustainability) and in the mural that the activists created during the sit in. They concluded "the best of any of these movements has dimensions of all three (Block, Build, Be) and this event felt like this for me!"

Yale and Harvard (where I went to college) and many other leading universities have not been leaders when it comes to divesting in fossil fuels. They are finally taking steps, after over a decade of student led protests along with the prompting from hundreds of pioneers (Bill McKibben and Naomi Klein come to mind along with pioneering schools and institutions, foundations, pension funds and institutional investors who divested much earlier. You can learn more about the proactive steps at the Global Fossil Fuel Divestment Commitments Database at divestmentdatabase.org).

Harvard President Lawrence Bacon sent a message to alumni seemingly boasting about the divestment commitments they were making when in fact the credit should be given to the student led divestment movement and the Attorney General of Massachusetts. Together they held Harvard accountable to have to consider the public good, charitable purpose and prudence of its investments given that it gets significant tax benefits as a non-profit organization. Besides marking progress, which is always a good thing however late in the game we come to the table, one thing that stood out to me about Bacon's message was the compelling and perplexing statement that "any problem caused by people can be solved by people too." On one level, that being the vast potential of the human spirit, this is a hopeful concept. The idea that we as a society can rise to the occasion and come together to address man made climate change once and for all is encouraging. But on another level, at the level of our fundamental disconnect with Mother Nature, this is a very worrisome way of thinking. If people go on thinking conventionally, the way we have been doing all this time and the way we have been taught by the schooling system, including these so called "great" United States educational institutions, we likely will go on perpetuating rather than solving the climate crisis. As humankind, in order to right the course, we need to learn both how to step back and how to get out of the way, allowing nature to be a regenerative solution, and how to fundamentally transform our way of thinking.

Vandana Shiva, a very effective and delightful activist from India, makes this case in her presentation called "Earth Democracy: Connecting the Rights of Mother Earth and the Well Being of All." In it she encourages us to consider the roots of our flawed way of thinking. She says a "structure of disconnection" has been engrained into our modern society dating back to the so called "great" teachers like Descartes and Bacon who espoused separating the mind from the body and controlling nature which gave rise to dominion. She says it is vital that we free ourselves from "imperialism over the mind." Shiva suggests the best ways to liberate ourselves from an oppressor mentality are to: (a) learn from Indigenous Peoples, who are deeply connected with nature to the point where they consider themselves children of the Earth and Sky; (b) raise our consciousness (which is akin to developing soul force like Martin Luther King Jr. and Gandhi encouraged us to do) which will foster quality—rather than quantity—of life; and I add, (c) act in consonance with the Beloved Community which fosters the convergence of being humble (knowing we aren't the end all be all) and being brave (stepping out of our comfort zone for the sake of caring for the common good).

So we need to think differently (which brings to mind Apple's early advertising slogan) and, more importantly, we must act differently. As far as a company that really thinks and acts differently, compared to the majority of corporations out there, Patagonia stands out. They care that their original clothing lasts a lifetime and they make it increasingly with responsible materials. They also make climate change a priority at every level of the business, including sourcing and integrating what they do. The CEO Ryan Gellert says, "It's not that complicated. Figure out what your north star is. Figure out what you think you can do to contribute to that, acknowledge that there's no end point to this, and continue to push yourself to do more. Existential threats require that level of commitment, and that level of systemic change. These are the issues that we've created as people, and these are the obligations we have to solve them. If you're not up for it, stop pretending" (Reference). He has no patience for the green washing that companies spew, and a case in point he said are the countless companies in the United States Chamber of Commerce who claim to be sustainable but who are anonymously lobbying against the Build Back Better Bill because of opposition to the corporate tax hikes to pay for it. We are witnessing hypocrisy and spinelessness at such a dangerous and crucial moment in history. Imagine if in World War II, United States companies lobbied secretly and successfully for us to not be involved in the military Nazi resistance just so they could chase their greed and avoid higher taxes (back then federal corporate tax rates were as high as 50% where as now companies are balking at federal minimum tax rates of 15%; and individual high income tax rates back then exceeded 80%—and Roosevelt even lobbied for the most well off to pay rates of 100% during the war effort—when now the top rate is below 40%).

The corporations meddling in government and the government doing their bidding are breaking us apart at the seams. There is now virtually no moral consensus, no north star, no civility, no lasting bipartisanship. I heard the funeral service of Bob Dole, who served in World War II, became paralyzed on his left side, and later served as the Republican leader in the United States Senate. He voted for the Civil Rights and Voting Rights Acts; can you imagine Republicans doing that today? Unlike today, Dole worked together with the other party on issues of common sense including ensuring services for those with disabilities. When he was in agony recovering from his war injury, he listened to a song over and over again called "You'll Never Walk Alone" by Gerry and the Pacemakers (Appendix 2). It goes like this:

When you walk through a storm
Hold your head up high
And don't be afraid of the dark

At the end of a storm
There's a golden sky
And the sweet silver song of a lark

Walk on through the wind
Walk on through the rain
Though your dreams be tossed and blown

Walk on, walk on
With hope in your heart
And you'll never walk alone

In Dole's final message to the nation before he passed away he said, when something is really important, sit down and listen and then stand up and do something about it.

18
CASCADING CLIMATE CHANGE VS. A SEA CHANGE

Well let's sit down and consider how our very life is being torn apart by human caused climate change. Water is life, as they say, and yet out west our water supply is shrinking dauntingly. According to Billy Barr, who has manually recorded weather measurements in the mountain outpost of Gothic, Colorado over the last fifty years, the number of days temperatures have stayed below freezing has plummeted. "In the seventies, there were winters where we had well over a hundred days in a row where it didn't get [above] freezing. Last winter, the most was nine," Barr said. Well over fifty million people rely on this water from the Rockies and with less freezing, there is direly less precipitation, more snow melting, greater avalanche hazard, less water retained, more run off and evaporation. Adding to the mix is "dust on snow," which hampers the sunlight's reflection, perpetuating the melting of ice and snow even more. This is happening increasingly with less secure soil (less aggregate stability) and more intense winds (including more tornados).

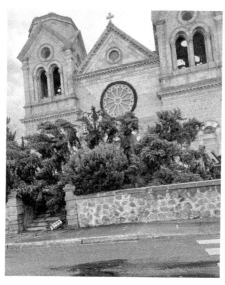

A Norwegian spruce tree blown down over the steps of the St. Francis Cathedral.

And on the topic of more intense winds, I woke up this December at dawn to a weather warning on my cell phone and minutes later sixty mile an hour winds swept through town (normally shielded by all the surrounding mountains here). Panels on my roof blew off and on the way into town to bring Holden to school we passed a giant Norwegian spruce tree that had been blown down directly in front of the St. Francis Cathedral. Well the same storm system picked up speed and intensity by the time it hit the plains where the winds grew as strong as one hundred and twenty miles an hour, ripping off entire roofs, turning over semis on a dime and shaking the whole region. The link between climate change and tornados is less studied than other weather events but the known fact is that climate change is majorly contributing to a dramatic increase in extreme weather, which like the water situation is compounding negatively against us. We are in the midst of a prolonged drought, severe dryness, mixed with high winds, creating a dramatic wildfire hazard, which sets aflame the forests that store so much carbon releasing so much more CO_2. And the cascading crisis continues to gain momentum.

Worldwide the reverberations from climate change are mounting including, as was announced recently, a destabilization of the earth's poles that not only puts the Arctic and Antarctic regions in jeopardy but places the whole planet in peril. Temperatures have been rising twice as fast at the poles than the rest of the globe. The resulting feedback loops are dire including melting of permafrost, which leads to greater methane emissions, on top of glacier and sea ice disintegration, which leads to greater heat absorption because of darker water exposure (instead of ice which reflects sunlight back into the atmosphere)—all together these phenomenon are changing global weather patterns, creating sea level rise and throwing entire ecosystems off balance.

We can see the ramifications in our own backyards. We can sit down and learn the increasingly daunting stories about extreme weather events and the cascading impacts of climate change until we're blue or red in the face. We can try to block it out of our minds, let it all bounce off us like reflecting sunlight and pretend everything is normal. Or we can begin heeding the warnings, standing up together and doing what is right in response. One way to do what is right in response is by sharing more—unlike the corporations who don't want to pay higher taxes to help solve the problem and more like the native groups in the Arctic region for example like the Inupiaq community. They are living in the melting permafrost region, facing major impacts including troubling shortages of traditional foods and wildlife they depend on for survival and instead of burying their heads in the shrinking snow, they are responding resoundingly by deploying a profound food sharing network and deepening their already strong resiliency.

Twila Moon a glaciologist at the National Snow and Ice Data Center and co-editor of the Arctic Report Card said "There is such a big range and difference in the future of the Arctic and the future of what anywhere on our globe can look like. It all depends on human actions" (Reference). Our future depends on whether or not we can find it in ourselves to renew a sense of community across the land. On a Zoom meeting recently with members of the New Mexico Healthy Soil Working Group, the First Nations Development Institute, the Intertribal Agriculture Council and the State Land Office, about ways to advance regeneration in this region, everyone agreed that "The problems we face require community solutions!"

On an accurate but cynical level, we have an increasingly dysfunctional government that is forcing people and communities to make needed changes for themselves because we can't necessarily depend on our government for answers. We have a perilous situation at all three branches of our government, where advancing climate action and the common good has been increasingly hard to come by. In fact some like Aziz Huq argue, understandably so, that we are facing a *Collapse of Constitutional Remedies* (Reference), meaning our government, our constitution and our court are not addressing the fundamental challenges of our time because they are so gummed up with corruption and divisiveness. On one hand this supports the point that community action is something we must resort to to solve our problems, because our prominent institutions are not delivering. But on the other hand there have always been so called "intractable" problems in our society. Segregation was an example of an "intractable" problem for so long and finally, in the mid 1960s, there was genuine improvement from the passing of the Civil Rights Act. This improvement was not necessarily due to our governmental institutions being more enlightened than before and now. The more compelling reason for federal action on segregation and delivery of democratic rights to people of color was the mass movement led by civil rights activists: from over ten years of struggle and direct action, the people non-violently forced the agenda on our resistant government to the point where vital change making took place in this country. The beloved community rose up and prevailed over the status quo, and it forced our government to respond, which is what we must do now in the face of the "intractable" climate crisis.

On the federal level—it did seem more and more intractable. On December 19th I woke up to the news that Joe Manchin, on Fox News no less, declared he was a "no" on the Build Back Better bill which effectively killed the legislation that is so needed to honor a meaningful US commitment to addressing climate change. What a Christmas gift Manchin delivered to the fossil fuel industry, plus to all the other complicit corporations and wealthy campaign donors that did not want their taxes raised. And what a lump of coal he gave to the rest of us. This was a huge blow. With the presidency and the slimmest of slim democratic majorities in the House and Senate, and with the likelihood of Republican gains in the midterm elections, this was and remains a make or break moment as a nation.

We then and still now face parallel threats: cascading climate change and the threat of an increasing authoritarianism and creeping fascism infringing on the right to vote, especially the voting rights of minorities, infringing on our democratic elections and infringing on freedom and the responsibility we have in freedom. Manchin was not only corruptly standing in the way of the Build Back Better social and climate legislation (Reference), but he was also standing in the way of vital federal voting rights protection by not being willing to change the arcane filibuster rule that requires 60 senators for non budgetary bills. We can, we must, fight this transgression against democracy and the co-equal threat of human climate change by deploying the very Bill of Rights (freedom of speech, freedom of press, the right to assemble and protest) that are at risk if we remain dormant. The very Bill of Rights Martin Luther King Jr. ultimately called for must not be taken for granted but rather must be used adamantly, nonviolently and decisively for the betterment of humankind and the stewardship of our one Earth. The empowering deployment of the Bill of Rights is indeed an essential ingredient of a flourishing civil society, flourishing to the point where we can turn the tide of inaction by our federal government into a tidal wave of possibility.

Speaking of possibilities, the holidays were upon us, which meant participating in a few empowering family and friend traditions. One of them was eating dinner at the famous Shed restaurant and then walking together over to the Plaza to see all the Christmas lights aglow. At this year's dinner our good friend Charles stood up to give his customary Man of the Year announcement, which he has done every year for over a decade. During his toast he stated that this is his favorite night of the year. This year, to my surprise, he awarded the Man of the Year to me of all people for the good spirit I showed walking to Chaco. Charles then made it explicitly clear however that there is no criteria to winning and that going forward anyone else can't just expect to win the award by walking long distances.

Charles Doerwald's annual man of the year toast at the Shed Restaurant.

When I stood up to receive the honor I said how "I never thought this day would come because Charles had always told me I would never win this award, so I have been humbled for many years, but now I feel like I'm on top of the world!" The Man of the Year Award is done purely in good fun and playful sincerity. But I am glad the walk inspired my friends and earned me this honor because at fifty-one years old, on the backside of my life journey, who knows when I will get the chance again. It's not every day, in fact it's not any day since I've known Charles, which is over twenty years, that I would have qualified.

Rest assured, I was not going to rest on my laurels. There was organizing work to do, but before I got back to it I will mention another tradition my family and I participated in: the Christmas Eve Walk up Canyon Road. Back in the day this was a very rustic and charming event, with bonfires burning in many of the little alley ways, hot cider offered by the neighborhoods and flying farolitos floating up to the sky. The wildfire risk put an end to flying candle lit paper bags but the other traditional aspects remain. Every year people come from near and far to participate and it's usually jam-packed. This year though it was raining all afternoon and into the evening and even though snow would have been nicer and better of course, the rain ironically made the walking event a bit calmer and less crowded.

My family feeling the warmth at the Canyon Road Christmas Eve Walk.

The most compelling thing was spending this cheerful occasion walking with my whole immediate family. Tabatha was back home from her first year at college. Fisher, who loves traditions like this one, had just been accepted into Wesleyan, his first pick, so he was in an especially good mood. Holden was sporting a Santa cap and was full of spirit as was Numi in her shiny red parka. Being warmed by the little fires along the way reinforced in me the sense that warmth we receive ignites in us a warmth which we reciprocate back into the greater community. In a beloved community there is a virtuous cycle: love begetting more love, truth bringing about further truth, warmth giving rise to greater warmth. This rippling resounding force can spread out across the land and thaw what is frozen in us.

A poignant example of darkness subsiding and the healing force spreading is the life and work of Maya Angelou. Maya Angelou was born in 1928 on April 4th (the same calendar day that Martin Luther King Jr. died). She came from a divorced family, and witnessed in Arkansas brutal racial discrimination and yet she learned a deep sense of faith and values from her grandmother and a traditional African American family, community and culture. Tragically, at the mere age of eight years old, she was raped. Afterwards her rapist was killed, and Maya thought it was because she told her brother about the rape that the rapist died and so she subsequently went mute for almost six years. A teacher helped her regain her voice, her self belief and her life force…She went on to become a magnificent writer, poet, civil rights activist and teacher. Her literary works and her teachings have inspired so many people, young and old alike, encouraging us to overcome adversity, right wrongs, and join the Beloved Community.

Her wondrous poem "Still I Rise" is a testament to the deeper powers prevailing over the pain of history.

STILL I RISE

You may write me down in history
With your bitter, twisted lies,
You may trod me in the very dirt
But still, like dust, I'll rise.

Does my sassiness upset you?
Why are you beset with gloom?
'Cause I walk like I've got oil well
Pumping in my living room.

Just like moons and like suns,
With the certainty of tides,
Just like hopes spinning high,
Still I'll rise…

You may shoot me with your words,
You may cut me with your eyes,
You may kill me with your hatefulness,
But still, like air, I'll rise…

Out of the huts of history's shame I rise
Up from a past that's rooted in pain I rise

I'm a black ocean, leaping and wide,
Welling and swelling I bear in the tide.

Leaving behind the nights of terror and fear I rise
Into daybreak that's wondrously clear
I rise

Bringing the gifts that my ancestors gave,
I am the dream and the hope of the slave.
I rise, I rise, I rise.

Maya Angelou aptly said: "Develop enough courage to stand up for yourself and then stand up for somebody else." And that's the whole point of why we need to fight the racial crisis and the climate crisis with the Beloved Community, because like true courage which extends from one to another, it extends beyond the limitations of our selves into the rippling and unbounded realm of the collective. It also tends to our past and helps us proceed with clear conscience toward the future. She said "History, despite its wrenching pain, cannot be unlived, however, if faced with courage, need not be lived again." Something we should heed as some in our society are going back to an ugly time of censorship when it comes to learning the truth about slavery and racism in our past. Maya Angelou is a walking hero for her uplifting truth and rippling light in the face of darkness (Appendix 1).

Another hopeful embodiment of the potential for a sea change, through the limitless possibility of community, is in the realm of biodiversity—the mighty strands of nature all around our world that are teeming with life. E.O. Wilson who passed away at the end of 2021 has been a remarkable spokesman for the vast restorative potential of biodiversity. He was a highly regarded biologist, endearing professor and prolific writer who built his career on the study of ants and culminated his storied life by encouraging humanity to protect at least half of the earth for species conservation and rejuvenation. Wilson's first research breakthrough back in the 1950s showed how ants communicate by excreting a certain substance that prompts their interaction. Later he studied and then demonstrated how the variety of life on an island can be fully replenished by nature even after we tragically cause lifelessness there and everywhere. This shows how strong the force of renewal is among living beings beyond just our human kind, down to the smallest microorganisms which are so essential to the well being of all. Ultimately, if and when we do really value biodiversity and work to safeguard and revive it, the healing power unleashed will be unstoppable. As E. O. Wilson poetically said, we would be living out our most inspiriting purpose "to begin the age of restoration, reweaving the wondrous diversity of life that still surrounds us" (Reference).

We are not living up to our potential in this department. In fact we are falling woefully short when it comes to safeguarding biodiversity. One example is Brazil's Cerrado, the world's largest most species rich savanna, called an "upside down forest" because of the extensive root systems of plant life there, where deforestation has reached dire levels like the precious Amazon rainforest nearby. With deforestation comes not only dangerous deterioration of the root system resiliency, but the loss of innumerable invaluable species and the proliferation of greenhouse gas emissions. A problem is the world community not valuing biodiversity enough to sufficiently invest in offsetting the economic insecurity that leads people to burn down these precious lands for inopportune ranching and farming lands. Another problem is the encroaching imperialism from outside economic interests.

Vandana Shiva, the sage environmentalist from India, has been warning the world community not to allow imperialists to dominate and mistreat these sacred realms of biodiversity any longer. The imperialism comes from monopolization, legal encroachment, claims of private property and intellectual property from the likes of Monsanto and so many other predatory multilateral corporations. They act as if they own the diversity of life and invented the life giving properties there. They claim the surface and sub surface rights of the rain forest and these other natural kingdoms. The stakes have never been higher and the threat never greater because as Shiva says "this time colonization will end in the extinction of biodiversity, including the human species" (p. 305). Instead of letting our selves and our natural allies down, which perpetuates cascading climate change, we could be making amends and forming alliances with the realms and vast species of life to become a greater functioning collective. Like the Rebels in Return of the Jedi joining forces with the Ewoks to defeat the Dark Side (please excuse the cinematic analogies from my childhood), we can align our lives in collaboration with the vast other species of life—from microorganisms in the Cerrado soil to polar bears in the Arctic—and in doing so more successfully restore the commons.

Countering the grave narrative of colonization is a burgeoning grassroots movement featured in Vandana Shiva's *Reclaiming the Commons: Biodiversity, Indigenous Knowledge, and the Rights of Mother Earth* (Reference). This book, which Tabatha gave me for Christmas, traces the 30+ year journey to safeguard nature's precious realms and the people who depend on them. It starts back at the 1992 Rio Summit leading to the Biodiversity Treaty and the Convention on Biodiversity (which I worked on when I worked at the State Department years ago). Shiva says "Diversity is life and the very basis of ecological stability. Diverse ecosystems birth diverse life forms and diverse cultures" (p. 270). She says the commons is the genuine article, a universally applicable system and an appropriate caretaking mechanism for biodiversity, unlike the exclusive system of property rights (p. 302). She says only in community are we the true guardians of biodiversity (p. 300). This is because the commons is rooted in cooperation, in sharing and in decentralized democratic decision-making (p. 299).

Shiva emphasizes that the commons preexisted and will outlast both the market and state's paradigm of controlling natural resources (p. 263) and she sees a shift from exploitation to common good guardianship (p. 281). Manifestations abound including in our local food system with the rise of community seed banks, urban gardens, Community Supported Agriculture (CSAs), food coops and farmers markets (p. 253). Compelling factors are the growing realization of our collective human rights to clean air, available water, healthy food and a livable climate as well as a growing awareness of Mother Nature's rights to health and well being irrespective of us. By reclaiming the common good of biodiversity (and climate stability) there is the "double effect" both in expanding protection of the commons and expanding consciousness that we have much more in common than not (p. 270). Elevating our common humanity and our commonalities as people is essential to addressing the climate crisis and to healing our torn relations.

Thank goodness Vandana Shiva is not alone in the quest for the commons. Archbishop Desmond Tutu, who sadly just passed away at the end of 2021, was and remains a quintessential humanitarian who helped bring together the human race not only in his country at the end of Apartheid through the Truth and Reconciliation Commission but also well beyond South Africa's shores. I had the good fortune of meeting him twice, once in New York City at a massive protest against the Iraq War and a decade earlier when my mom brother and I visited Cape Town. My brother recalled that wonderful encounter as follows: "Meeting Bishop Tutu was truly an incredible experience—we really got to interact with him…his famous joyful spirit, playfulness and infectious sense of humor were all on display. We popped into Saint George's on a whim, hoping to perhaps see a glimpse of him, never expecting such an intimate encounter. That became a highlight of our African adventure with Mom. It seems even more special now." Building on what my brother said, what I remember was his hospitality, serving us tea even and making us feel like family. It is that sense of kinship and 'the brotherhood of man' that we need now.

The hospitality of Archbishop Desmond Tutu on display
at St. George's Cathedral in Cape Town, South Africa.

Going forward we can honor him by coming together in pursuit of a purpose greater than ourselves. Archbishop Desmond Tutu was previously honored, fittingly, by the Beloved Community Project, the mission of which is to promote the concept of the Beloved Community as inspired by Martin Luther King Jr. and as described by the King Center in Atlanta, Georgia. In the dedication are a beautiful selection of statements from Bishop Tutu on a number of relevant and vital topics. The one that stands out to me is as follows: "If we could but recognize our common humanity, that we do belong together, that our destinies are bound up in one another's...then a glorious world would come into being where all of us live harmoniously together as one family, the human family...In truth, a transfiguration would take place."

19
ORGANIZING

Over the holidays and at the outset of the new year of 2022, I started organizing in earnest a community event to walk together and rally for brave climate action. I knew, with the breakdown of the Build Back Better legislation at the federal level and with the corrupt convergence of the oil and gas industry and government at the state level, that we cannot just sit back and hope that our elected officials will do the right thing when it comes to transfiguring our economy and our society around resolving the climate crisis. No, we the people will have to do the heavy lifting of demanding and ensuring climate justice on a broad scale. On one hand, obviously I know that our little community here in New Mexico is not the end all be all driver of world events. But on the other hand, everyone's communities all over the country (and beyond) acting together, collectively standing up for full scale climate leadership on a state and national level would cause reverberations worldwide. Turning the United States, the leading culprit, would hasten a turning of the tide globally.

I was not naive. I know that I am just a drop; but then again, we are much greater than a drop. We together are a sea change. And if we stand up, stand together and stand firm there is nothing that can stop our flowing waters. One community can inspire another, especially in this information age when news and events—including epic stands of humanity—travel so fast. So our community can act in concert with other communities, giving and gaining inspiration and drawing on those who have come before. And if we lead by example from where we are, we can encourage others to do the same and so on and so forth.

So I set forth to organize a community event calling for human and environmental restoration. I worked through the small non profit I founded called the Climate Change Leadership Institute. I involved the board which is comprised of creative and cheerful friends. I brought on a student intern named Araceli as well as a local professional named Amanda who specialized in communications and event planning to help in general and specifically with social media which is not my forte. I am good at taking action and facilitating but I am not so good at promotion. I don't do selfies, I don't have social media accounts. You could say I'm old school or you could call me a cave man, I like the former description but I know these days it's an Achilles Heal to resist these vogue ways of interacting and organizing social change.

So, in conjunction with the ultimate prong of my four foundation walking journey—the Beloved Community—I came up with the idea that on Martin Luther King Day, the wider community would walk from Four Directions and at high noon converge at the State Capital building, the "Roundhouse," fittingly shaped as the Zia Sun symbol (see illustration below), to rally for brave action to combat the climate crisis. Martin Luther King Day was the right day to plan this being that it is a day of service when we hopefully evoke the spirit of the Civil Rights Movement, which was the epitome of non-violent change making. The first thing we did was contact the local branch of the National Association for the Advancement of Colored People (NAACP) to make sure we were not conflicting with a planned MLK Day event of theirs which they often put on at the Roundhouse. Because of COVID they were not doing a Roundhouse event on that day. And so not only were we not conflicting, we were actually converging because, upon our invitation and their thoughtful consideration, joyfully for me and so many others, they agreed to participate in our event as collaborators and partners, which meant they would notify their members and of course be given the opportunity to speak at the Rally. We worked to establish a lot of partners in collaborating on the event, as I will share, but none made me as happy as the budding partnership with the local NAACP branch because the synergy of the movements is so important.

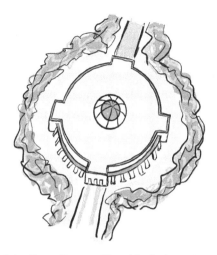

A drawing of the Roundhouse, New Mexico's state capital building designed after the Sun Zia symbol. (Illustration by AuPalette)

It was also a perfect day to put on this event on January 17th because that was literally the day before the state legislature commenced so it would help send a message to the elected officials that we have had enough of equivocating on such a vital matter as safeguarding our future. Sadly I had to make sure, given the stench from the January 6th 2021 insurrection, that outside democratic events at the New Mexico state capital were going to be permitted, which I soon learned they would be. I also had to check with the city permitting regarding walking through the city to the roundhouse from four directions including from three nearby city parks. And while I submitted the permit request to be proactive, I learned that as long as walkers stayed on the sidewalks and used cross walks that there was no issue. Of course we were and are always allowed to practice our constitutional rights to demonstrate, but we just wanted to make sure we covered our bases in terms of any permitting required.

Once those bases were covered, we zeroed in on the event itself, starting with the name of the event. Walking Four Directions for Climate Leadership was the lengthy concept in my brain: of course I tend to be long winded in my wording. Amanda cleverly broke it down and came up with "Walking 4 the Climate," which is a great play on the number four. I reached out to the Zia Pueblo to make sure as the originator of the Zia Sun symbol they were okay with us using it for this event. With that honorable image along with our relevant additions we and the talented illustrator AuPalette developed the logo featured at the start of this section.

I then reached out to the All Pueblo Council of Governors to invite them and all interested Pueblo community members to participate. Furthermore I reached out to the Pueblo of Tesuque, the Pueblo nearest to Santa Fe that has historical roots here before the Spanish invasion, to give a land acknowledgment and invocation. They were all going through the final transitions of their annual government, the establishment of new governors and new personnel so it wasn't the best time for them to participate, not to mention COVID flaring up again.

Walking 4 the Climate

Sign up here to join this MLK Day January 17th event walking from one of the four directions to the Roundhouse, arriving together at noon, to encourage New Mexico to take brave action to combat the climate crisis.

Getting out the word about Walking 4 the Climate on MLK Day.

We developed an event page at www.takeresponsibility.us where people could go to learn about the event and sign up on a Google form if they wanted to participate (the header of the Google form is pictured here). Amanda developed a Facebook event and an Eventbrite page. And then we started to get out the word. Araceli, who was a senior at a local charter school and also a Breakthrough student, one of the first in her family to be going to college, and I recorded a Public Service Announcement (PSA) and went on the local radio station called Hutton Broadcasting to promote the event. I sent out a blast to the Climate Change Leadership Institute's network with about 2,500 contacts. I sent at least 50 emails to organizations I knew, and many I didn't, to encourage involvement. We reached out to schools, churches, civic groups and beyond. I also of course notified friends and people I knew and asked Araceli to do the same.

And then, by around the second week of January, less than a week before the event, we started getting some good feedback. What's more is that some organizations (the Sierra Club Rio Grande Chapter, Universalist Unitarian Church, New Mexico's 350.org, New Energy Economy, local branch of the NAACP, Wood Gormely Elementary School, where my son Holden goes to school, the local Green Chamber of Commerce, the Temple Beth Shalom and others) forwarded the event page to their respective networks and so the word traveled. And the most heart warming aspect about planning this event were the sign ups from people I didn't know that wanted to participate in the walking event. Students, teachers, parents, grandparents, small business owners, church goers, the whole gambit were getting involved. I received a message from a veteran with the local Veterans for Peace organization asking if it would be okay if they joined in and carried signs featuring their message; it was very sweet of them to ask and of course the answer was yes. Bring it on! A woman named Linda emailed expressing her feeling of urgency about the climate crisis and inadequacy that so far she was only able to recruit five people in her neighborhood to come along. I emailed her back asking if she would captain the South Direction, which meant wearing one of the "Walk 4 Climate" tee shirts that our board member Erin designed, carrying a sign made for the event and leading the south community of walkers safely to the Roundhouse. Of course, being the go getter that Linda is, she said yes!

It evoked emotion in me to be interacting with the community while planning the event. I was touched every time a young person signed up, knowing how down the road they bear the brunt of this struggle. It was likewise stirring when older people signed up, including an eighty year old woman, given the significant walking that was involved. I received a call from a gentleman named James who was on crutches and wanted to know which direction would be easiest to navigate to get to the State Capitol. He said he had recently had a hip replacement and was recovering but wanted to still participate. I told him that I had had a hip replacement also. He asked me where and with whom and I told him Dr. Matta in Santa Monica at the St. John's Hospital. James then sadly told me that his daughter had cancer treatment there over a period of three years and passed away there a few years ago. I expressed my sincere condolences and he said "it's never something you get over really, but being involved in the community helps." It was moving that he shared his personal situation with me and that he was locally taking a stand for climate action and other causes despite his ailment and loss.

Amanda put the event on all the local event calendars, and sent out press releases to the local media. From one of the collaborative email blasts the partners and I sent out, we got a response from Roz with the New Mexico

News Connection who did an interview with me and put out the story to all the radio stations statewide on the day of the event (Appendix 3), and hopefully it would draw more attention. Another local radio show had me on. And so on, to the point that word was getting out there and the event was taking shape. I arranged for "Walking 4 the Climate" buttons to be made. I also got a banner made to use for the rally. We organized speakers from the group of partnering organizations. I got a microphone and battery powered amplifier. We didn't want to talk people's heads off but once everyone arrived from all sides to the capitol by foot we could have about thirty minutes to rally for climate justice, enough to get the message out but not too much to overwhelm the participants.

A few days before the walk I got a call from a staffer named Matt who worked for our local Congresswoman, who said she wanted to attend and speak at the event. At first I was reluctant because this was about the community leading the charge and pressing our elected leaders to be bolder; not about spotlighting our elected officeholders. But after thinking about it and talking it over with my wife and colleagues at work, we decided not to turn anyone away. We thought it was nice that she took the initiative to be involved. Plus it would add bravado to the event and perhaps attract more media attention. Another matter that came up was an organization that was partnering with us, the local New Mexico branch of 350.org, who wanted to pass out flyers at the event about state policies they supported and one of the policies was net zero emissions by 2050 which I didn't support because I thought it was too little too late of a commitment. I said so to them and there was an uncomfortable back and forth over the email that wound up getting worked out. I thought we needed to act bolder much sooner, they thought it was a very significant first step. We respectfully agreed to disagree. Then a women on the thread named Judy emailed me personally (off the group thread) and said "I agree—2050 is far too late. But how to move foreword with the urgency you suggest is not clear to me." Then came the kicker: "Building community seems to be key." She added "these days especially, I find the need to revisit the basics. Often."

There is nothing more powerful and basic than community mobilization. That was what the "Walking 4 the Climate" was all about and I appreciated Judy's insightful reminder to get me back on track. I spent a good amount of time (leading up to the morning of the event) responding personally and uniquely to everyone who signed up. There was over one hundred people signed up, mostly on the website accessed Google form, and some of the other forums, but that didn't include many other people planning to come but not being formal about it. Anyways, I believed that every person who registered was making a meaningful commitment, not to mention the others, and it was incumbent on me to acknowledge each and every community member that was taking these steps of participation. It was a form of relationship and community building to email the folks who signed up, and like I said, unlike past CCLI events, most were people I didn't know who were getting involved.

On the eve of Walking 4 the Climate I was nervous. I told Holden in the kitchen about my feelings and Holden was sweet about it, asking me if I needed anything to feel better. Holden then told me a relevant statistic: the number one anxiety people have is before public speaking. I did have to speak, which sometimes I do from the heart or off the cuff but this time I prepared something. Trying to strike a balance of saying all that was on my mind while being concise worried me. What worried me more was I felt responsible for the whole event. Not just responsible for it going over well: for the logistics, people's safety and the overall flow. But deeper down, I felt responsible for the community event being successful in helping solve the climate crisis. I wanted our little event in our little town to spark a fire that would sweep the nation. And I was sure it was wishful thinking but I went to bed hoping. Of course, with all this pressure, I didn't sleep so well.

20
JOURNEY 4,
WALKING 4 THE CLIMATE ON MLK DAY

I am not nervous any more, partly because I put the things out-standing in order: I sent out a final blast on constant contact reminding everyone of the details for the day (enclosing a climate justice statement by NAACP to generate more awareness regarding MLK Day); I made a few changes to, and tightened up my remarks; I parked the car with the sound system, banner and stand, and other supplies in the short term parking by the Roundhouse (I left a note saying: "please do not ticket or tow this vehicle, it is here for a special event that was approved by the state capitol;") I was outfitted and ready; I ate a banana and a Bobo bar; Jesse, our friend who was coordinating the West Direction walkers, was on time dropping off his then ten year old son so he and Holden could walk in the event together. But the main reason I am not nervous anymore is because I realize that in teamwork no one person is responsible for the well being of all. Rather, in community all of us are responsible for the whole! This notion, now resounding in me, takes the pressure off me and puts it on us. There is still personal pressure, perhaps even more so because you don't want to let the team down, but this realization eases my anxiety: I cannot solve the climate crisis; we can solve it together.

Holden holding up the sign with Gary and Company on our way to the Climate Walk.

At five minutes before eleven, I along with Fisher, Holden, his friend Calder, Numi and Gary (our French Bull Dog who is wearing his red argyle sweater and climate pin) all walk out the door. Coaster, our beloved black lab, is not with us (mainly to spare her from any ligament soreness which she gets if she walks too long). And our daughter Tabatha is not with us either because she is with her college classmates living the dream. But she is thinking of us (and I have proof of that in a phone message she left).

The sun is shining—It's a "Brand New Day," I sing the title of Joshua Radin's song (Appendix 2)—but it's still a little brisk out. As we walk about a half a mile down the dirt and then paved road to the North meet up location at Ft Marcy Park, some cars honk and drivers wave, seemingly at the sight of our sign and the message on our shirts ("Walk 4 Climate"). When we arrive at Fort Marcy Park and make our way to the parking lot, we are impressed with the turn out. Friends and strangers are gathering up together. I walk around saying hello to everyone, I thank folks for participating and one by one hand out the

"Walking 4 the Climate" pins. Before the departure at 11:30 we take a picture on the field. By the time we start walking south toward the capitol there are over 40 people from the North walking together and the good news is that there are three other directions of people coming, plus many people inevitably going to the Roundhouse on their own. Holden is leading our group and holding up the sign above his head for all to see. The Congresswoman Teresa Leger Fernandez joins me just behind Holden and we get to catch up—she reminds me that one of the first times we met was in association with Nahum Ward Lev who teaches the Beit Midrash group. She's a genuinely kind and uplifting presence. I'm really glad she's with us.

A stream of marchers from the North,
rounding La Fonda Hotel on Old Santa Fe Trail.

Some of the walkers rallying and gathering
at the East meet up spot.

We sail along, staying on the sidewalks, using the cross walks. There are not many cars out today on this holiday Monday but at one busier intersection Numi stays back to make sure cars don't interfere with the stream of walkers. We pass the historic downtown plaza and continue along the oldest most famous route in the country, the Old Santa Fe Trail, for the remaining quarter mile or so to the Roundhouse. We also pass the oldest church in the country, the San Miguel Chapel. We arrive in what feels like no time and the good news is we are right on time, just before high noon. Even better news is that there are a lot of people at the State Capitol. The South and West groups have already assembled, and together they comprise more than twice the amount of folks we have. And so there really is a good turn out! Just before the East group arrives, I have time to set up the amplifier and banner in front of the main entrance to the capitol, right at the base of a prominent statue of a Native American woman facing east, greeting the sun. Camilla, who is one of the partners, is leading everyone in a chant: "What do we want!" People say, "Climate Justice!" "When do we want it?" People respond "Now!" I join in next saying, "let's hear it for the West"—the walkers cheer. "Let's hear it for the South." More walkers cheer, and so on as the East arrives and I say "welcome walkers from the East and welcome walkers from all four directions." Everyone cheers.

In solidarity I begin my remarks with a land acknowledgement.

As I take hold of the microphone I say: "What a beautiful sight!" I then introduce myself as the founder of the Climate Change Leadership Institute. I take out my prepared remarks and continue: "I first want to acknowledge the power of our community! Thank you all and all our partners for making this happen. Teamwork is on display! It's vital now to acknowledge that the land we are standing on is not ours, this was Pueblo land and likewise throughout this country is land that Native American tribes belonged with. We are guests on the land and we should act in that manner!" People applaud. "We should also acknowledge that here in the US we are the highest historical and per capita emitter of greenhouse gasses—and since we've contributed the most to the problem, we need to step up and contribute most to the solution." People cheer.

"Today is all about the community standing up to achieve a successful solution to the Climate Crisis. And that means here in New Mexico, ending the delusion that we can keep on pumping oil and gas to fund our state and public services; we need to phase out of fossil fuel, leave it in the ground where fossils belong, and demand elected officials stop taking contributions from the fossil fuel industry—if they don't we need too vote them out of office. That's what we must do to solve the climate crisis!" People yell out in agreement.

"We also must increasingly act responsibly as consumers by boycotting fossil fuel related products and choose instead the growing alternatives in the marketplace. One alternative you have demonstrated today is to walk instead of drive. Way to go! That's a way we will help solve the climate crisis: not by being paralyzed, cynical and silent, like the special interests want us to be, but by participating in a positive and powerful mass movement to ensure collective health and our life on earth!

Half measures and delaying tactics are not the answer. The UNIPCC, the world's leading scientists say we must transform our economy and eradicate man made greenhouse gases by 2030 in order to keep warming below 1.5 degrees, so if we are going to solve the climate crisis we must insist elected officials take bold action now, not put it off to the future when they won't be in office any longer.

We as a civil society must drive the agenda on federal climate legislation. To be effective we should learn and apply lessons from the abolition and civil rights movements which for centuries have been making a way out of no way: vivid examples are enacting the emancipation proclamation after the dark period of slavery and civil war and enacting the voting and civil rights acts after deep segregation. That's what we must do in the movement to solve the climate crisis: all together dedicate ourselves for as long as it takes, with soul force, sweat, tears and our dignity in tact—until we get it done! We are holding this event on MLK Day because of the promising synergy of these two movements—which are really about the same thing: advancing a better relationship with each other and the Earth!

We are so proud today to be partnering with the Santa Fe branch of the NAACP which has been promoting this event to their members and beyond. Their director Cedrick Page wasn't able to make it today bc of COVID precaution but he wanted me to read a statement: 'Climate change, has a disproportionate impact on communities of color in the United States and around the world. The NAACP recognizes environmental injustice as the result of systemic racism. We must work for Climate Justice to address the harm being done to communities everywhere. Thru participatory democracy we can fight for the policies needed to rectify the injustices and advance a society that fosters sustainable, cooperative, regenerative communities that uphold all rights for all people in harmony with the earth. Furthermore, the NAACP declares that the right to live in a safe and healthy environment is a civil right that no person should have to sacrifice for economic security or employment.'" People applaud louder.

Hundreds gathered at the Roundhouse calling for equity and climate leadership.

"This strong, important statement relates to another way we're going to solve the climate crisis which is by reclaiming our rights to the common good and engraining in the constitution our fundamental natural and civil rights to clean air, quality water, healthy soil and a livable climate. Thankfully we have a champion here leading the people's movement for a green amendment, it's a people's movement because if the joint resolution is adopted this session, which we should all make sure it does, it will go on the ballot for we the people to vote on. So let's welcome Maya K van Rossum, Founder of the Green Amendment for the Generations." Participants clap and Maya energizes the crowd.

I then continue, "We will also help solve the climate crisis by coming together, young and old, cross culturally, business and non-profit, dare I say Democrat, Independent and Republican alike." I literarily stumbled on the word Republican and people grumbled when I said it but I persevered: "This is necessary and this is possible, unity is possible, at least a governing majority is possible, because we are not about attacking people, we are about combating pollution. We need a big tent, which means people can come to climate action for different reasons: economic reasons, justice reasons, health reasons, moral reasons—all are relevant and needed. In the spirit of collaboration we welcome Camilla Feibelman with the Sierra Club Rio Grande Chapter, who has helped a lot on this event and she is someone that treats everyone with civility." Camilla leads people in another rally cry, and then calmly and methodically informs everyone how to be involved in citizen lobbying listing all the relevant bills for this session.

I proceed to introduce and invite our next guest, "Another way we succeed is by doing right and sacrificing ourselves for the well being of our children. It's great to see all of the young people here today. Young people are the future and deserve climate justice! Our endeavor today is all about safeguarding their future—and thankfully we have Elena Gomez from the Youth United for Climate Crisis Action (YUCCA) who is a champion of the movement inspiring us to be brave." Elena proceeds to blow me and everyone away. She speaks passionately and articulately for climate justice, and she speaks truth to power, calling on

 us not to be fooled by the Governor who is in cahoots with the oil and gas industry. Elena urges us not to support some of her touted legislation, most notably her Net Zero Emissions Act by 2050 which Elena says is a smokescreen that kicks the can down the road and doesn't deliver the strong climate justice desperately needed.

Elena Gomez with YUCCA demanding climate justice.

The program continues, as I invite Mariel Nanasi, who exquisitely heads New Energy Economy, to speak on her resolution calling for a public utility to replace the corrupt utility we have now. She calls for people power and for public power to combat the climate crisis and she evokes Martin Luther King Jr.'s "fierce urgency of now" to encourage our community to take a stand right away.

I then thank the elected officials who had come to the rally and I introduce one of them to be our final speaker: "We are here today to demand and encourage elected officials to be brave. Our member of congress, Congresswoman Teresa Leger Fernandez is listening and wanted to be here today to honor this cause, so let's give her a big welcome." She proceeds to talk about the John Lewis Voting Rights Act which she says is so crucial to the environmental and racial justice cause and crucial for the advancement of the common good. She also spoke on Martin Luther King Day about his vision of the Beloved Community which very much includes caring for everyone and our one Earth as one combined endeavor. The Congresswoman proceeds to invite young people to stand beside her and read off the posters they made for the event. They are all beautiful and the one that stands out most to me reads as follows: "If you can't fly, then run. If you can't, walk. Then crawl. Whatever you do you have to keep moving forward!"

School children standing up strong with Congresswoman Teresa Leger Fernandez.

After thanking the kids and the Congresswoman, I proceed: "I want to end this event like it started by honoring, as the Congresswoman eluded to, the Beloved Community reflected by all of you who took the time out of your lives to come together and stand up for a cause much greater than our selves. In honoring your collective efforts I want to share some of the statements you made when you registered about why you are doing this. Here are a sampling of your answers: Carlos Trujillo from the North says "Climate change is the most important issue facing humanity;" Liz McGrath from the East says "Let's show our government how much we care about climate change!" Marcia Valdez from the West says "I am doing this because I love Mother Earth and have beautiful grandchildren who need to have her in good shape;" Mary Burton Risely from the South says "I am a believer in non-violence and I want to do whatever I can to prevent climate catastrophe." Richard Mark Glover: "It sucks that New Mexico is the cheapest state in the country to drill for oil and gas." Karen Anderson: "We are out of time!" Esther Kovari: "I am a high school teacher and am going to try to get some students to participate." A high school senior, Nick Farrell: This is an awesome effort from everyone, my generation thanks you for doing it! Barbara Conroy who is 80 yrs old says one word: "Life!!" Jane and Bill: "we always do something together on MLK Day and this year we choose climate action." Rebecca: "all other progressive efforts depend on climate!" Dominique Mazeaud: "Walking with intention is a great way to speak on an issue and develop community." Rachel Kelly: "We have to do everything we can to combat climate change." And finally, Linda Wilder Flatt: "Taking action on the Climate Crisis is serious and must be addressed. I hope our legislators will pay attention to this effort, take steps and take action! Nothing else matters more than this. Nothing!"

So "In closing," I say, "thank you all for participating in this first critical step to build community. Next up is to join and grow a civil society wide mass movement that will sweep the nation and together solve the climate crisis!" When my speaking wraps up, I experience (a) the exhilaration of not speaking anymore and (b) the joy of meeting some of the many participants. First, an old man holding a Veterans for Peace flag introduces himself saying not enough attention is given to the fact that the US military is one of the worst polluters on the planet and the Department of Defense gets trillions of dollars which he said is diverting funds from more truly constructive causes like solving the climate crisis. He is absolutely right and on top of that no other issue is making the world community less secure and more in turmoil than climate change. Next, I meet James Moss who is the man who came on crutches. He too is a veteran, like his father in World War II before him, who now believes in the power of community action as well as the integration of the climate change and MLK movements. He says he is feeling sore in his hip after walking as far as he did so I asked my son Fisher to use the supply car to drive him back to where he started. He is appreciative and promises to be in touch. The third person I meet named Dave, tells me he will retire soon from the New Mexico Health Department and would like to volunteer for climate efforts because he says "there truly is no more important issue facing the human race." I encourage him to reach out when he is ready.

There are folks from the media covering the event that come over and I answer questions they have for me. KRQE 13, one of the leading statewide news stations is filming the event for their afternoon and evening news coverage. They take video footage of the attendees and of me holding the sign. I'm glad they are here. Also a photographer from the Albuquerque journal asks me a few questions. I'm happy for the tv and print news coverage but what excites me even more is the radio coverage this event is receiving. According to Public News Service over twenty media outlets picked up the story with cumulative audience circulations of hundreds of thousands of listeners from cities and towns across the state, which has only about two million people in total. I feel gratified that people in both urban and rural communities across the Land of Enchantment are being reached and hopefully moved to some form of action in their lives (Appendix 3).

Afterwards I take the Climate Change Leadership Institute (CCLI) board out for lunch at Rio Chama which is a restaurant next to the State Capitol. I want to show appreciation for their participation and for their organization in promoting Walking 4 Climate. We toast our glasses, have some lunch and then go our own ways back home. Gary, Fisher and Holden catch a ride home in the supply car, but Numi walks home with me. As we retrace our steps, she flatters me by saying the program went off without a hitch (no injuries, good turn out, lovely walk, nice rally, great radio coverage) and she says that my public speaking skills have noticeably improved. That's good because I have had a few doozies over the years, not least was Numi's fortieth birthday when I stood up in front of all of our friends and compared her to a statue of a beautiful naked woman.

Numi wasn't the only one to give positive feedback. There were dozens of folks who sent emails and texts, uplifted by the event. It was reassuring. Of course I responded to each kind gesture, and I also sent out a huge thanks to the whole network with pictures and highlights from the day and mainly with the message of deep gratitude for the lovely demonstration of teamwork. The one email I received with criticism said that we have to do much more than walk and rally; we have to engage in broader non-violent civil disobedience. I agree with this person. This was just a warm up, hopefully a spark, for the brave community and civil society action to come.

That evening my good friend Andy came by and we played some backgammon by the fire. We use the doubling cube and play for low stakes. He was on a roll (no pun intended) that night and got the best of me. Unfortunately, Andy had recently learned from his doctor that he had cancer in his leg. Fortunately, it turned out to be contained and treatable. But it made me think: first not to take walking, the sports or other activities we enjoy for granted; also it made me think about our vulnerabilities and the sad truth that there's a lot of struggle on earth. I've been lucky to have more happiness and health in my world than hardship but I'm not immune. This month in fact is my least favorite because my mom, dad and grandma all died in January, not to mention other things that happened. To help get through the dreary season I grow a beard and when it's burly enough I shave it down to a mustache, which my wife likes so that's a plus. Like playing backgammon—it provides some relief, comic and otherwise, to take our mind off dread that can surface.

What I am getting at is we all have hurt (to varying degrees). Ironically as a human race, though, we are aggravating the hurtfulness through our role (to varying degrees) in the climate crisis and in systemic racism. We could be alleviating the pain by addressing these twin injustices head on. Of course there would still be loss and sadness in a climate safe and racially just world but the important difference is we wouldn't be causing the grief as much as we are now and that would be rejuvenating and spring true peace of mind. We would more often summon light from our ability to care for and connect with one another, rather than live in the shadows of inadequacy and shame from our harmfulness. The Beloved Community provides a key opportunity for us to heal, one which certainly needs to be explored much further than I do in this chapter and applied much farther than simply by holding a community walk and rally. In the whole foundational realm, which I am aiming for in this book, it is one of four cornerstones needed for our collective restoration.

The story for statewide radio coverage (Appendix 3) emphasized correctly that the walk to the Capitol was pragmatically important to encourage elected officials to lead, but our walking there from four directions was also symbolically important because as PNS reported, "the Capitol, known as the Roundhouse, was designed to represent the sun's rays, as well as the four directions, four seasons and four phases of life." So then what does it mean for our greater health to journey to the sun's rays or to walk four directions? I will devote the last section of my exploration to answering this question. I suspect there is meaningful integrity that comes from assembling the four direction foundations into one whole way of being. And I venture to say, in the spirit of the man holding up this simple sign, if we carry out and bring together the four directions at once, we can "heal our world!"

If we carry out and bring together the four directions at once, we can "heal our world!"

SECTION VI
WALKING HOME

"We're all under the same sky and walk the same earth."
—Maxine Hong Kingston

It would have been my mom's 78th birthday today, February 7th 2022. I mentioned this to Holden on my way to drop him off at school this morning and he said, serendipitously, that he had a dream of Nama early this morning. She was driving us, he said, down the coast of California in a convertible and she looked "especially young." Tabatha, when I texted this to her at college, responded: "I was just reading this walking to my class. Have to stop to appreciate how special that is. I almost just started crying. Thank you. Owl always love [we associated my mom with an owl and so we often will say 'Owl Always Love You']." Fisher added, "That is really amazing and touching. Her spirit lives on!" It's true how compelling it is that she carries on, mobilizing her offspring and getting younger in our collective memory.

I said originally, before I set out on this journey, that if I walk four directions—with each direction representing four regenerative cornerstones consisting of Human Spirit, Mother Nature, Heritage Values, Beloved Community—maybe they will become concrete enough to assemble them into the wholeness we need. Now having done it I'd like to see if this holds up, if it's easy to assemble the pieces into a whole. What better way, I thought, to assess the merits of this prospect and realize the meaning of walking four directions, than to take my dogs on four short walks from my home in order to reflect on each of the directions I have been. In other words, to use an alpinist analogy, it's important to scale where we have been, with an eagle eye review of the foundational sections of our climb, in order to fully appreciate where we stand and visualize where we now may be capable of going together. In Plain English, dogs have a way of making sense of things so I am going to walk with them to help put my ideas together.

So the dogs and I took little walks from our home on different days of the upcoming winter week (in contrast to the different seasons of the year) and we went in each of the four directions in confluence with the previous year's adventure. The walks were only for about 30 minutes a pop, and all were in the neighborhood for the most part. Much of the time I reflected on where I had been according to the direction we were going, and each time we encountered something new and insightful before we turned back home.

21
NORTH

In the north direction, I reflect on what the CEO of Patagonia said, that it's important to have a North Star, something of deep principle that we aim for (Reference). I think of the Prophets and how they kept reminding us to do the same. Micah's message percolates, "walk humbly, pursue justice and love mercy." Humility and equity demand that we step back while others step forward, acknowledging the harm we are causing and actively turning in a new direction. Mercy being something we all need because we're all fallible. Love being what actualizes our epic transformation. The lyrics of "Love Train" by The O'Jays play in my head: "People all over the word, join hands, start a love train, love train..." (Appendix 2). I kneel down to give affection to the dogs, knowing how affectionate they are to us. They eat it up and then run off ahead. Dogs raise morale with their good cheer. Raising up our human spirit, which we must do to solve the climate crisis, means building character as much as it means drawing on soul force. Being as we are one part feeble and another part expansive beyond measure, as I learned on my pilgrimage to Chimayo, why not embrace the boundless realm of possibility within us? John Francis, the Planet Walker, comes to mind, particularly his extraordinary example of defying conventional limits, and his clear articulation of our problem: the environmental crisis is, he says, "a crisis of our mind and spirit" (Reference).

On the way to pick up Holden from school today I drove passed the St. Francis Cathedral and just as I passed the south-side of the building, loud and beautiful church bells sounded. It was a wake up call if I ever heard one, on my mom's birthday no less. I was reminded then and there of the Prayer of St. Francis as well as the African proverb from John Lewis, 'When we pray, let's move our feet." The two together converge as one that we need to respond to any lethargic condition of our people and to any degeneration of our planet, with what is lacking: a robust display of spirit and regeneration.

The person I can think of who best exemplifies this virtue of giving it her all and providing what is sorely missing is Harriet Tubman. She is a walking hero for sure (Appendix 1). Holden, for Black History Month at school, has been reading with me aloud her incredible biography. Her story along with other vital truth teachings of our history are being censored in a Nazi like manner throughout many southern states. It makes it all the more important to learn the folly of our past so we never repeat it in the future. The biography (Reference) discusses her upbringing as well as aspects of the utter inhumanity of slavery, including the brutal whippings, the torture, the horrifying conditions of slave ships, sickening auctions, among the other dehumanizing illustrations, which all together make me feel deep anguish.

With my head bowed and tears welling up, Holden proceeds to read the chapters featuring Harriet Tubman's courage: first helping a man escape to freedom at the expense of her physical health; then risking death to achieve her own freedom by walking over several nights—initially from Maryland to Pennsylvania, and ultimately on to Canada (which is a total of 1,322,157 steps and about 650 miles!); taking her father's advice to follow the North Star and getting help from the brave kindness of Quakers and other abolitionists who took her in along the way; and then devoting her life as a lead conductor of the aid network that was the Underground Railroad, helping at great risk, not only her family but dozens upon dozens of others gain their rightful freedom and dignity. The reason this is so important to the current climate crisis as well as the persisting crisis of systemic racism is that it shows the vast healing power and potential of the human spirit, which Harriet Tubman and all her compatriots of the Underground Railroad exhibited in droves (Reference). For combating dehumanization with utmost courage and compassion. Putting ones' lives on the line to honor life itself by upholding the right of liberty and the hope of human decency for all. This is something we are all now called on to do if we are to prevail as a people, no less prevail as a planet.

At the half way point of our north walk when the dogs and I are about to turn home, we come to a drive way featuring an outpost of solar arrays. Usually in residential areas you would see solar panels on rooftops, but these are neighborhood scale solar arrays that are ground mounted and turning toward the sunlight. It occurs to me that this is a fitting symbol of our greater endeavor. Yes, on one level of course, we need to fully replace our harmful energy sources with clean, renewable power. And we've only scratched the surface of the vast potential for solar, geothermal and renewable power. In 2021, renewables made up 30% of the world's energy sources, which is significant, but we have the capability to achieve 100% renewable energy, if we make the commitment, modernize the grid and utilize energy storage. We should do all of this as soon as humanly possible.

On another level this picture of panels facing the sun is symbolic in the quest for restoration because the sun gives us life. Neither humans nor plants would survive without its light and energy. In fact the sun gives the opportunity for health and vigor throughout the whole global community. Prana is the Sanskrit word for breath, and for "vital principle" as well as for "life force." In Hindu tradition life force originates from the sun and the connecting elements. In Maori tradition, "mauri" means the life force abiding in us and in everything from rocks, trees, waterways, creatures and the sun alike. Appreciation of life force is essential to our well being and that of the earth, and for many the sun is what gives this possibility. I think of Nelson Mandela's optimism even as he was wrongly imprisoned for decades, how he always kept his head pointed toward the sun. We can raise the level of our spirit and the human and environmental condition if we honor the sun, protect access to healthy food and clean water, and make sure everyone has fair claim to the commons and other healing sources critical for survival. Instead of bowing our heads, we can hold our heads up (like my dogs are doing in this picture) with curiosity and respect for the life forces that bind us and sustain us all.

The dogs are wisely intrigued about these ground mounted solar arrays located at the north side of our neighborhood.

22
EAST

Inaturally am inclined in this direction of thinking, which is why in the mornings I instinctively turn toward the sunrise with a feeling of gratitude. The next little walk that I take with the dogs, for reflection and insight, is in the east direction from our home, and this time we have a special guest joining us. Holden Gerald Hirsch for the time being is right by our side, and soon he's leading the charge. East, compared with the other three directions from our home, is the most natural of all the terrain near us. This is especially true once we climb over a not so neighborly fence that was put up to keep us and others out of the private property portion of these parts. But it's the only access point from where we live; so I lift Holden and then the dogs over the fence, and once we are on the other side we are smiling bigger and striding faster. We're well on our way now into this little Adventureland well behind our home. There are sandy hills, piñon forests and a prominent arroyo running through it with a slight prospect of witnessing coyotes who frequent these parts. I used to take all the kids back here regularly, when they were all young, before the neighbor barricaded us and others out.

It's the prefect place to reflect on the Mother Nature foundation of my journey. Perfect because nature abounds. In fact this is the gateway to the Sangre de Christo mountains. But it's also perfect because a clear trace of humankind is present too in the forms of hidden trails, dirt roads, homes that blend into the surroundings and...tire swings. I recall my two pronged journey on the Winsor Trail and remember the overriding message: once we restore our relationship with the land, we and the land can be restored at once. But like the erected fence, we keep separating ourselves out from nature as if by being separate we can manipulate her and control our destiny, and thereby be better or more mighty somehow. But we're not. We are little pequeño, and more to the point, we are our own worst enemies. Nature will go on, however damaged or mangled by our harmfulness, but we may not survive ourselves.

Holden says, "Mother Nature is like Coaster, too kind to us" even when we don't deserve it, and we don't deserve it! But I hope for his sake we rise to the occasion to the point where we deserve and earn Mother Nature's kindness. I think of Cold Play's song called "Humankind" (Appendix 2) with the emphasis on kind. In the lyrics it goes: "Today I had the strangest feeling that I belong, Before, I was dying...now I'm flying, I say I know, I know, I know We're only human...How we're designed, yeah...We're only human, But from another planet, Still they call us humankind." I wonder what would it take for us to be the envy of life from another planet. More to home, I wonder what will it take for us to heal and soar, and then restore our relationship with Mother Earth? Going into nature and observing and listening to her is one definite way, as I learned personally from my journey. Another way is to consider the advice of Sue Van Hook, a naturalist and mycologist who recovered from stage three breast cancer. She said, "We don't have to fix anything. Nature can heal and restore on its own. We just have to get out of the way" (Reference).

That's all important and true. But I know too, beyond emulation and wisely modeling ourselves after her, and beyond stepping back and giving her center stage to perform widespread regenerative miracles, there is a third way. The third way is through symbiosis, which means forging a mutually beneficial relationship. Read Dr. Daniel Benor's paper called "Web of Life" (Reference) about symbiosis between people and the environment for an excellent understanding. The gist is that we as humankind can perpetuate our parasitic relationship with nature, which will rapidly burst the carrying capacity of the earth leading to mass species extinction including our own, or we can forge a symbiotic relationship, an on-going interaction with the natural world that makes us each grow better and thrive together in concert.

A great example is the symbiosis going on in our bodies, and especially in our gut biomes, with the presence of bacteria and friendly micro-organisms. We host them, they feed off us and thus they need us. And, on our end, we wouldn't survive without them. The kicker is that we thrive when they are healthy, and they are more healthy when we eat more unprocessed foods, less artificial flavors, more diversity (including multi-colored vegetables and fruits), less monocultures, more food grown without gut and planet harming pesticides and fertilizers. The take home point is that if we restore our gut health through a full embrace of regenerative agriculture, we can, together with nature, restore health on earth. There is mutual vitality and genuine hope, versus doom and gloom, when there is symbiosis. It's a give and take. A back and forth.

The beloved tree swing east from our home, upholding the prospect
for a healthy relationship between humankind and nature.

Holden and I have arrived at the acclaimed tree swing portion of our dog
walk together. Again, this is the half way point of our outing, right before we
commence the second half of the loop back home. There is a tire swing earlier on
that all three kids have enjoyed over the years but the rope has frayed precariously
to the point of it being temporarily decommissioned. This other current tree
swing, further along the way, between the dirt road and the arroyo, is much
sturdier. It appears like it will endure through the ages, which is good because
it has something important to teach us: how vital it is that we interact with
and play in nature. Why? Because, as I learned from my walking journey, from
the encounter with MacGregor the volleyball, God wants us to play outdoors.
The Giving Tree also wants us to—because there is a sense of innocence and

integration that come alive when we do. I think our dogs already know this because they are having a ball. In Coaster's case today she's having (chewing on) a stick, but normally she likes balls; and Gary likes whatever Coaster is enjoying—stick or ball, it makes no difference as long as he's stealing it from her (Gary is parasitic, Coaster is symbiotic).

I recall what the young woman Lucy from Australia and her dog Wombat said that when you are walking major distances you see that the divide between humans and the natural world is just a myth. That we are, in truth, boundary-less and fence-less. We are one. This is the kind of transformative thinking that Buddhist Zen Master Thich Nhat Hanh embodied. He was born in Vietnam in 1926, became a monk and later on was exiled, but not before influencing eastern and western societies alike in the centering power of mindfulness. He taught meditation, which he famously said "is not to escape from society, but [a chance] to come back to ourselves and see what is going on. Once there is seeing, there must be acting." He more recently founded "Wake up" schools which train young people how to get up out of sleep walking and into "the art of mindful living." Perhaps our sleep walker Fisher would be interested in this.

I bring up Thich Nhat Hanh not only in remembrance, because he just passed away in the beginning of 2022 (at the ripe age of 95), but more because of his uplifting nature oriented and humane temperament which is instructive for our wide-scale health and longevity. He wrote the book *How to Walk* (Reference) encouraging calm walking that focuses on our in and out breaths and enables present mindedness. I read the book with delight and then gave it to Tabatha because she is taking a class on mindfulness and I thought it could be handy as she is already making bounding strides in this direction. She knows, as my mom knew before us, that meditation can contribute significantly to our vitality; and "walking mediation" as Hanh coined it can be immensely helpful to our well being as well as to the nature under our feet. Thich Nhat Hanh is a walking hero of mine and so many others (Appendix 1). He said, "Dear Mother [Nature], I make the promise today to return your love...by investing every step I take on you with...tenderness. I am walking not merely on matter but on spirit" (p. 117). He also stated, "only love can save us from climate change."

Right now I am loving Holden, the dogs, and the land that we're lucky to be in synch with, as we make our way back the round about way: first on the "Coyote Trail," then through the 'tunnel" between houses, and finally on the dirt road home.

23
WEST

Ironically, or perhaps fittingly, when I took the dogs for a walk to reflect on Heritage Values and honor the west direction of the journey, it was the shortest of all the little walks from my home even though the western walk to Chaco was by far the longest of the four directions. Maybe this brevity is important, so I can't and shouldn't re-tell the lengthy experience. It stands on its own. But perhaps I can and should share, in a nut shell, what it meant to me, like I shared my feelings about Leslie Marmon Silko's extraordinary Ceremony story without retelling it. Thinking back, what comes to mind was the moment half way through the long slog to Chaco when I felt broken and that I couldn't do it anymore, not on my own. A flood of emotions ran through me to the point of resolve when I realized then and there that I needed help. I needed to draw on the warm thoughts from my immediate family, the well wishes from my friends, the supportive energy from the Great Spirit and all the remarkable acts of kindness from good Samaritans throughout western New Mexico. And, equally importantly, I needed to draw on the collective force of our ancestors! That's where we find ourselves now as a civilization. We've reached a pivotal breaking point—in terms of the climate crisis and the crisis of human relations—where we direly need help. We can't fix our crisis alone. Yes we need to turn to nature and elsewhere for help. Yes we need to rise up our spiritual resolve. But we also need to summon the heritage values of our ancestors and take to heart the sacredness of life.

As my dogs are bounding down the dirt road ahead of me, rhymes of remembrance stream out like versus of a walking poem: step on the ground with the sound of drumbeat, leave no trace from the soles of my feet; it's oh so hard but simple see, put one foot in font of the other, as my grandmother taught me; dance and chant, like a Soldier Beetle aiding a plant; act not frail but bold like a burro conquering a cliff trail; relay a cactus's staying power, don't fade away;

enter the zone and become, like the Apache, a people of backbone; like Po' Pay don't act alone, make sure thieves and pillagers are overthrown.

The dogs head off the road, and go seemingly in hiding, presumably they don't appreciate my poetry. I don't blame them. I call them several times, finally promising that if they come out of hiding I will stop rhyming. And, as they do on so many occasions, they joyfully forgive me, joining up with me back on the road.

Fisher told me last night about a real poet named Arthur Sze who lives in the Land of Enchantment and works on poetry with Native American youth among others. Sze, who is of Asian decent, visited Fisher's school and Fisher said how captivated he was by Sze's reveal of the old Chinese language, how the symbols used are so steeped in nature imagery. He said Sze showed them that the symbols for the moon and the sun when placed back to back mean "bright." And he appreciated the brightness of Sze's poetry. One poem of Sze's called "Before Completion" asks "what is it like to catch up to the light?" Another ponders "When does matter end and space begin?" Walking along I can answer the latter question by saying: when walking whenever my feet leave the ground!

There are many questions that linger with me from my journey—like: will I be forever changed, or just go back to my old self? For the time being at least, I am changed. So many cross currents of insights and feelings circulate in my brain and in my soul. If all of this energy is brought together like a poem, hopefully it will illuminate human experience, empathy and our shared potential for restoration. One illumination I experienced is the sense of struggle. I learned it the hard way during the long walk, but also from Fisher's wise suggestion, that it's important to "seek discomfort." When we feel deep anguish—in our body, mind and spirit from people and the planet being harmed—we step out of our safe divided zones and into a place of compassion; and if we act on our compassion we can enter the realm of kinship, where personal transformation and societal change-making is possible. Another illumination I realized, like yin and yang, is the exhilaration of life. I experienced it in the distance walking itself. I also learned it from the Pueblo and Native American way of balancing "this is the place"—therefore plant roots in the ground, be hospitable and find belonging on earth—and "the sky is our father" so gain a greater understanding of our close connection with the cosmos around us.

I think of my father and his refrain 'somebody up there likes me.' I feel that way too. I feel my dad's love shining down as well as love from a Force much greater than my comprehension. It's all gently guiding me to a path of integrity, which is not only a personal quest toward some semblance of uprightness but more a meaningful adventure together to the state of being whole and undivided.

Someone who is a walking hero for doing this exact thing—creating wholeness, uprightness and belonging out of anguish—is a young Kenyan activist and humanitarian named Elizabeth Wathuti (Appendix 1). She says that climate change induced drought in her country means that so many go without food and water. She has watched children cry in despair after walking twelve miles for water only to find the river dry. She says: "over two million of my fellow Kenyans are facing climate-related starvation…the decisions you make [as a world community]…will help determine whether children will have food and water." She herself has responded to her call for action, and in doing so has brought pride to her ancestors. She founded the Green Generation Initiative, a youth led endeavor that has planted over 30,000 trees, which among other things provide shade and hold water in the ground instead of perpetuating run off and run away drought. It is now our turn to respond in kind.

Elizabeth Wathuti from Kenya implores the world to thwart the hunger and water emergency being caused and exacerbated by our exorbitant greenhouse gas emissions. (Illustration by AuPalette)

The dogs and I come to the point of turning around. But not before we encounter and ponder a new and old symbol of the journey: a charmingly painted stagecoach, fitting because we are at the very end (or beginning) of the dirt road named "Stagecoach." The image of course has the anguishing association of western colonialism so harmful to the Native American Tribes and so shameful to our Nation. But, on the other hand, if that painful history was somehow reconciled to the extent possible—through a full truth and reconciliation commission; by returning ample sacred lands back to the rightful original people; by fully honoring the sovereignty of the Tribes; by ending the on-going exploitation of natural resources including all the illegal pipeline crossings, oil and gas extractions and other industrial development incursions; by halting the wider society's egregious pollution of air, water and soil in and around tribal communities; by embracing co-management of lands in common; by federally honoring Indigenous Peoples Day and treating everyday as an opportunity to honor the sacredness of life and respect one another...and by countless other steps of acknowledgement of the pain and destruction we caused, and still cause today, and the restitution we owe in return—the stagecoach symbol could be turned into a more hopeful one. We could imagine a new pioneering spirit, not about Manifest Destiny, but actually about ingenuity and problem solving, facing and overcoming the grave challenges in our civilization and developing a clean, empowering and fair economy that doesn't pollute the earth or enable the few to get ahead at the expense of the many.

Gary rides in the stagecoach heading west.

Two companies come to mind, one is a California based company called Brimstone Energy (full disclosure I don't know enough about them to vouch for them). They have patented an alternative to cement. The global society's widespread use of cement is responsible for 8% of worldwide greenhouse gas emissions. But their patent is actually carbon negative because it uses clean energy in place of fossil fuels for the heating process and, instead of making cement by using limestone which emits CO_2 when heated, it uses a different rock called calcium silica which when heated produces magnesium which absorbs CO_2 from there air. So it's a two pronged solution and example of a new kind of pioneering spirit that is hopeful.

The other company that comes to mind, based right here in New Mexico, called Public, PBC, is an all woman owned public benefit corporation that specializes in home design and building. Not only do they use innovative materials (carbon absorbing rather than emitting) and accomplish holistic sustainability as well as energy conservation, they do so with equal priority on social justice, affordable housing and fair labor practices.

All I can say is the dogs and I adamantly favor reconciling and turning a new leaf of pioneering spirit. As we walk home we reaffirm the plan, contemplating the new and old keys to the kingdom. We opine, if our society can apply lessons from those who have come before us, and establish new paradigms of innovation, if we learn from Indigenous communities and step onto cross cultural pathways emerging before us, it's possible to both develop new habits of the heart and utilize age old fortitude enough to save the day.

24
SOUTH

On another day of the week, the dogs and I journey down the arroyo toward town. We're heading south and descending in elevation, both of which you'd think would make us warmer. But it's a cold winter's day. Warmth is hard to come by except when we appreciate diversity while acting in unison and except when we stand strong as an unbreakable Beloved Community! I recall John Lewis' story "Walking with the Wind" and one of his concluding statements: "I believe" he said, "that the next frontier for America lies in the direction of our spiritual strength as a community." (p. 461) This implies that we all have spiritual strength, especially in community, and if that's true (which I believe it is) then the question becomes in what direction are we going to apply our spiritual strength? Or in other words, what is our society going to use our strength to lift up? Are we going to use it to lift up material wealth for the few, with the many chasing in vain from behind—is that what our legacy will be? Or will we use our 'exceptionalism' for a legitimately great purpose? John Lewis thought, and I agree, that we should use our strength to lift up and inspire all of our people, the whole American family, in the direction of integrity. He goes onto to say: "What…is…right? If we keep out hearts and minds constantly focused on that single question, and if we act on the answer with courage and commitment, we will overcome all that stands between us and the glory of a truly Beloved Community" (p. 473).

We encounter a coyote running across the way. Gary goes crazy wanting to chase after him but thankfully Gary is on a leash for the time being. I imagine what would happen if Gary got his way and I let him loose: he would act the part: bull dog tough, barking and running roughshod up to the Coyote; but meanwhile there would be a whole pack of coyotes cleverly waiting for him around the bend; he'd be toast; a braggart who turned up to a gun fight with only a nail clipper. Even big strong mankind has had an impossible time trying to capture and exterminate coyotes; they have not only survived our onslaught but they have come back stronger and more widespread. It makes me think that resiliency—for animals and humans alike—will be one of the most important traits we can have in this century. So we better start learning from the experts.

Another character trait that will serve us well this century is humility, the counter part to resiliency. Simply by acknowledging when we make a mistake goes a long way to us being able to fix it. There is a statement I like to tell Numi on the seldom occasions when she is off base—and of course we all know that more of the time in our marital disputes I am to blame. But when she is I say: "admit that you're wrong and let's move on!" Well that's what we need to do as a society in the face of climate catastrophe. We need to admit we are walking in the wrong direction and if we do then we create an opportunity to either turn around or turn a corner to the point where we can renew ourselves. I heard Anne-Marie Slaughter—president of a "think and action tank" called New America—interviewed on the radio about her recent book called *Renewal* (Reference). She had a reckoning in her professional life and once she faced up to it she not only turned the page, she wrote this important story about our widespread potential for renewal, something she describes as a healing process that "looks backward and forward at the same time." Likewise, Michael Phillips, who is a pastor of a black church in Maryland, wrote a hopeful book called *Wrong Lanes Have Right Turns* (Reference), featuring the second chance he got in life to escape the prison pipeline which he used to embrace empowerment and education for at risk youth. This is on my mind because it speaks to the virtue of having the courage to make the best out of any situation, something important no matter what but increasingly important in this century ripe with immense challenges and immeasurable opportunities.

We can make the best out of our situation. If we led the world in solving the climate crisis we would gain tremendous competitive advantage in desirable clean technologies. We would save and overtime build up American treasure from ensuring a more stable future by fixing the problem head on (versus steadily and drastically losing national economic wealth from putting out mounting emergencies in vain by maintaining the status quo of denial). More importantly, if we tackled the challenge head on, we would live up to our promise as a nation. What's the point of the Declaration of Independence, the Revolutionary War and our whole democratic experiment if we are going to use our republic simply as a guise for pursuing private property and preserving the powers that be. What a lame and uninspiring existence that is. But it's also just plain wrong considering we have built this republic on the backs of slaves as well as at the eradication expense of Native American people and their way of life. To be true to our promise we could make amends and make our democracy for which it stands—of the people, for the people and by the people. We could make it seminally all about the advancement of liberty and justice for all. This could be epitomized if we built our society around solving the climate crisis, if we ended systemic racism and if we modeled free enterprise with equal opportunity (welcoming *the tired, poor and huddled masses yearning to breathe free* and concluding the reign of a few haves over mostly have nots). Building such a Beloved Community would be something to be deeply proud of, something that would enable us to hold our head up high like the Statue of Liberty, to the point where we could have invigorating purpose brightening our day and we could sleep, me included, soundly at night.

This promised land, this Laguna (aka oasis), is not going to just fall on our lap. We are going to need the foresight and daring to make it happen. We will have to be involved like never before. We will have to stand up steadfastly against the tyranny that's holding us back. And in this case tyranny means the conglomerates profiting most from pollution, the greedy forces degrading the earth and the people on it, and the power structures dividing us up so we don't come together and change the power structure. We must deploy the full force of our God given, inalienable, civil and constitutional rights to the nonviolent overthrow of this tyranny. Our duty is beckoning and it's time we answer the call. The Beloved Community and life force itself, more than our lives alone, depend on it.

And as for the civil right to vote which we must use like never before to hold politicians accountable, I should mention I'm Independent in terms of my voter registration because in the long run I believe in profiles of courage and collaboration and don't think the entrenched two party system has lately proven effective at achieving the common good solutions we direly need. Money in politics is destroying our democratic principles, no matter the party benefiting from it, and we must address it on a non partisan basis. But I'm not crazy to think the two parties are equally harmful. The Republic Party has gone totally off the rails by aligning itself with tactics of racism, climate nihilism, authoritarianism and borderline fascism. All companies and special interests including the fossil fuel industry who are donating to the RNC and to Republican Party elected officials or candidates that have subscribed to these dangerous positions—including infringing on BIPOC voting rights, censoring education pertaining to our history of slavery and racism, standing against climate and environmental stewardship, not supporting the January 6th Commission and not federally safeguarding free and fair elections—should be called out by investigative journalism and on social media and effectively boycotted by our information age capabilities as well as by mass movements of people collectively utilizing our consumption choices, organizing abilities and powerful protesting tools.

Protesting is necessary as well to counter the dangerous tide of the Supreme Court which at the end of February heard a case called West Virginia vs. EPA, putting in jeopardy the ability to regulate carbon dioxide under the Clean Air Act. The best way to protest this ghastly move, which is as harmful as the Citizens United Case, is for an overwhelming majority of Americans to demand—through voting, non violent direct action and all the change-making means at our disposal—that Congress enacts domestic legislation that not only sanctifies the right to be regulating greenhouse gasses under the Clean Air Act but vigorously calls on the EPA to go ahead and thoroughly regulate greenhouse gasses at all levels of the economy to ensure a livable climate. That would be the gift the American people can give that would get us on a serious footing in solving the climate crisis.

Speaking of gifts, it's Valentine's Day and Numi explicitly told me not to get her anything. That's not surprising given my history of gift mishaps. On our most recent anniversary I was smart, taking her queue on jewelry rather than selecting something myself. I wasn't as wise when I proposed to her. I infamously got her what friends later described as a "CanArdly" which meant that Numi and everyone could hardly see the jewel in the ring. Numi was as sweet as can be about it throughout the engagement but since then my gift giving didn't improve, and then her patience ran thin. For example, one year I gave her a massage table as if I were a professional masseuse. She got mad and told me to send it back immediately. Another time, in front of her and our three kids, I misspoke saying "this year my gift to you is an oral gift" and everyone laughed as I blushed. What I meant to say was "a verbal gift:" I was going to say "yes" for a whole month to everything she asked for—whether she wanted to go out to dinner with me and our friends (I'm less social than she is), watch a particular show (I don't like all the shows she does), or renovate the house. No more needs to be said, but for anyone reading, if you're going to take anything away from this book, take my advice and don't give an "oral" gift to your better half because your house will get renovated.

So fast forward to Valentines Day 2022, when Numi told me not to get her a gift, not flowers either. I listened (I'm becoming a better listener). Instead I got her a card with a picture of a bouquet of flowers on the cover. In the card—which she later affectionately termed "a love letter"—I went on and on in truth telling her how crazy I am for her. I also mentioned my grandparents who were married on Valentines Day in 1935 and how I hope and trust we can experience the sweet longevity they shared (they celebrated their 70th anniversary). Ultimately I told her how much I appreciate her for putting up with me all these years and I thanked her whole heartedly for keeping me on my toes!

It happens that I have walked well over 2000 miles in this last year on my quest for human and climate restoration. Included in this are the walks I took in four directions as well as the dog walks and other outings averaging 12,500 steps/day. I still like walking, and I'm ever committed to the climate cause, knowing that I along with my fellow citizens have to ramp it up. At the same time I'm also so personally committed in my marriage with Numi and in raising our family together. These matters of the heart aren't mutually exclusive. In fact, my love has deepened after this journey, and she was there for me when I was at my most vulnerable, to the point where our relationship is ever closer. Likewise with my children and my relationship with the wider community. They are in a good place, partly because I find myself living with, and seeking out, more humanity…and humility. Don't get me wrong. My life is far from nirvana. I have conflict and my old self will rear its bald head on too many occasions. Just the other day Numi was talking to me repeatedly in a loud tone of voice, upset at me for something, and after a while I couldn't take it anymore and I yelled at the top of my voice "stop yelling at me!" But of course my abrupt scream was ten times as loud as her mild angry tone in that moment so my hasty reaction was not only not constructive, it was self defeating, as is often my downfall.

What's undefeated is the joy and admiration I have for the dogs. We make it to town to the point of turning back, but not before I take a picture of them under a new symbol we stumble on for the south direction—a giant silver iconic dog statue. I realize, what could be more fitting at the end of this journey than to honor my dogs and dogs in general. They are the ultimate walking heroes (Appendix 1), and for so many reasons. They get us off the couch and onto our feet. They get us out of the house and into the outdoors. No peloton or smart phone could do that trick. Dogs get us interacting with others (in my case sometimes merely to apologize for Gary's aggressive behavior around other dogs, but other times actually to greet people in reciprocal kindness). Dogs show us how to love unconditionally, by tending to us when we're hurt and enthusiastically greeting us even when we've been gone for long. By wagging their tales as they do so often, especially with our attention and affection, they reveal the importance of kinship. They model how to be present, fully using their senses. They teach us the art of symbiosis, giving and receiving for mutual benefit: we feed them, they nurture us, we both are happier and better off together than alone. As Coaster, Gary and I make our way back home, I expand the list of the many accolades of dogs. What becomes clear to me is that dogs integrally embody the attributes that our world needs in order to heal. Not only are they our life long pals, they are prophets guiding us to the promised land.

In honor of our dogs who are walking heroes exemplifying
the traits of a beloved community.

In the interim, late in February 2022 and for some time thereafter, it felt like the promised land was out of reach. This is because Russia ruthlessly invaded Ukraine, which shook the world and brought us back to a dangerous time when might makes right and empires indiscriminately seized the sovereignty of independent nations. This was sheer authoritarian aggression against democracy and human rights. This was a needless loss of innocent life as well as a terrible refugee crisis. This was a brutal display of the utter inhumanity of war and it cast a dark shadow squarely on Putin, a war criminal, and indirectly on his supporting cast: the Russian oligarchy for not standing up to him, the Chinese government for looking the other way (with their eyes probably on gobbling up Taiwan), the cronies including a few politicians in our country for not uniting steadfastly against this tyranny but sowing division and doing the bidding of those who benefit from this egregious war, the oil and gas industry for complicitly profiting and capitalizing off this plunder as commodity prices soared.

But then, when the Russian people—at great risk of imprisonment, fines and surveillance—daringly protested in the streets (References), when Ukrainians demonstrated extraordinary resistance and backbone, the likes of which will go down in history for remarkable bravery, when Europe planted the seeds of full fledge—carbon free and renewable energy style—independence from Russia (Reference)…we realized there is hope in despair. Russia is the third largest oil and gas producer in the world behind the United States and Saudi Arabia and most of their production is exported to Europe. By invading Ukraine and threatening the whole NATO Alliance Russia ironically poked the European bear which is now committed more than ever to self determination through clean energy. We can help by implementing a lend lease type program delivering heat pumps in place of natural gas as Bill McKibben wisely advocated (Reference). The Soviet style regime will come undone from the outside eventually if Ukraine has her day and the rest of the world boycotts the fossil fuel energy receipts keeping Russia alive. Furthermore, what we saw initially as brute force by the Russian military was really a desperate attempt to cling to power and feebly hold on to the old world order. But the new world has taken root and is taking shape increasingly, as inevitable as the rising sun if the people keep standing up for it like the Ukrainian people have done decisively and young generations in Russia are starting to. Alexei Navalny, the brave Russian opposition leader, a walking hero (Appendix 1), said "I am against this war. I believe…[it] is being waged to cover up the robbery of Russian citizens and distract their attention…from the degradation of the economy." Navalny when free and healthy years prior would walk in demonstrations with his wife Yulia, but he was tortured, poisoned and unjustly imprisoned by the Russian regime to the point where he described himself as "A Skeleton Walking." But there is light at the end of the tunnel for him and all oppressed people, through courageous resistance, like Navalny himself encouraged in the fight for self determination: "each arrested person must be replaced by two newcomers." If there is sustained civil disobedience in mass, likewise in China, authoritarian regimes will topple from within.

These are lessons to heed by the United States, which has recently seen ominous signs of authoritarianism, corporate cronyism, polarization and isolationism. We the people should not ever take our democracy for granted, or be fooled, lulled to sleep or implicated. Rather, we must rise up with our rights in tact, wean ourselves off fossil fuels—and all the associated pollution, corruption and worldwide harm they are perpetuating. We must stand up strong, step forward boldly and carry the day, not only for democracy, but for diversity, widespread prosperity and the Beloved Community.

25
WALKING FOUR DIRECTIONS

It's time to bring this journey home. In saying this, it's important to acknowledge that an integral part of being home and being alive is being present in every step we take. As Thich Nhat Hanh says, "why not step in the direction of life, which is in the present moment" (Reference). Walking—in a synchronized motion with one foot firmly on the ground and the other gently lifting to the sky—is the act of being home and taking a journey all at once. Walking Four Directions—which I have done now for exactly one year since that sleepless night in February 2021 when I had my compelling dream to do this to begin with—sounds complicated. But it's really more fundamental than that. It means love force, life force, soul force and the force of our ancestry all combined in confluence. Upholding the integrity of life and our collective well being are synonymous with Walking Four Directions. This translates to "making a way out of no way" like civil rights activist Ben Jealous said about the grim prospects of enacting the John Lewis Voting Rights Bill with a 50-50 senate. It's what the epic heritage of our Nation's justice movements have all been about, and what the climate movement can become today. It means coming together—cross cultures, across life spans, from intersecting ways, and with rays of brightness like New Mexico's Zia Sun symbol—to fearlessly topple the status quo so we may restore the land and our humanity at once.

Walking Four Directions happens when we calmly and decisively walk into the intersection between brave ideals of our youth and the wisdom of our elders. This is where we lay the groundwork that may spawn a truly hopeful future. Native to the Land of Enchantment, and available everywhere with these common core materials, is the chance to build up the foundation of regeneration using (the fitting analogy of) adobe: with nature as the clay, spiritual fortitude the sand or 'holy dirt;' mix that with water which is the heritage of our ancestors and add grass or straw which is the binding of Beloved Community. These are the four tenets and interactive ingredients, we can use not only to make a place of belonging but also to safeguard the Earth and all the inhabitants who dwell here.

I am starting to wonder if my synthesis is sounding too abstract and otherworldly like the "Meanwhile" segment of Stephen Colbert on the Late Show. So I remove myself from typing on the computer and I take a walk with my furry friends, trying to break free from hyper philosophizing. But as we are walking from south to north, the sun hovers above the Jemez Mountains, just before setting in the west, while the full moon, aptly called the snow moon, has already risen just above the Sangre de Christos in the east.

The sun and the moon and all four directions are aligned,
ready for us to step into being.

In that moment, standing in between these orbs of brightness, four occurrences cross my mind. And it's not lost on me that four, like Diné, is sacred. First, the importance of the Human Spirit occurs to me, both at once being someone that emanates warmth like the Sun and like my faithful dog Coaster and being someone that reflects light like the Moon and Snow.

Second is Thich Nhat Hanh's notion (Reference) that we walk with our ancestors healthily beside us, and with those we can think of presently who can't walk. I think of Maria Lisa who was in a wheel chair at the Chimayo Chapel, and—as far as my ancestors go—I think of my parents. A smile comes to my face as I step forward carrying forth their enduring wellness. Yes our body and mind may restrict us from time to time and brake down eventually, as happened more abruptly to my parents due to their respective diseases. But that's not the end of the story. The deeper truth is that our brokenness is only temporal, involved with getting us from point a to point b. It does not last. It is outlived by more uplifting forces including Heritage Values and the subsequent generations' rejuvenating dreams (mine and Holden's come to mind). I realize and remember, on top of the steps we take in solidarity, that what lasts and enables us to be whole, springs from our soul which is unbreakable. While I am still caught in a dance of contradiction and I still wake up too early, sometimes (but less often) not falling back asleep again. I am letting go of angst and inadequacy. Because I am not alone carrying the burden. We collectively share in the responsibility. And therefore I believe in us and the prospect of walking to the promised land together in our lifetime.

The third occurrence that crosses my mind relates to a series of studies indicating that when we practice acts of kindness our health improves (Reference). In a nutshell this suggests we can turn back the clock of our aging selves when we are in service to others. I close my eyes in the twilight and imagine how invigorating and redeeming it will be when we act boldly together—in Beloved Community—to heal the climate crisis and repair the racial divide holding us back.

And this leads to the forth and closing concept intersecting in me just before the sun dips down (offering a chance for rest before our epic renewal). My son Fisher, like the Moon, continued his luminous tradition of suggesting to me a worthwhile story to read, this time from his environmental literature packet. I took him up on it thankfully and came across this poignant phrase: "Old trees are our parents, and our parents' parents, perchance. If you would learn the secrets of [Mother] Nature, you must practice more humanity" (Reference). The four direction journey—concluding now for me alone and commencing anew for all of us in tandem—has felt this way: the more insights uncovered along the way, the greater the motivation to share them and lend a helping hand. In the greater journey of kinship embarking, it's likely that we will all be so inspired.

At home this evening, I untie my shoelaces, take off my boots and put on moccasin slippers. Only to put on my boots and retie them up early the next morning, but this time with anticipation of much greater collective purpose and camaraderie. It's time I fade out of the picture and we stand up together like never before. We got this! With every foot—among hundreds of thousands, perchance even billions—pacing over thawing ground, and our sights set to the sky, secrets of nature will soon be revealed. "Here Comes the Sun" (Appendix 2). So turn toward the life force, knowing revolution and the chance for redemption as well as wholesale restoration are upon us. Let's not let it pass us by.

AFTERWORD

Late in the summer of 2022—as my *Walking Four Directions* journal was being fashioned into this book for publication—the US Congress passed and the President signed the Inflation Reduction Act which included broad investments in public health and 370 billion dollars for climate stewardship. This was to date the single most important US domestic legislation to combat the climate crisis and consisted of meaningful incentives for renewable energy, electric vehicle affordability, heat pumps, regenerative agriculture, and much more. The bill was paid for by imposing a fifteen percent minimum tax on corporations that earn over one billion dollars.

Senator Joe Manchin, who had been initially reluctant to join those calling for climate leadership, quietly negotiated a last minute deal with Senate Majority Leader Chuck Schumer. Credit is due to these two senators in particular and to the whole Democratic caucus in general. Not a single Republican voted for this. President Biden worked some magic behind the scenes to get this bill done. Credit is also due to the American people who increasingly consider the climate crisis a priority issue; to the entrepreneurs and problems solvers showcasing how "going green" is good for people, the planet and for profitability; and especially, to those who for years have been out front on this matter demonstrating, creatively pushing and pleading to the point where legislators are starting to listen and take this seriously.

We celebrate this step in the right direction. But we must not let down our guard. We cannot be content making 40% reductions in 2005 greenhouse gas emission levels by the year 2030. To safeguard civilization and our children's future we need to get below 100% reductions from 1990 levels—and we need to do so as fast as possible in a way that is economically feasible and socially just.

We in New Mexico have experienced the effects of the worst wildfires in our history that raged in the spring and summer of 2022. And the whole world is continuing to cope with countless examples of devastation including that year's drastic flooding in Pakistan putting as many as a third of their population in jeopardy. There are so many unsettling stories, including the finding that sooner-than-expected ice melting in Greenland will cause worldwide sea levels to rise at least one foot by the end of the century.

All of this is to say that we don't have time to wait. We need a community wide, statewide, nationwide, and worldwide mass movement to oppose the extraction, development, production and use of fossil fuels. We need to see increased levels of voting for wide ranging legislation including: 1) a progressive carbon fee and dividend; 2) a clear stipulation that the EPA thoroughly regulate CO_2 and all other anthropogenic greenhouse gases throughout our economy; and 3) hard hitting policies like California enacted by setting an ambitious path to banning fossil fuel vehicles.

Like walking on the Earth, the ground is where this all happens. Movements on the ground make all the difference. It has been shown that without the abolitionist movement, slavery would have lasted much longer in our country. Likewise for the women's suffrage movement elevating women's rights and expediting the right to vote, and the civil rights movement prompting the end to segregation. The same goes for the human climate crisis. Once the more drastic climate changes are set in motion they become harder to reverse; greenhouse gas emissions remain in the atmosphere for extended periods of time, causing great harm even well after emissions could be significantly reduced.

We can overcome and we can reach our destination by walking four directions, by ceasing our emissions altogether, plus sequestering CO_2, while at once healing our relations and empowering our lives through the transformative power of love.

Godspeed!

REFERENCES

(A-Article, B-Book, P-Podcast, S-Speech, W-Website)

Section I / Finding Stride

B: *Keep Sharp: Build a Better Brain at Any Age*, Sanjay Gupta, Simon & Shuster hardcover edition, January, 2021
A: "More Evidence That Physical Activity Keeps Depression at Bay" Christopher Bergland, *Psychology Today*, January 24, 2019
A: "Give your ideas some legs: The positive effect of walking on creative thinking." M. Oprezzo and D. L. Schwartz, *Journal of Experimental Psychology: Learning, Memory, and Cognition*, 2014
B: *PlanetWalker: How to Change Your World One Step At A Time*, John Francis, Elephant Mountain Press and *National Geographic*, 2005 and 2008

Section II / North, Human Spirit

A: "The Decoding of the Human Spirit: A Synergy of Spirituality and Character Strengths Toward Wholeness," Ryan Niemiec, Pinnate Russo-Netzer and Kenneth Pargament, Frontiers in Psychology, July 2020
B: *The Liberating Path of the Hebrew Prophets: Then and Now*, Nahum Ward Lev, Orbis Books, 2019
B: *Staying Awake, the Gospel for Changemakers*, Reverend Tyler Sit, Chalice Press 2021
B: *Draw Down*, Paul Hawken, Penguin Books, 2017
B: *Global Green New Deal* by Robert Pollen and Noam Chomsky, Verso Books,

2020

B: *Walking with the Wind: A Memoir of the Movement*, John Lewis, Simon Shuster, 1998

Section III / East, Mother Nature

B: *Sapiens, A brief History of Humankind*, Yuval Noah Harari, Harper Collins, 2015

B: *The Giving Tree*, Shell Silverstein, Harper Collins, 1964

P: "On Being," Krista Tippett, New York Times Podcast featuring Robin Wall Kimmerer, August 2020

B: *Braiding Sweetgrass: Indigenous Wisdom, Scientific Knowledge, and the Teachings of Plants*, Robin Wall Kimmerer, Milkweed Editions, 2013

A: "Vital soil organisms being harmed by pesticides, study shows," Damian Carrington, Guardian, May 2021

B: *Who Was Cesar Chavez?*, Dana Meachen Rau, Penguin Random House, 2017

B: *Who is Greta Thunberg?*, Ann Leopard, Penguin Books, 2020

B: *Brown University's Slavery and Justice Report*, 2021

W: Conner Divine's site for Hike the Continental Divide: http://www.hikethedivide.com/film

W: Lucy Barnard's site on walking from one pole to the other: http://www.tanglesandtail.com

B: *Thousand Mile Walk to the Gulf*, John Muir, Houghton Mifflin Harcourt Publishing Company, 1981

A: "Return the National Parks to the Tribes," David Treuer, *The Atlantic*, May, 2021

A: "The Unintended Consequences of Returning the Parks to the Tribes" Readers responses, *The Atlantic*, June, 2021

B: *Kindling Tikanga Environmentalism: The Common Ground of Native Culture and Democratic Citizenship*, Robb Hirsch, University of Otago, May, 1997

A: "How Returning Lands to Native Americans is helping protect nature," Jim Robbins, Yale School of the Environment, June 2021

B: *We Are Water Protectors*, Carole Lindstom, Roaring Brook Press, 2021

Section IV / West, Heritage Values

A: "In the Bag: Why being green comes naturally to US Latinos," Evette Cabera,

The Grist, February 2020

B: *Long Walk to Freedom*, Nelson Mandela, Little Brown and Company, 1994

B: *Braiding Sweetgrass: Indigenous Wisdom, Scientific Knowledge, and the Teachings of Plants*, Robin Wall Kimmerer, Milkweed Editions, 2013

B: *Gathering Moss: A Natural and Cultural History*, Robin Wall Kimmerer, Oregon State University Press, 2003

B: *Ceremony*, Leslie Marmon Silko, Penguin Classics Delux Edition, 2006

A: "Can Nuclear Fusion Put the Brakes on Climate Change," Rivka Galchen, New Yorker, October 2021

A: "The Other Afghan Women," Anand Gopal, *The New Yorker*, September 2021

W: Spirit Farm, James and Joyce Skeet at https://www.covenantpathways.org

W: Pueblo Action Alliance at https://www.puebloactionalliance.org

B: *Hope and History*, Bill vanden Huevel, Cornell Press, 2019

B: *The Comfort Crisis: Embrace Discomfort to Reclaim Your Wild, Happy, Healthy Self*, Michael Easter, Penguin Random House, 2021

B: *Coyote America: A Natural and Supernatural History*, Dan Flores, Basic Books, 2016

Section V / South, Beloved Community

S: Martin Luther King Jr., speech "Facing the Challenge of a New Age," 1956

B: *The Essential Writings of Mahatma Gandhi*, Raghavan Iyer, Oxford University Press, 1996

B: *Braiding Sweetgrass: Indigenous Wisdom, Scientific Knowledge, and the Teachings of Plants*, Robin Wall Kimmerer, Milkweed Editions, 2013

A: "New Mexico Wants it 'Both Ways,' Insisting on Environmental Regulations While Benefiting from Oil and Gas," Maya Leachman, Inside Climate News, February 2022

A/W: "Casey Harrell: the climate activist taking on Wall Street – and the muscle-wasting disease that's killing him," Patrick Greenfield, the Guardian, November 2021 (https://blackrocksbigproblem.com)

A: "Methane leaks are far worse than estimates, at least in New Mexico, but there's hope," Andrew Myers, Standford Earth Matters Magazine, March 2022

A: "Bison are back and that benefits many other species on the Great Plains," Matthew Moran, The Conversation, January 2019

A/P/W: "Three Pillars of Great Turning," Joanna Macy; "Embody Fierce

Compassion," Annie Mahon (https://www.rawmindfulness.com); "Wisdom and Activism," Kate Werning with Katie Loncke (Podcast November 28, 2017, https://www.healingjustice.org)

A: "A special place in hell for companies not fighting climate change," Jeff Beer, Fast Company, December 2021

A: "Climate Change has destabilized the Poles, imperiling the planet," Sarah Kaplan, *Washington Post*, December 2021

B: *Collapse of Constitutional Remedies*, Aziz Huq, Oxford University Press, 2021

A: "Manchin's Coal Corruption is So Much Worse Than You Knew," Jeff Goodel, *Rolling Stone*, January 2022

B: *Half-Earth: Our Planet's Fight for Life*, E.O. Wilson, Liveright Publishing Corporation, 2016

B: *Reclaiming the Commons: Biodiversity, Indigenous Knowledge, and the Rights of Mother Earth*, Vandana Shiva, Synergetic Press, 2020

Section VI / Walking Home

A: "A special place in hell for companies not fighting climate change," Jeff Beer, Fast Company, December 2021

B: *PlanetWalker: How to Change Your World One Step At A Time*, John Francis, Elephant Mountain Press and *National Geographic*, 2005 and 2008

B: *Who Was Harriet Tubman*, Yona Zeldis McDonough, Penguin Random House, 2019

W: Sue Van Hook at http://suevanhook.com

A: "Web of Life," Daniel Benor, Wholistic Healing Publications, May 2014

B: *Walking with the Wind: A Memoir of the Movement*, John Lewis, Simon Shuster, 1998

B: *How to Walk*, Thich Nhat Hanh, Parallax, 2015

B: *Renewal: From Crisis to Transformation in Our Lives, Work, and Politics*, Anne-Marie Slaughter, Princeton University Press, 2021

B: *Wrong Lanes Have Right Turns*, Michael Phillips, Crown Publishing Group, 2022

A: "Invasion brings rare sight in Russia: protests against Putin" Robyn Dixon, *Washington Post*, February 2022;

A: "Russians Continue Anti-War Rallies Despite Protesters' Arrests," Vladimir Isachenkov and Irina Titova, AP, February 2022

A: "E.U. to unveil new energy strategy in wake of Russia-Ukraine crisis," Michael

Birnbaum and Stephen Mufson, February 2022;

A: "Heat Pumps for Peace and Freedom," Bill McKibben, The Crucial Years, February 2022

A: "The Health Benefits of Random Acts of Kindness," Sandee LaMotte, CNN, February 2022

B: *The Overstory*, Richard Powers, W.W. Norton and Company, 2018 ("Now is the Time of Chestnuts," Nicholas Hoel)

APPENDIX 1: WALKING HEROES

Doris Haddock ("Granny D"), p. 243

Thich Nhat Hanh, p. 296

Casey Harrell, p. 241

Leonard Coe Hirsch (My Grandfather), p. 121

Delores Huerta, p. 119

Isaiah the Prophet, p. 42

Martin Luther King Jr., p. 235

John Lewis, p. 62

Nelson Mandela, p. 123

Alexei Navalny, p. 309

Peace Pilgrim, p. 18

Po' Pay, p. 230

Tarantulas, p. 200

Harriet Tubman, p. 290

Archbishop Desmond Tutu, p. 261

Elizabeth Wathuti, p. 299

APPENDIX 2: WALKING SONGS / PLAY LIST

Alive, Pearl Jam, p. 218

Blue Sky, The Allman Brothers Band, p. 65

Brand New Day, Joshua Radin, p. 272

Canyons, Tabatha Rose, p. 99

Four Seasons, Antonio Vivaldi, p. 98

Here Comes the Sun, The Beatles, p. 314

Humankind, Coldplay, p. 294

I've Always Been Crazy, Waylon Jennings, p. 131

Like a Rock, Bob Seger, p. 140

Love Train, The O'Jays, p. 289

Redemption, Nathaniel Rateliff & the Night Sweats, p. 50

Ripple, Grateful Dead, p. 206

Rock Around the Clock, Bill Haley & His Comets, p. 203

Rocky Mountain High, John Denver, p. 229

APPENDIX 3: PUBLIC NEWS SERVICE RADIO STORY

Public News Service (PNS) Radio Story 1/17/22
NM Environmental Groups Mark MLK Day with Climate Walk

New Mexico climate activists commemorate today's Martin Luther King Jr. Day by walking to the State Capitol in Santa Fe from four directions, calling on lawmakers to take bold action to combat climate change.

The Capitol, known as the Roundhouse, was designed to represent the sun's rays, as well as the four directions, four seasons and four phases of life.

Robb Hirsch founded the Climate Change Leadership Institute nearly 20 years ago and is now its executive director. He said it's appropriate for people to rally on MLK Day.

"It's really perfect on Martin Luther King Day to have the community rise up in a nonviolent, peaceful manner," said Hirsch, "but rise up strongly, to demand action on this critical, vital issue for our lives."

Hirsch said the walkers will convene outside the Roundhouse at noon.

The National Association for the Advancement of Colored People - Santa Fe branch, the Green Amendment for the Generations group, 350 New Mexico, the Sierra Club Rio Grande Chapter and many others will participate. Organizers of today's "Walking for the Climate" event in Santa Fe say the crisis should not instill paralysis, but rather invoke a mass movement, much like the 1960's Civil Rights Movement.

New Mexico has long relied on oil and gas to fuel its economy, but Hirsch said the event is less about demanding specific policies during this year's short legislative session than ongoing, unequivocal action.

"There's a lot of equivocating going on," said Hirsch, "because a lot of the elected officials, unfortunately, are taking campaign dollars from the very industries that we need to be regulating."

Hirsch said he believes climate change is a civil rights issue of our time—because while it affects everyone, those most likely to be affected are people of color and of lower income.

"Martin Luther King Day is so vital for this," said Hirsch, "because the Civil Rights Movement—the brave citizens who participated in that—showed us a course of action to get things done when people thought there was no way to get the Civil Rights Act and the Voting Rights Act passed."

Printed in the USA
CPSIA information can be obtained
at www.ICGtesting.com
JSHW012035130823
46472JS00005B/16